Sunset

NORTHEASTERN
LANDSCAPING
BOOK

Edited by Ken Druse

SUNSET BOOKS INC. · MENLO PARK, CALIFORNIA

Sunset Books Inc.
VP, General Manager: Richard A. Smeby
VP, Editorial Director: Bob Doyle
Production Director: Lory Day
Art Director: Vasken Guiragossian

Sunset Northeastern Landscaping Book
was produced by:
Editor: Ken Druse
Managing Editor: Janet Cave
Photography Editor: Jane A. Martin
Art Director, Design and Production Manager: Alice Rogers
Computer Production Manager: Linda Bouchard

Senior Editor: Carole Ottesen
Writers: Jean Benedett, Catriona Tudor Erler, Mimi Harrison,
    Jocelyn G. Lindsay, Jeffrey S. Minnich, R. C. Scott, Robert Speziale,
    Mary-Sherman Willis
Editorial Coordinator: Britta Swartz
Editorial Assistants: Tishana Peebles, Barbara Brown,
    Bridget Biscotti Bradley

Production Coordinator: Patricia S. Williams
Copy Editor: Anne Farr
Proofreader: Jarelle S. Stein
Index: Lina B. Burton
Computer Production: Joan Olson
Illustrators: Ron Hildebrand, Lois Lovejoy, Rik Olson, Mimi Osborne,
    Erin O'Toole, Mark Pechenik, Reineck & Reineck, Wendy Smith,
    Jenny Speckels
Supplemental page layout: Elisa Tanaka

Principal Consultant: Robert S. Hebb is a horticulturist, garden designer,
author, and frequent lecturer on gardening. He wrote the pioneering
book *Low Maintenance Perennials,* and has been director of horticulture for the Mary Flagler Cary Arboretum of the New York Botanical
Garden and executive director of the Lewis Ginter Botanical Garden in
Richmond, Virginia. He is a recipient of the Massachusetts Horticultural
Society Silver Medal for leadership in American horticulture.

Foreword

For over half a century, West Coast gardeners from novice to expert have relied on Sunset's comprehensive gardening library to help them solve landscaping problems. *Northeastern Landscaping* builds on Sunset's reputation as the premier publisher of regional gardening books and brings that approach east, where the climate and topography are dramatically different. What works in San Diego or Eugene may not work in Buffalo or Baltimore, even though the goal is the same: to make a functional and beautiful outdoor space.

But the country's northeastern quadrant itself varies from place to place. Rocky New England presents a gardener with different challenges from those found on the seashore of New Jersey or by the Great Lakes of Ohio, or in the hills of West Virginia. I've always believed that we must look to the natural world for design cues when planning a garden—in particular, that our local natural world determines the form and success of our landscaping designs. That means looking carefully at your region to experience it and get a sense of the place. Even if you live in or around a city—and many of us do in the Northeast—I advise gardeners to go to a nature

preserve and form a picture of it. This book will help you to assimilate what you see and get you started on your own landscape by showing you what worked for other gardeners in your area.

What defines the Northeast? The area covered in this book spans a diverse region, from southern Quebec and the New England states to Virginia and west to Ohio. To understand this region, it is helpful to learn about its past, beginning with the events that shaped its character. Arctic glaciers that had buried the Northeast for millions of years began to recede about 10,000 years ago. What emerged was the northern division of the Appalachian Mountains, blunted and scraped clear of vegetation, and lowlands strewn with rocky debris—which gardeners can still find today. These geological conditions affect your soil, its drainage, and what plants will grow best in it. In this book, we'll look at ways to make the most of what you have, whether it's Maryland clay, New York schist, or New Hampshire granite.

Your area's more recent history—the history of its agriculture, the development of your neighborhood, and the architecture of your house—will guide you in choosing a style of landscaping. If you are starting with a clean slate, such as an open lot around a new house in a suburban development, or if you want to revive an old garden that has established plantings, this book will fire your imagination and provide all the information you'll need to get started. We asked professionals—garden designers and landscape architects—to draw up plans for different types of gardens appropriate to a variety of home styles and lifestyles. The result is planting diagrams suitable for a row house or a summer cottage, a patio or a rooftop, a family garden or a kitchen garden, to name a few.

Gardening in the Northeast is also about the seasons, which so transform our gardens and affect how we use them throughout the year. The floral exuberance of spring pulls us outdoors for hours, as do the fiery colors of a crisp autumn. But in winter, cold and snow conspire to keep us indoors. Some days, all you might see are the bones of your garden embossed in the snow; it takes the evergreens and a glimpse of the first crocus peeking through that white blanket to reassure us that life goes on in the frozen soil. Soon the warm months roll around, and even the hot, muggy summer has

its charms. You can sometimes forget about drought and the blistering sun when you sit back on a summer evening, breathing in the scent of nicotiana and moon vine.

After you have an idea of what you'd like to do in your landscape, it's important to know how to do it, even if that includes hiring professionals to participate. We'll show you the nuts and bolts of garden construction, or hardscaping—building the framework upon which you add the finishing touches. In the Northeast we have become mindful of the effects of a steadily growing population on the environment. As gardeners we'll look at conserving resources, including water; at fertilizer alternatives to limit the runoff polluting streams; at controlling invasive introduced species that are crowding out native plants; and at ways of dealing with deer and other animal pests.

We give our thanks to the many garden designers and construction experts who contributed their knowledge to this book, and to the dozens of gardeners who shared their visions for a perfect union of setting, structure, and plants in the Northeast.

Ken Druse
Ken Druse
Editor

THE NORTHEASTERN DIFFERENCE

Geologically, the Northeast is the oldest region in the United States. It is dominated by the ancient Appalachian mountain range, its peaks and hills worn smooth over millions of years by the action of glaciers that extended as far south as North Carolina. The Northeast also is home to the earliest European settlements and is the most densely populated region of the United States; gardeners have been planting here for almost 400 years. Their gardens reflect a deep sense of tradition, influenced particularly by the landscaping styles of Great Britain and Europe. The partitioned cloister garden and the cottage garden, the formal French parterre, and Dutch bulbs bursting forth in spring are part of northeastern garden vernacular. But so are such distinctly American landscaping features as the backyard patio or deck, the lawn, the swimming pool, the front porch festooned with vines and hanging plants, and the shrub border along the house foundation.

The Northeast's greatest distinction, however, has less to do with garden styles and decks than with its natural seasonal beauty, from spring and summer's floral abundance to autumn's fiery foliage and winter's snowy stillness. Gardeners in this region, and rightly so, must weigh all the elements that affect their plant choices and where they site them. Among the elements to consider are:

TOPOGRAPHY. From Nova Scotia to West Virginia and further south, the Appalachian mountain system rises up and forms a natural barrier between the eastern seaboard and the expansive lowlands of the continental interior. The Appalachians don't reach soaring heights—Mt. Washington in New Hampshire, the highest mountain in the northern division of the Appalachians, is a relatively modest 6,288 feet. But these mountains pervade the northeastern

sensibility, giving it a flinty endurance. Rivers and deep, glacier-carved lakes, including the Great Lakes, dot the North and serve as conduits and reservoirs for rain and melted snow. On either side of the mountain range are plains. The coastal plain stretches to the east from New Jersey to the Chesapeake Bay and south, and has sandy, sometimes boggy soil. To the west, from western New York, Pennsylvania, and West Virginia and through Ohio, runs the hilly Allegheny Plateau, which descends into prairie in western Ohio and the fertile Ohio River Valley in southern Ohio. Long barrier islands, such as Long Island in New York and Assateague Island in Virginia, stretch along the Atlantic coast.

CLIMATE. Northeastern gardeners can expect cold winters, hot, muggy summers, and drier autumns. Rainfall is plentiful, from 30 to 50 inches per year, with much precipitation taking the form of snow in the Great Lakes, Hudson Bay, and St. Lawrence River areas. Drought, therefore, is generally less of a problem than the cold. In much of the Northeast—northern Maine, New Hampshire, Vermont, New York, and southern Canada—winter temperatures range from 0 degrees Fahrenheit to −20 degrees Fahrenheit. In the warmer Chesapeake Bay area of Maryland and Virginia the coldest winter temperatures hover between 0 and 10 degrees Fahrenheit. In late summer and fall, a coastal storm season begins as tropical storms from the Gulf of Mexico track up the Atlantic coast; "nor'easters" from the North Atlantic batter the coast in winter.

POPULATION. The Northeast is home to almost a third of the population of the United States, much of it living in the milder zones in urban areas and in the suburban corridors running north from Washington, D.C., to Baltimore, Philadelphia, New York, and Boston. Urban gardeners claim what space they can in front of and behind townhouses, on rooftops and balconies, and around the bases of street trees. Besides the lack of space, their chief landscaping challenges are pollution and shade produced by tall buildings. In recent

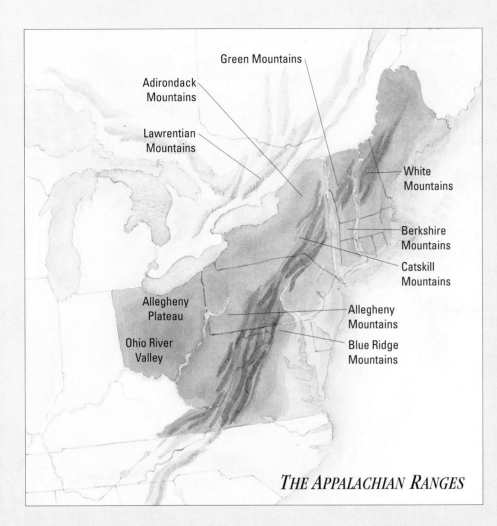

Green Mountains

Adirondack
Mountains

Lawrentian
Mountains

White
Mountains

Berkshire
Mountains

Catskill
Mountains

Allegheny
Plateau

Allegheny
Mountains

Ohio River
Valley

Blue Ridge
Mountains

THE APPALACHIAN RANGES

The Appalachian Mountain range and its branches dominate the Northeast. The region is covered by the largest broadleaf deciduous forest in the world, giving way to a mix of conifers farther north. Deposits of sand and gravel—brought down from mountains during the Ice Age—lace the soil of the coastal plain, and rivers and glacier-carved lakes dot the entire region. Temperatures are modulated along the coast, where the land flattens and meets the sea.

Canadian hemlock, thrive only in the cooler zones and languish in the warm coastal areas. But imports from Europe, and especially those from Japan and East Asia, have enriched the diversity of ornamentals. Protection from the cold in sheltered locations and from temperature fluctuations under mulches helps the marginally hardy exotics to survive; heat-sensitive plants, however, do best in partial shade or on north-facing slopes.

How to use this book

The *Sunset Northeastern Landscaping Book* is a companion to the *Sunset National Garden Book*. To find out more about the plants mentioned throughout these pages—where they perform best, their growth habits, and how to care for them—refer to the encyclopedia section of the *Sunset National Garden Book*.

years, gardeners in the roomier suburbs and rural areas have been experimenting with replacing their lawns and foundation plantings with low-maintenance, natural landscapes of grasses and native plants. Gardeners in the mountains and along the coast must adapt their landscaping plans to account for poor soil, high wind, and salt.

PLANTS. In the woodlands, spring brings a dazzling wildflower display, with ephemerals such as spring beauty *(Claytonia virginica)*, Dutchman's-breeches *(Dicentra cucullaria)*, trillium, bloodroot *(Sanguinaria canadensis)*, and wild geranium. Meadows burst into bloom in late summer with asters, goldenrod *(Solidago)*, Joe-Pye weed, and grasses. In fall the trees come to the fore in blazing shades of red, orange, and yellow. Winter also has its rewards, after the foliage has dropped to expose the skeletal structure of trees and shrubs. The infusion of sunlight reveals a tracery of shadows on the snow, brightly colored berries on the branches, and the rich texture of tree bark.

Native plants give the northeastern gardener a wealth of material for landscaping; indeed, some of the most beautiful plants, such as paperbark birch, balsam fir, and

CONTENTS

FINISHING TOUCHES 264

REGIONAL PROBLEMS AND SOLUTIONS 300

LANDSCAPE PLANS 334

MATERIALS AND TECHNIQUES 360

PLANNING YOUR GARDEN

When you want to create a beautiful and functional place for outdoor relaxation, the reality of your bare or overgrown yard may seem utterly daunting. So before you turn your first shovelful of soil, close your eyes and picture your dream garden. Does it have a spacious deck or patio for parties? Is it serene and secluded, with roses and a wisteria-covered gazebo? Or is it a lively dooryard garden with a profusion of flowering plants blooming in exuberant disarray? Whatever your fancy, make a wish list of your favorite garden styles and plants. Then use the information on the following pages to help you plan space for your activities, choose the right plants, and work with your soils and microclimates. The result will be a garden that reflects the reality of your site—and also your dreams.

PLANNING WITH A PURPOSE

H ow you design your property can greatly enhance the pleasure of living in your home. When it is thoughtfully planned, landscaping does far more than merely beautify. It can provide recreation areas and places to entertain. Well-placed trees, shrubs, and arbors temper the weather and cut down on heating and cooling costs. A good design can also add much-needed living space to your home in the warm seasons and provide a window on the natural world throughout the year.

Explore your garden's potential

Think of the spaces between the exterior of your house and the edges of your property as potential outdoor rooms. For example, a house that lacks a foyer gains a welcoming entry with the addition of a well-designed front garden. An entrance garden also improves the appearance of your house and signifies the return to a comforting haven for you and your family.

Space behind the house or along its sides can become an outdoor room, spacious enough to host large gatherings. Paving or decking defines the room's dimensions. Planting or fencing around it ensures privacy and lends a comforting sense of enclosure. Furniture—for dining or lounging—further defines its identity.

A garden room of your own

You can also make room in your garden for sports and hobbies. A swimming pool is great for family entertainment. A large deck or patio can double as a dance floor or an exercise room, while a sunny bit of ground can be transformed into an herb garden for an enthusiastic chef. For the artist in the family, a shady grove may serve as a sylvan studio.

Even the narrow strips on the sides of a house can be put to good use. On the shady side, consider a garden for strolling, bright with spring bulbs and lush with ferns and wildflowers in summer. A sunny strip is perfect for growing vegetables such as tomatoes and beans, which can be trained to grow vertically, and fruit trees that can be espaliered against a wall. Or turn your sunny side garden into a nursery or a cutting garden. Where privacy is an issue, the side yard may be the place to plant a privacy screen.

For those times when it is too cold or too hot to spend time outside, the garden, viewed through windows, extends the house visually outward. A living tableau of plants that monitor the seasons can be enjoyed from inside as well as out, and planting for wildlife will enliven your vistas with birds and butterflies.

The potential uses of spaces around houses are as individual as the people who live in them. When you begin designing your garden, don't be bound by convention. Think of what you and your family want and need and proceed from there.

A WELL-DESIGNED LANDSCAPE

NORTH ▶

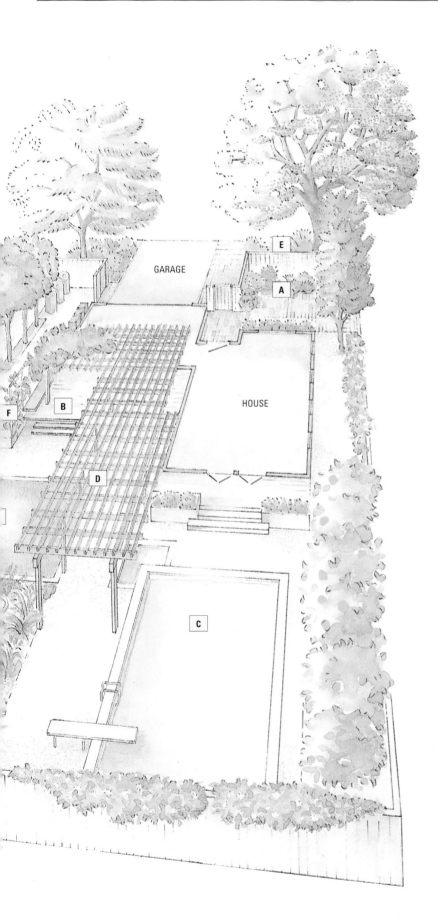

GARAGE

E

A

HOUSE

F

B

D

C

LANDSCAPING GOALS

A. Create privacy. The walled patio is really an extension of the living room. It creates an enclosed space and conceals the front yard from passers-by. The fountain masks traffic noise.

B. Invite entertaining. A broad deck wraps around the family and dining rooms to offer plenty of outdoor space for dinner, parties, or simple relaxation in view of, but removed from, the swimming pool.

C. Provide recreation. The swimming pool is a great way to cool off on hot summer days. A trellis—creating a transition between house and garden—provides privacy, a sense of enclosure, and shelters the spa.

D. Modify the climate. Draped in deciduous vines, this arbor shades southern exposures from the summer sun. In winter, when the vines are dormant, it allows the low winter sun to shine through and warm the interior. Around the pool, plantings along the fence filter strong winds.

E. Beautify the property. Lush plantings between the sidewalk and the patio wall create an attractive view from the street, soften the lines of the house and wall, and add color.

F. Grow a kitchen garden. Raised beds along the south side of the rear yard offer an ideal spot for raising herbs and vegetables, and are convenient to both the kitchen and the garden work area next to the garage.

G. Attract wildlife. Wildlife plantings and a birdbath, sited to be visible from inside the house and from the deck, lure birds and butterflies to the garden.

H. Reduce water use. A small lawn saves more water than a large one would; other features that lower consumption are an irrigation system, the grouping of plants with similar water needs, and liberal mulch throughout the garden.

A WELL-PLANNED GARDEN

A. Edible and ornamental plants share a bed in this colonial-style garden. The straplike leaves of leeks, rough-textured Italian kale, beans, and white-flowered garlic chives mingle with nasturtiums, orange gem marigolds, red zinnias, and tall spider flowers in a ground cover that is as beautiful as it is utilitarian.

B. An ivy hedge encloses one side of this low-maintenance garden, which includes robust pink-flowered *Anisodontea,* yuccas, mullein *(Verbascum),* and myrtle *(Myrtus)* trimmed into tree form. Paving eliminates the need to maintain lawn and the sturdy plants need little looking after.

MEETS A VARIETY OF NEEDS

C. Beautiful and easy to care for, the perennials in this New York garden create a meadow effect. In the foreground, mounding lemon yellow 'Moonbeam' coreopsis contrasts with succulent house leek *(Sempervivum)* and dazzling petunias *(Petunia parviflora)*. In the background, daylilies *(Hemerocallis)*, lilies *(Lilium* spp.), and yucca contrast with low spreading plants.

D. Recreation takes place in naturalistic splendor in this swimming pool set into a wooded hillside. Rustic sandstone coping around the pool and rocks flanking a waterfall enhance the natural look. Plantings include a Japanese maple, juniper, cotoneaster, rhododendron, and a weeping white pine, which blend with the forest setting.

E. Relaxation and enjoyment of the luxuriant borders come with a leisurely stroll through this garden. An edging of Vermont stone neatly separates grass from perennials and doubles as a retaining wall that steps down the slope and keeps the lawn level.

COLD-AIR POCKETS

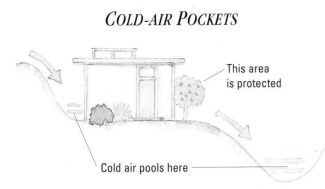

This area is protected

Cold air pools here

Cold air flows downhill like water, and "puddles" in basins. It can be dammed by a barrier such as a house, wall, or fence. So if you build a sunken patio or planting area, you may find yourself shivering, even when higher or more protected surroundings are balmy.

AIR FLOW

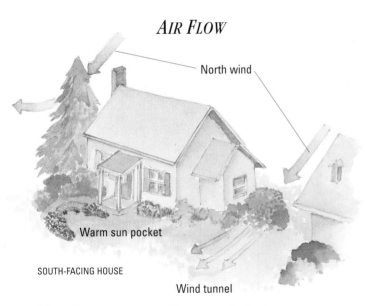

North wind

Warm sun pocket

SOUTH-FACING HOUSE

Wind tunnel

Microclimates are created in your garden by the way your house sits upon the land. A house casts its own shade patterns and can hold warmth. It shelters one side of the garden from the prevailing wind, forming a warm sun pocket to support tender plants that would perish in colder sites. While the windward side of the house will be colder, plants that need good air circulation, such as lavender and lamb's ear *(Stachys)*, stay healthier there. Landscaping—evergreen trees and shrubs in particular—can further influence microclimates. In the "wind tunnel" areas between houses these plants filter and soften winds.

THE EFFECT OF

In planning a landscape, it's important to consider the weather and climate in both your region and your garden. The path and angle of the sun, the seasons of the year, and the wind patterns around your property all affect your opportunities for outdoor living, your choice and placement of plants, and the overall design of your landscape.

Have you ever wondered why, in a warm, south-facing garden, the flowers of a star magnolia are ruined by a late frost while, just down the street, the fuzzy buds of another star magnolia—this one facing east—have yet to open? Microclimates are responsible. Most gardens have several microclimates—areas that are a little warmer or cooler, wetter or drier, more or less windy than others. Microclimates are created by a combination of factors, including sun angle, wind direction, and the exposure and topography of your site.

Air temperature and movement

Because warm air rises and cold air sinks, cool air tends to pool in low places and to back up behind obstacles such as hedges and houses, creating frost pockets. Slopes are the last features in a landscape to freeze, because cold air constantly drains off them, mixing with nearby warmer air as it flows. Flat areas, by contrast, cool off quickly as heat radiates upward, especially during nights when the air is still and skies are clear. Any overhead protection reduces this loss of heat.

In most gardens, the house influences the garden's microclimates. A house blocks the wind, creating warmer, protected pockets on its leeward side. In these warm microclimates, plants not generally hardy in the area may survive the winter. Alternately, beds in the teeth of the northwest wind won't support marginally hardy plants: their colder microclimate may slow plant maturation, and the appearance of flowers may be as much as a week behind gardens in milder situations.

Other influences

Keep in mind, too, that structures and materials influence microclimates on your property. The presence of water—a swimming pool, pond, or water feature—can slightly cool the air. Certain hardscape materials reflect sun and heat better than others. Light-colored masonry paving and walls spread sun and heat and can be uncomfortably bright; wood surfaces are a little cooler. On the other hand, dark masonry materials retain heat even after nightfall. And plants and buildings can filter or block wind.

Sun and shade

In summer, the morning sun rises in the northeast, arcs high across the southern sky, and sets in the evening to the northwest. This long passage means extra hours of daylight. By the time of the summer

MICROCLIMATES

solstice in June, Philadelphia enjoys about 14½ hours of daylight. Points north will experience a few minutes more of daylight and those south, a few minutes less. By contrast, the winter sun rises in the southeast, passes low across the southern sky, and sets to the southwest. Days are much shorter at winter solstice in December, when Philadelphia receives slightly more than 10 daylight hours.

That shifting sun angle means longer shadows in winter when the sun is low in the sky—leaving a greater part of the garden in shade during the dormant season and more of it in the sun when plants are growing. The pattern of sun and shade also varies depending on the time of day; at noon, when the sun is highest, there is little shade to be found.

SUN ANGLES

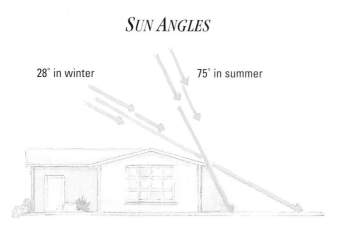

28° in winter   75° in summer

In winter, the sun crosses the sky at a lower angle than it does in summer. The effects can be pronounced, especially on north-facing exposures. The illustration above shows how the ground is shaded by the house at noon in summer and winter.

Exposure

Slopes that drop to the south or southwest get more heat during the day than those that drop to the north or northeast. Similarly, walls that run east and west reflect extra heat and sunlight onto plants on their south sides. Walls that run north and south reflect extra heat to plants growing on their west sides, but cooler microclimates are created on their east sides. Sunny locations are best for heat-loving plants, but the soil is also affected, drying out faster and requiring extra irrigation and soil amendments.

SUMMER AND WINTER SHADOWS

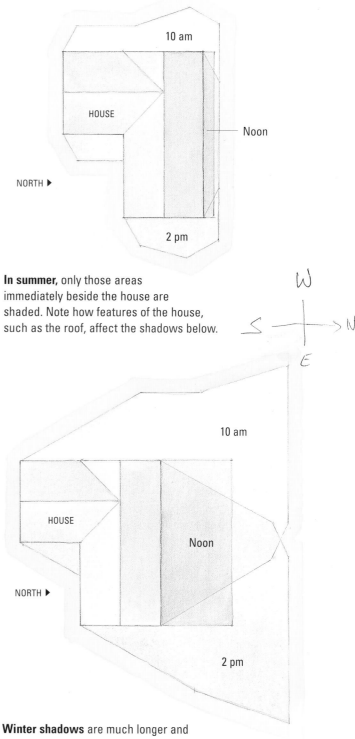

In summer, only those areas immediately beside the house are shaded. Note how features of the house, such as the roof, affect the shadows below.

Winter shadows are much longer and can shift dramatically within the space of a few hours. Compare the shadow cast at noon with that cast at 2 pm.

MONTH	−40°F 90–160 FROST-FREE DAYS
January	Use pine boughs to protect plants from frost heave; spread wood ashes.
February	Brush snow from evergreens to prevent breakage; prune dormant woody plants, berries; order seeds.
March	Avoid walking on frozen grass; force forsythia inside; check evergreens for bagworms.
April	Prune evergreens before new growth starts; set out bare-root plants as soon as available.
May	Set out hardy annuals; prune forsythia after bloom; fertilize lawns.
June	**In bloom:** columbine, iris, lilac, moss pinks, peonies, poppies, roses, spirea, tulips.
July	Divide and transplant daffodils; deadhead annuals and perennials.
August	Divide irises, daylilies, bleeding heart, lily-of-the-valley.
September	Plant evergreens, balled shrubs and trees; start new lawns; plant bulbs.
October	Water and mulch newly planted shrubs, trees; mound earth around roses, tie stems.
November	Water garden; clean up dead plants, mulch.
December	Mulch bulb beds; wrap trunks of flowering and fruit trees against rabbits and mice.

SEASONS

The best gardens mirror the seasons. Old blooms pass, and new ones magically take their place. The plant palette never fades, it just evolves. When flowers are gone, foliage sets the garden alight with dazzling fall shades of red, plum, orange, and gold. Then the fiery berries of shrubs and trees take over, followed by winter's striking silhouettes and colored bark.

Good gardeners make sure that their gardens have some interest every day of the year. Some feature flower color nearly year round, from the earliest spring bulbs to the latest fall mums. Others fill the air with ever-changing fragrances, starting with the earliest spring hyacinths and lilacs and lasting through the winter with the crisp scent of cedar and pine. Still other gardens are eclectic, filled with blooms for cutting in spring, fragrance in summer, fiery leaves in fall, and fascinating peeling, striped, or colored bark in winter. In any garden, you can put all these things together—and give your garden its own unique personality in the process. The secret is knowing what to plant and when to plant it.

Find the column for your area in the chart at right, then use it as a design tool to help you choose plants with seasonal interest. The chart is organized by minimum temperature; you can learn the minimum temperature in your area by contacting your local county Cooperative Extension Service. For each month, you'll find planting and bloom times for a sampling of favorite landscape plants. These are guidelines only; include your own favorites in your four-season plan. The *Sunset National Garden Book* provides further details on the regional adaptability of plants.

Chart key

ANNUALS: Cool-season annuals develop during winter and bloom in spring. Warm-season annuals bloom in late spring, summer, and early fall.

PERENNIALS: Most perennials flower once a year for weeks or even months. They die back in winter, then grow back from the roots or woody top growth the following spring. Regular deadheading can extend their period of bloom.

REGIONAL MINIMUM TEMPERATURE

−30°F 160–180 FROST-FREE DAYS	−20°F 180–200 FROST-FREE DAYS	−10°F 200–220 FROST-FREE DAYS	0°F 220–250 FROST-FREE DAYS
Use pine boughs to protect plants from frost heave; prune woody plants.	Use pine boughs to protect plants from frost heave; feed birds.	Use pine boughs to protect plants from frost heave; feed birds; order seeds.	Use pine boughs to protect plants from frost heave; feed birds; order seeds.
Brush snow from evergreens to prevent breakage; order seeds.	Brush snow from evergreens to prevent breakage; order seeds; start seeds of hardy annuals inside.	Start seeds of hardy annuals inside; force forsythia.	Start seeds of hardy annuals inside; force forsythia. **In bloom:** witch hazel, hellebores.
Start seeds of hardy annuals inside; force forsythia inside; set out bare-root plants as soon as available.	Force forsythia inside; fertilize lawns; set out hardy vegetables.	Begin major lawn work; set out hardy vegetables; prune forsythia after bloom. **In bloom:** crocus.	Fertilize lawns; set out hardy vegetables; prune forsythia after bloom. **In bloom:** crocus.
Set out hardy vegetables, bare-root roses; begin major lawn work; enrich soil with compost.	Plant bare-root roses; prune evergreens before new growth starts; begin major lawn work. **In bloom:** crocus, snowdrops.	Plant bare-root roses; prune evergreens before new growth starts. **In bloom:** daffodils, cherries.	Plant bare-root roses; set out tender annuals. **In bloom:** daffodils, cherries, columbine, star magnolia, camellias.
Prune evergreens before new growth starts; prune forsythia after bloom. **In bloom:** daffodils, moss pinks, tulips.	Set out tender annuals. **In bloom:** columbine, moss pinks, poppies, tulips.	Set out tender annuals. **In bloom:** columbine, iris, peonies, poppies, roses, tulips.	Deadhead annuals; feed roses; divide daffodils. **In bloom:** azaleas, magnolias, peonies, roses, tulips.
In bloom: columbine, iris, lilac, mock orange, peonies, poppies, roses, spirea, tulips.	Feed roses after first flush of bloom. **In bloom:** lilac, peonies, roses.	Divide daffodils; deadhead annuals, perennials; feed roses. **In bloom:** roses, bee balm, daisies, rhododendron, sweetbay magnolia.	**In bloom:** bee balm, butterflyweed, daisies, hydrangea, rhododendron, sweet bay magnolia.
Feed roses; divide and transplant daffodils; deadhead annuals and perennials.	Divide and transplant daffodils; deadhead annuals; divide irises.	Divide irises; deadhead perennials. **In bloom:** bee balm, coneflower, yarrow.	**In bloom:** bull bay magnolia, coneflower, lilies, sweet bay, magnolia.
Divide irises, daylilies, bleeding heart, lily-of-the-valley; start fall vegetables.	Divide daylilies, bleeding heart, lily-of-the-valley; start fall vegetables.	Water during dry spells; harvest vegetables; start fall vegetables.	Harvest tomatoes, cucumbers; water during dry spells. **In bloom:** cardinal flower, goldenrod.
Start new lawns, feed established ones; rejuvenate perennial beds.	Start new lawns, feed established ones; rejuvenate beds.	Start new lawns, feed established ones; divide and transplant perennials.	Feed established lawns; divide and transplant perennials. **In bloom:** asters.
Transplant trees, evergreens; plant spring bulbs; water permanent plantings.	Plant evergreens, balled shrubs and trees; plant spring bulbs; water the garden.	Plant spring bulbs; rejuvenate beds. **In bloom:** ornamental grasses.	**In bloom:** camellias, ornamental grasses; dogwoods in fall color.
Mulch; clean up dead plants; mound earth around roses; clean, oil, sharpen tools.	Mulch; clean up dead plants; mound earth around roses; start Paperwhites for the holidays.	Clean up beds; finish planting bulbs; start Paperwhites for the holidays.	Plant spring bulbs; spray broadleaf evergreens with antidesiccant. **In berry:** callicarpa, winterberry.
Pot amaryllis; feed birds; avoid walking on frozen grass.	Clean, oil, sharpen tools; pot amaryllis.	Mulch beds; mound earth around roses; clean, oil, sharpen tools.	Mulch beds; mound earth around roses; clean, oil, sharpen tools.

BULBS: This term refers to plants that grow from bulbs, corms, tubers, and rhizomes. Fall-planted bulbs flower in spring, spring-planted bulbs bloom in summer or autumn.

TURF GRASSES: Most are available as either sod or seed. Their period of dormancy varies from one region to another (see pages 222–223).

BARE-ROOT PLANTS: These are typically deciduous plants (roses, vines, trees, shrubs, and even some perennials) that go dormant in winter and are sold then with no soil around their roots. They're inexpensive, easy to transport or buy through the mail, and adapt easily to most garden soils.

BEDDING PLANTS: These may be annual or perennial flowering plants used for massing in flower beds. They are typically sold in small pots or packs.

SOILS OF THE NORTHEASTERN UNITED STATES

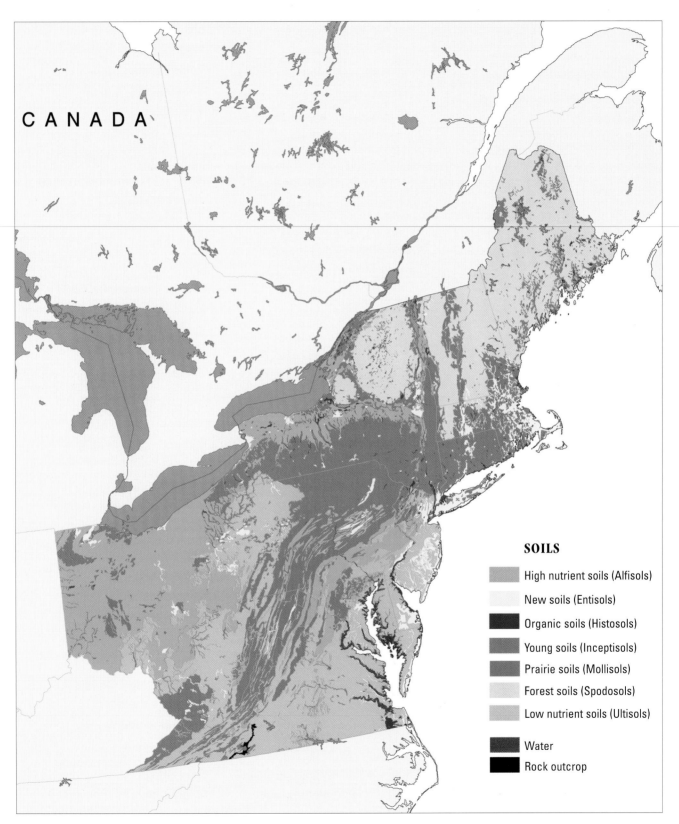

CANADA

SOILS

High nutrient soils (Alfisols)

New soils (Entisols)

Organic soils (Histosols)

Young soils (Inceptisols)

Prairie soils (Mollisols)

Forest soils (Spodosols)

Low nutrient soils (Ultisols)

Water

Rock outcrop

SOILS OF THE NORTHEAST

More than any other factor, your soil will determine which plants will thrive in your garden. Although you can modify your soil to expand the range of plants you will be able to grow, you can never completely change it.

The map at left, prepared by the Soil Survey Staff at the USDA's Natural Resources Conservation Service (NRCS) in Lincoln, Nebraska, shows the various soil types distributed across the Northeast. These include *forest soils*, which have a generally more acid pH, sandy texture, and a high organic subsurface layer; and *young soils*, which often occur on the stony, wooded foot slopes of mountains and have low clay content. *Low-nutrient soils* have an acid pH and are leached of nutrients, while *high-nutrient soils* tend to have a more basic pH, and may be derived from high-lime glacial tills. *New soils* are found on steep slopes, flood plains, and in sandy areas and recently disturbed landscapes such as those in urban areas. In the western part of the region, *prairie soils* are high in organic matter in their surface layers.

The reason experts speak of "modifying soil" rather than changing it is that the provenance of soils is ancient. It has taken eons for the soil in any one place to take on its distinctive characteristics. Glaciers have moved across the land, skimming off the surface in some places and depositing rocks and minerals in others. Rivers have deposited silt, vegetation has grown up and decomposed, and wind and rain have weathered rock. Human civilization has also had an impact on the development of soil character. Rather than try to change a soil that has developed over thousands of years to suit your plant choice, chances are you will be more successful if you choose plants compatible with the existing soil type.

To find out the composition of your particular soil, it's a good idea to have it tested. This service is typically available for a small fee through your local county Cooperative Extension Service.

Determining soil texture

One of the ways garden soils are characterized is by their texture, described as sandy, silt, or clay. Sandy soil has relatively large particles, drains quickly, and usually doesn't hold nutrients well. Silt has intermediate-size particles that fit together more tightly and hold more water and nutrients. Clay has tiny particles that hold nutrients and water well, but little air reaches plant roots. When clay dries, it becomes as hard as brick (which is why it was used to make the many bricks in colonial Williamsburg, Virginia). The perfect garden soil is loam—a light, crumbly mixture of approximately equal parts of sand, silt, and clay, with at least 4 percent organic matter by weight (which can translate to 25 percent by volume). Organic matter does a good job of holding what plants need—water, nutrients, and air—and it is loose enough for roots to penetrate easily. Most gardens don't start out with loam, but you can develop it by adding organic amendments such as compost.

Soil pH

Soil pH is another trait that can influence what can or cannot be grown in your garden. Every plant has a preferred pH, which is measured on an acid-to-alkaline scale of 0 to 14. The preferred pH will be the same as that in the plant's native region, which is why choosing plants native to your area almost always results in successful growth. However, many plants are adaptable enough to grow in soils ranging from pH 5.5 to 7.5. Soils with a pH measurement above 8 or below 5 restrict plant growth, though, because it becomes difficult for plants to absorb nutrients at these levels.

While you can amend soils to alter their pH—for example, make them more alkaline by adding lime or more acid by adding peat or acid fertilizer—it will be only for the short term. If you live in an area with naturally acid or alkaline soil, it will be necessary to repeat the amendment periodically.

It's easier to go with the flow and suit plants to the pH you already have. For example, where there's abundant rain and snow, as in New England, soils tend to be more acid. Mountain laurel *(Kalmia latifolia)*, native azaleas, and rhododendrons grow well in acid soils, which tend to contain plenty of organic matter.

No matter what the general soil type in your area, you may be surprised to find pockets of quite a different type in your backyard. The lime from concrete walks or foundations may leach into adjacent garden beds, raising their pH. Decomposing pine needles or oak leaves tend to lower pH. Experiment with different plants in problem areas. The plants themselves will tell you whether they are in the right soil.

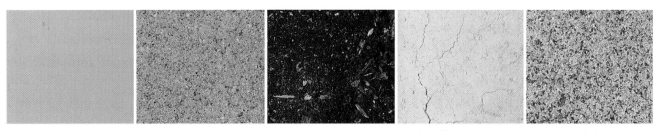

| Clay | Sand | Loam | Clay loam | Sandy loam |

NORTHEASTERN GARDEN STYLES

Northeastern gardens have their roots in the styles of Europe and colonial America. The old-style gardens are generally symmetrical, with geometric designs that reflect the desire to exert control over nature and to have an efficient, easy-to-care-for garden.

Today, however, many gardeners are employing designs that complement the site as it is, rather than opting to clear and grade the land to fulfill the homeowner's vision of an ideal garden plot. Instead of cutting down trees, gardeners are creating woodland gardens filled with shade-loving plants. Those lucky enough to have a stream or pond on their property are fringing the edges with water-loving bog plants. In sunny spots, some gardeners are replacing clipped lawns with meadows or massed plantings of ornamental grasses and native flowers such as black-eyed Susans.

The marrying of nurture with nature often extends to the garden structures. If local stones, rather than imported ones, are used to create hardscapes in the garden, they link the

Clipped hedges, geometric lines, and statuary such as that shown above are hallmarks of the formal garden style.

property beautifully with the surrounding landscape, affording it a sense of place.

Of course, the architecture of your house and your lifestyle are also factors in your choice of garden style. Some types of architecture strongly suggest a particular style of garden. For example, a formal garden would be well suited to a large Georgian home, but less so to a modern or contemporary one. And sometimes the building's materials will have the strongest influence on garden style. A house constructed of natural stone or brick, for example, may call out for an informal or naturalistic garden rather than a precise, formal one.

If you will be gardening at a weekend home—or if you simply want to minimize the time you spend on garden chores—your plantings will need to be practical and low maintenance, as well as beautiful. You might choose native plants that require little in the way of shaping or fertilizing, or consider container gardening—changing plantings as the seasons change, or as the mood strikes you.

A. Water abounds in the Northeast, and adds a marvelous dimension to gardens. Bog plants, including water-loving iris and *Iris laevigata* 'Variegata', with its striped foliage, grace the margins of ponds and streams, while hardy water lilies float on the water surface. In this garden, a stand of Japanese iris (bottom left) overlooks a pond where pale green duckweed intermingles with the lily pads. To add water music to a garden, homeowners incorporate fountains and even waterfalls into their designs.

B. Cottage gardens are characterized by exuberant plantings of flowers, herbs, vegetables, and even small trees and shrubs, all mixed tightly together in a harmonious medley. Vines scrambling around windows and doors or over an arbor are another charming feature of cottage gardens. In this garden, foxgloves, *Crambe cordifolia,* and a myriad of other flowering perennials share the space without one plant competing for center stage. A narrow path gives access to the plants, while the enclosing fence defines the space.

C. Avant-garde designs take traditional garden motifs and present them in a new and often startling way. In this garden, a classic reflecting pond and focal point are given a modern look with the grid pattern in the pergola and the screening hedge of ornamental grasses and bamboo. Instead of a formal bench centered on the view, the homeowner has strung up a hammock,

creating an exciting tension between the old and the new. Jungle-like gardens are a trend that can be adapted to the Northeast with hardy plants that have a tropical look, or with tender tropicals grown as annuals.

D. Woodland gardens are a beautiful solution to landscaping a forested region. Tall trees are pruned up to let in light and open up the space. Understory trees, such as dogwoods and redbud *(Cercis),* and woodland shrubs (rhododendron, mountain laurel) are planted beneath the trees as a second layer. Finally, delicate woodland plants cover the available bare ground. In the Long Island garden shown here, drifts of bleeding heart, accented with primroses and bluebells, make a colorful spring display.

E. Naturalistic or informal gardens look to echo nature with curving lines and plants that blend with the local scenery. While native plants are often incorporated into the design, they are not essential—some gardeners simply want to create a relaxed setting where plants are allowed to grow in their natural forms without excess pruning and shaping. In either case, flowers look best if they are planted in naturalized drifts. Here swaths of colorful flowers, including yellow *Ranunculus repens* 'Flore Pleno', and orange and yellow primroses punctuated by purple Siberian iris light up the gently sloping hillside and emphasize the curving lines of the lawn.

F. Urban gardens are studies in making the most of a limited amount of space. Window boxes and containers provide planting space where most surfaces are paved. On deep, narrow city lots, as shown here, the design focuses on using all the space effectively while disguising the narrow prospect. A seating area at the end of the property draws one into the garden, while diagonal lines and plantings that screen parts of the garden help reduce the tunnel effect. Multiple points of interest, including the ponds and stone slab bridge, also keep the eye moving and entertained.

G. Traditional garden style is hall-marked by plantings of shrubs and small trees tucked up against the house foundation and a lawn dotted with a few specimen trees and perhaps an island bed. To give front gardens a more personal, private feel, some homeowners plant a low hedge or perennial border along the perimeter of the property to create an enclosed garden room without excluding the neighbors. Here a brilliant swath of pink astilbe along the property boundary is echoed by a similar planting near the house, thus separating the garden from the street while at the same time drawing the eye to the house.

H. Colonial gardens hark back to the country's roots and reflect the European heritage of the Pilgrims. Here geometric beds are arranged in a symmetrical pattern, tidily edged with brick, and planted with matching clipped boxwood balls and daffodils. In some cases, the beds may be outlined with low-growing plants or a boxwood parterre. Paths running along-side the beds provide easy access to the garden and add to the pleasing pattern. Often a feature such as a sundial, bird-bath, statue, or woven straw beehive is placed in the middle of the garden as a central focal point.

I. Formal gardens, such as the one shown at left, are characterized by straight lines, geometric shapes, and a symmetrical layout. The overall structure—the bones of the garden—is immediately apparent, delineated by evergreen hedges, parterres, paths, and walls. Focal points, such as a bench, a statue, or a pruned plant, are key features of formal gardens, placed either at the end of a walkway or as the centerpiece of an enclosed "garden room." Most formal designs have a central axis, generally referenced to the house. In a large garden, there may be several axes that link different garden spaces.

THE LANGUAGE OF LANDSCAPE DESIGN

Whatever landscape style you choose, your plan will be most successful if you observe some simple principles of design, which in turn requires that you become familiar with the terms used by landscape professionals. Some of these terms are used throughout the broad field of design. Focal point, symmetry, and asymmetry, for example, are used by architects, interior designers, and graphic artists alike. Other terms, such as berm and borrowed scenery, are specific to landscape architecture. As you go through this book, you'll see these terms used to describe the features of various gardens. And as you follow the process of creating a successful garden, you'll have an easier time communicating with professionals if you use their lingo.

A focal point is an object that draws the eye. This moongate is a double focal point because it functions from both inside and outside the garden fence. In informal gardens such as this one, a focal point may appear anywhere, but its distinctiveness will attract attention and encourage movement toward it. In formal gardens, the focal point is usually at the end of an axis.

Borrowed scenery is a concept adapted from Japanese gardens in which views beyond the borders of the gardens are incorporated into the design to make the garden seem larger. Here the sea and the lighthouse on a point of land are obviously not part of the property, but make it feel more spacious because they are a part of the view.

A. The texture of plants and other elements is enhanced by the play of light and shadow on their surfaces. Textures may be fine or coarse, delicate or bold. Here, a coarse-textured hosta and lacy-textured ferns stand out against the bold texture of the boulder.

B. An axis is the centerline of a view or walk. In this garden, it begins between columnar shrubs next to benches and travels past the sundial to the end of the path. Box hedges and herbs align on either side of the axis, emphasizing its formal pattern. In a less formal garden, the axis may be a visual line between two significant elements.

C. Berms and swales are landscape features, usually man-made, that let you make changes in grade for privacy, for wind control, to deflect runoff, or simply for beauty. A berm is a low mound; a swale is a depression. Here, the position of the azaleas on the top of the berm greatly accentuates their effect.

D. An accent adds variety and depth to a composition or emphasizes a particular spot in the landscape. Here, a dwarf papyrus (*Cyperus* 'Haspan') rises above the flat surface of pool and water lilies, contrasting vertically with its horizontal pool mates.

E. Symmetry exists when matching elements are balanced on either side of a central axis, most commonly seen in formal gardens like this one. Asymmetry occurs when those elements are different; this may be found in both formal and informal gardens.

DESIGN BASICS

Experienced landscape professionals work with several basic design principles; after years of practice, they have absorbed these guidelines so completely that they apply them automatically when designing a garden. Design principles apply at all levels of landscaping, from the most elaborately constructed feature to the simplest of planting compositions.

You can learn a lot by studying gardens that you visit or see in magazines, as well as from those illustrated here and throughout this book. Note the application of the principles explained here and keep them in mind as you flesh out your landscape plan.

In well-designed gardens no one plant, structure, or feature stands out too much, but rather all the parts work together to establish a sense of *unity*. Note how plants or construction materials are used with *repetition* or placed for dramatic *emphasis*. All the elements should be in *proportion* to the rest of the garden and in *scale* with the size of the house, the property, and the people who live there. Also, note how *harmony* is achieved by balancing *simplicity* (in form, texture, and color) and *variety* (in materials and plants).

A. Simplicity reigns in the landscaping of a summer home on the island of Martha's Vineyard. A ground cover of a single plant—native sweet fern *(Comptonia peregrina)*—was added to neaten the edge of woodland. The only other addition was a low retaining wall of local fieldstone.

B. Repetition and emphasis draw a visitor down the path of this Long Island garden. An inviting white arch, repeated in the distance, emphasizes the path's progress through masses of pink astilbes. A delicate color combination of pastel pink roses, astilbes, and variegated plants—dead nettle *(Lamium)* and gardener's garters *(Phalaris)*—repeats throughout the garden.

C. Unity and harmony create a restful oasis in this Maryland garden. A single shade of red in the roses, lounges, and umbrella unifies these elements. Contrasting shapes of decking and river rocks are unified in their earth tones and harmonize with the manicured lawn and boundary planting.

DESIGN TRICKS

In addition to basic design principles, professionals have an array of tricks at their disposal—techniques that help overcome typical challenges or simply make the garden more attractive and livable for occupants and visitors alike.

Some of these ideas are very basic, such as understanding the dimensions of the human body in designing the height and size of structures in the garden. For example, the best ratio for stair risers and treads is based on dimensions that are the most comfortable for people to climb (see page 392). Similarly, pathways are the most comfortable when they are more than 4 feet wide, and built-in seating for decks or benches should be 16 or 17 inches deep.

Other techniques involve altering the perception of space by manipulating materials, colors, and textures; by taking advantage of

Steps with broad treads and low risers meander down this hillside garden, allowing for slow, comfortable movement and time to enjoy the plant delights along the way. A landing marks a change in materials and creates a stopping area.

a hillside or other changes in the garden's elevation; or by placing elements in such a way as to mask the size and shape of a space.

Bring your garden design to life by incorporating some of these tricks. They can be particularly helpful if you are renovating or upgrading an existing landscape or if there is a particular area of your garden with which you have never been especially pleased.

As you develop your ideas, refer to your bubble plan and the basic design principles to make sure you haven't forgotten your original intentions amid the flurry of other considerations. There will be plenty of opportunity to add whimsy and interest to the garden as you choose plants, structures, and accessories to complete your garden's design.

A. Use different levels to enlarge space. Creating distinct, contrasting levels that engender different experiences on each one enlarges the apparent space in this New Jersey garden. Viewed from above, the stone patio seems a distant, inviting destination.

B. Conceal part of the garden. In this Baltimore garden, not all is revealed at first glance. The visitor walks through a series of spaces—some hidden, others only partly visible. This gradual revelation of a series of garden rooms makes the garden seem much larger than it is.

C. Use elements to suggest space. The walls of raised perennial beds, the steps leading up to the arch, and the arch itself all suggest that this area is an entryway to a larger area. However, the arch only suggests additional space beyond: the garden ends at the hemlock hedge.

D. Create a perspective. A large element in the foreground enhances depth. In this rural Virginia garden, twisted tree trunks force perspective and make the background appear deeper than it is.

FROM PLAN

Before drawing up your final plan, you may wish to consult a landscape professional to assist with some element of the design or its implementation. Although many homeowners prefer to tackle the entire design and construction of their garden themselves, others rely on various professionals to help with some of the steps along the way.

The role of the landscape architect

Creating a garden can call for the addition of patios, decks, dining areas, play yards, shade structures, drainage systems, and perhaps a pool or spa. Designing such structures and relating them to a coherent plan for your outdoor environment is where a *landscape architect* comes in.

In addition to determining the most effective use of paving, planting, and lighting, landscape architects are licensed to design exterior structures, solve site problems such as ungainly slopes and poor drainage, and give advice on siting a house and locating service lines, entries, driveways, and parking areas. A landscape architect is familiar with landscape and building materials and services, and can suggest cost-saving options.

For individual services or for a simple consultation, landscape architects usually work at an hourly rate. More commonly, however, a landscape architect provides a complete package, from conceptual plans to construction drawings and supervision of an installation; fees will depend upon the complexity of the project, its length, and the degree of supervision required.

Other professionals

Landscape architects are not the only professionals involved in the creation of fine gardens. The terms *landscape designer* and *garden designer* apply to professionals who may be self-taught or may have the same academic credentials as landscape architects but may lack a state license. The focus of their work is more likely to be residential gardens, and if you are not in need of a complex deck construction or high retaining wall, they may well serve your needs. Their fees may be lower than those of a landscape architect. A landscape designer usually works in conjunction with a licensed *landscape contractor,* an important professional, especially when major construction—beyond the limits of do-it-yourself projects—is involved. A licensed contractor is trained in methods of earthmoving, construction, and planting.

TO REALITY

You may work directly with a contractor, or your landscape architect or designer may select and supervise the contractor. In either scenario, the contractor will submit a bid, either as a lump sum or as a figure based on the estimated time and materials. The latter approach allows more modifications during construction.

Finally, there are professionals who work primarily with plants. *Horticulturists* are trained in the selection and care of garden plants; many have some design training as well. If you are merely looking for plants to complete a design, you can work with a horticulturist. *Arborists* are trained in the care of trees and other woody plants; although not usually able to prepare a design for your garden, they can guide you in the handling of existing trees on your site, identifying healthy ones and those needing pruning, shaping, or removal. Local nurseries may also offer design services and may have talented designers on their staffs; but beware of free design services, as the designer may be obligated to work only with plants and other materials offered by the nursery employer.

Finding the right professional

Begin by identifying the professional services you need. Be realistic in assessing the amount of work you want to do yourself. Collect names from friends and neighbors—even if it means knocking on doors when you spot a good design. Then call each of the designers or contractors whose work you like to set up an interview either at your home (there may be an hourly fee for this) or at their offices (often free). Inquire about the nature of their work, their workload, and their fees. Most important, ask for references—other residential clients whose gardens may give you an idea of the range and quality of the designer's work or the caliber of the contractor's construction. Above all, you must feel a rapport between yourself and the professional; you will be working closely on the design and installation of your garden and need someone with whom you feel comfortable.

When the designer of your choice makes the first visit to your site, use the time wisely. Prepare in advance a list of wishes, needs, and problems that must be dealt with in the design, making sure everyone in the household has had a chance to participate in this step. Give serious consideration to your budget and your time schedule. When a design is complete, meet with the contractor and the designer to make certain that the contractor understands the design and is comfortable working with the materials proposed.

To protect yourself from any surprises, be sure to request a contract from any professionals you hire. This legal agreement should spell out the services to be provided, the schedule to be followed, and the fees to be charged.

Computer-aided Design

Of the several dozen landscape CD-ROMs and software programs currently on the market, most are for Windows-compatible computers and are similar in format: you must first electronically render your site by means of the program's computer-aided drafting tools, and then you must experiment with the placement of structures, plants, and accessories.

Some programs allow you to work from a scanned image of your property; others require you to position shapes to create an electronic design. Some programs can manipulate elements, such as slopes, or provide a three-dimensional view of the design.

Once the plan is accurate and to scale, you can start to place various elements in the digital landscape. Although many programs offer choices such as perennials and annuals, trees and lawns, and even special effects such as lighting, shade patterns, growth rates, or seasonal changes, none offer extensive databases of plants. Some allow you to print out your final plans to show to a landscape or nursery professional.

Landscape programs can be fun to play with, but they can't give you good design advice. The best electronic garden design tool may be a plant encyclopedia that helps you select plants for your garden on the basis of specific search criteria, such as flower color, bloom time, growing conditions, or regional adaptability.

THE DESIGN MOCK-UP

Whether you have completed the design of your garden yourself or have in hand a professionally rendered landscape plan, the next step is to translate the design to your property. If you are having difficulty visualizing the finished garden or can't quite decide on the specifics of certain elements, you may wish to mock up the design on your property. Seeing an approximation of the layout on site in the form of stakes, strings, and markings will help you to determine the exact dimensions necessary for some features, such as decks, terraces, and walks. Even if you feel your paper plan is final, be prepared to make some adjustments as you lay out the design on site until the arrangement of spaces and elements feels just right.

There are a variety of methods for staking out your design. Choose the one that works best for your situation; the choice will be likely to depend on which features predominate—straight lines

A flexible boundary. Where your design is mostly curving lines and free-form shapes, snake a garden hose to lay out the lines to your liking. The hose can be curled at nearly any radius, especially if it is warm. As an alternative, use PVC pipe that you will later use for your irrigation work; the pipe can be softened in the warm sun and gently bent to mark your design.

Colored powder. Limestone or gypsum, common soil amendments, can be used to lay out free-form designs such as the outlines of beds and borders. Powdered chalk of various colors is useful if you have overlapping elements. Measure corner or end points, then dribble a line of powder along the outlines. To make changes, simply turn the powder into the soil and start again.

or curving lines, geometric forms or free forms. Use materials that you have on hand or that can be found at your local hardware store or garden center, such as bamboo or wooden stakes, kite string, clothesline or garden hose, powdered gypsum, lime, or even flour.

Live with your design layout for a few days before making any final decisions or beginning construction. Walk through or sit in your "mock garden" several times to be sure that it provides you with the spaces you need, circulation paths that are comfortable, and garden areas that suit your interests and the time you have to spend maintaining them. When you are ready to begin construction, mock-up techniques will also come in handy. Staking is often used to mark an area of concrete to be poured; colored powder can show the true boundaries of planting areas in borders and beds, and a hose snaked along a pathway can help guide the placement of pavers or bricks.

Strings and stakes. For straight or gently curved lines, mark each corner with a short stake and connect them with strings to outline paving areas, deck construction, pathways, hedges, and planting beds; use taller stakes to mark fences and walls. Then test how they affect traffic circulation through the garden and whether they block any important access points or views.

A mock garden. Tall stakes can stand in for trees or elements like fountains, sculpture, or posts for overhead construction. Large pieces of cardboard on the ground can indicate paving or decks; cardboard can also represent fences and walls. Note any shadows cast by your planned vertical barriers. The neighbors may stare, but you will get a much better sense of how your design is shaping up.

REAL-LIFE DESIGN

It was with a respect for tradition that landscape designer Junghi Epstein approached the renovation of a garden in the historic Old Town district of Alexandria, Virginia. In an area of 18th-century rowhouses and single-family homes set close together, this small patch of yard led from the back of the house out past a carriage house to the street. The garden had been long neglected: the existing shrubs were misshapen boxwoods overgrown with vines; ivy had choked out much of the remaining vegetation (above). The low brick wall along the property line provided scant privacy from the neighboring house, and the few plantings gave little visual relief from expanses of brick. And the narrow brick walkway, Epstein says, "was so uneven, it was dangerous."

The designer first cleaned up the garden, then turned her attention to the walkway. She decided to renovate some of the original brick path, and went about having the bricks lifted, leveled, and reset. She then made an asset of "an awkward transitional space" by expanding the paving and giving it a pattern. With bricks and triangular flagstones, Epstein formed a "four-square garden" pattern, a neoclassical form that complemented the 18th-century home. To further emphasize the four-square design, Epstein placed four identical black cast-iron pots in a symmetrical pattern within the beds. She then gave the garden a modern, asymmetrical twist by filling these pots with a variety of plants.

Adding structural plantings

To create the framework of the garden, Epstein first went to work on the two misshapen boxwoods, pruning, fertilizing, and nursing them back to health. New, large boxwoods were placed on the other side of the walk for balance, and hawthorn trees gave instant screening and a sense of separation from the neighboring house. A newly planted hedge not only provided a backdrop to the perennial border, it also helped balance the relationship between the plantings and the house. "On the vertical plane," says Epstein, "the amount of brick was overwhelming. We needed something at the level of the hedge. It's like a chair rail."

A–B. Once vines and weeds were removed and ivy cleared from some beds and severely cut back in others, the structure of the garden emerged **(A).** The boxwoods were nursed back to health, and hawthorn trees and a cutleaf Japanese maple in a cast-iron pot provided vertical elements. Perennials, including *Sedum* 'Autumn Joy', *Hosta* × 'Golden Tiara', and fritillaria, filled in the border.

C. The garden's original brick path was lifted, leveled, and reset. To provide a focal point in the walkway and a stopping area for visitors to enjoy the plantings, Epstein created a four-square pattern using bricks and flagstone. Each corner of the pattern is anchored with a black cast-iron pot; three contain a mixture of 'Goldflame' spirea, apricot pansies, common sage, and bird's-foot ivy, while the fourth holds a cutleaf Japanese maple, tulips, and yellow creeping Jenny.

D–E. Designing plantings that would screen views of the neighboring house **(D)** was a priority for Epstein. Ivy and old-fashioned climbing rose cloak the top of the wall, and fast-growing hawthorn trees were planted at intervals along the wall to help provide privacy. New littleleaf box *(Buxus microphylla)* was planted opposite the rejuvenated shrubs for balance, and to create what Epstein calls a "box court" **(E, foreground).** 'Crown Rose' pansies echo the red of the climbing rose.

GARDENS OF THE NORTHEAST

The Northeast sets the stage for our gardens. Its mountains and plateaus, plains and seacoasts supply the backdrops for plantings—and increasingly they define the types of gardens homeowners plant.

Traditionally, whatever work a gardener had to do to achieve his or her vision for a garden was done. But as more and more gardeners recognize the futility of continually challenging the conditions of a site—be it soil studded with rocks in Maine, or the wind that whips along the coast in Connecticut or Delaware, or a narrow, shady row-house backyard—landscape designers and homeowners alike are turning to nature for inspiration. As a result, many of today's gardens echo or blend into the surroundings and reflect their region's heritage. Supremely adapted to the land and the climate that nurtures them, they touch the land lightly.

THE ROCKY NORTH

I use local stone in my garden designs to link the house to the surrounding woods and meadows, and to keep it in harmony with the larger landscape.

—Gordon Hayward, Putney, Vermont

Gardeners in the rocky North know a thing or two about rocks: the ground is studded with stones like nuts in a fruitcake. Prying the rocks out of the soil has bent and broken many a shovel and gardening fork, and explains those long stone walls snaking over the countryside.

And yet rocks are what give northeastern gardens their special beauty. Those rock walls and pathways, and the eye-catching boulders placed at a focal point all convey an air of permanence and age, of being linked to the landscape. A blue-gray shale outcrop, cracked and worn smooth by time, rises majestically from the earth like a whale from the sea. A skim of soil has collected on its top, and from it sprout ferns and wild columbine, and a tiny maple sapling. It is a garden unto itself.

How did the Northeast become so well endowed with rock? Nearly every state in the Northeast and eastern Canada contains part of the Appalachian Mountain range, which, with its transverse ranges, stretches 1,200 miles from Quebec to central Alabama. These are among the oldest mountains on earth. They are made of layers of hard, crystalline rock like granite and softer sedimentary rock, folded and lifted over millions of years. Then for 2 million years—up until about 10,000 years ago—shifting sheets of glacial ice 1,000 to 2,000 feet thick raked the mountain surface, grinding away the edges, heaving rocks, and scraping soil away. The receding glaciers gouged out a system of deep lakes and ravines, and deposited sheets of sand and gravel dragged from farther north.

All that geological churning and the activity of the subsequent 10,000 years have left the northernmost northeast region with a thin layer of topsoil over hard rock. Spruces and firs, which grow without taproots and can survive the bitter cold, cling to the shallow footing. From Maine to Connecticut, the coast is strewn with exposed chunks of lichen- and seaweed-covered granite, the bane of merchant ships. New Hampshire, the Granite State, has tall mountains that "curl up in a coil," in the words of poet Robert Frost.

Farther south, and in the central Northeast, the mountains are clothed in one of the largest deciduous broadleaf forests in the world. Here the sugar maple is king, attended by oaks, basswood, birch, and pine; it gives way farther south to tulip poplar,

sweet gum, and magnolia. Rain falls regularly all year, and in winter the snow is deep. In autumn the hills and mountains take flame as the temperatures drop below 45 degrees Fahrenheit. Maples, oaks, dogwoods, sumacs, and sourwood turn scarlet red to burgundy and orange, as do garden shrubs like the aptly named burning bush *(Euonymus alatus)*, viburnums, oakleaf hydrangea, certain deciduous rhododendrons, and vines such as Virginia creeper and poison ivy. Fields of blueberries and cranberries become vermilion. Poplars and birches brighten to golden yellow, their white trunks stark in contrast with their brilliant neighbors. Even some evergreens deepen to bronze or purplish burgundy.

As autumn's fiery colors sputter and the deep snows of winter cover the fallen leaves, the rocky North becomes a tone poem of white and gray. But there are splashes of color in the garden: the flashing red of a cardinal at a feeder, the red and orange dots of rose hips and crabapples, the metallic mahogany bark of a paperback cherry tree, the bright canes of yellowtwig dogwood *(Cornus sericea* 'Flaviramea'). The rocky North's long winter holds a hint of a vibrant spring to come.

A FREE-FORM FLOWER GARDEN
Nestled in the hills

Where corn once grew at Wisdom Farm in Litchfield County, Connecticut, masses of colorful blossoms now frame the view. The owner began gardening the land by planting tomatoes, zucchini, and Brussels sprouts—with just a sprinkling of flowers among them. Soon her passion for dreamy color combinations took over, and she was mixing delphiniums in purple, blue, and white with silvery red cabbage and orange nasturtiums.

And so the vegetables have ceded ground to grasses, flowering shrubs, rows of nodding sunflowers, and other self-sowing annuals and perennials that scramble for space. Such a

freestyle garden can be full of surprises. For instance, obedient plant *(Physostegia)* appears where the yarrow had once been, while the yarrow has hopped into the pathway.

The flower beds have been carved into the contours of the hillside surrounding the house. "I personally dug out everything, listening for the 'plink, plink' of rock against shovel," the owner remembers. Since stone is part of the landscape, it is also part of the design. Refurbished stone walls run throughout the property and enclose a pebble garden; slabs of granite hold up its raised beds and edge a lap pool surrounded by thick, irregular flagstones.

LEFT Terraced flower beds trace straight lines up the hillside, giving a sense of geometry to the lush growth spilling over their edges. Tall, frost-tender cannas, yellow black-eyed Susans and sunflowers, and a dominant grassy hummock of variegated feather grass *(Miscanthus sinensis)* flourish in the garden.

BELOW The house's high vantage permits a visitor on the porch to take in an abundance of contrasting colors and textures, including hostas, short grasses, and flower-filled planters. Beyond an expanse of lawn, a neighbor's cornfield recalls the farm's first purpose.

TOP LEFT In early fall, cosmos in varying shades of pink and rosy red obedient plant *(Physostegia virginiana)* run riot in this vegetable garden-turned-cutting garden. A rustic trellis laced with clematis on one side frames a misty view of trees beginning to change into fall colors.

INSET LEFT A cold-hardy panicle hydrangea *(Hydrangea paniculata)* is covered with showy white flowers, while blooming yellow and pink daylilies rise up to conceal its bare reddish brown stems.

BOUNTIFUL HARVEST
From a weekend retreat

A love of gardening and a weekend retreat in the foothills of the Berkshires in Millbrook, New York, presented gardeners Belinda and Stephen Kaye with a challenge: designing a bountiful kitchen garden that could survive on its own during the week. They chose a location conveniently close to the kitchen door—moving the driveway in the process—and brought in loads of good topsoil. A brick and fieldstone pathway divides the plot, which is hedged in by a row of herbaceous peonies on one side and by hardy *Rosa rugosa* on the other.

The Kayes' strategy is to plant as densely as possible to suppress infiltrating weeds. To control pests and diseases, they rotate crops each year, putting zucchini in the lettuce patch and broccoli where tomatoes grew. A good dose of organic fertilizer in spring and regular applications of compost during the growing season supply extra nutrients. The garden has been so successful that Stephen has branched out with a plot of his own, from which he supplies restaurants with specialty vegetables and 25 varieties of gourmet potatoes.

LEFT The path to a walk-through potting shed at the edge of the garden is flanked by a towering collection of ornamental plants, vegetables, and herbs. Scarlet-leaved *Amaranthus tricolor* 'Hopi Red Dye' at right, Mexican sunflowers, black-eyed Susans, and a purplish castor bean plant at left supply color; edibles include red cabbage and corn.

ABOVE As a bonus, the Kayes' *Rosa rugosa* produces decorative orange hips that make excellent jelly.

MONET IN MONTREAL
Romantic abundance

Henriette Miral, a doctor and former painter, moved to the farm country just south of Montreal more than 20 years ago to raise horses. But when a 1990 accident curtailed her riding, she turned her energies to planting a 7-acre garden on her property. She enlarged the existing pond, enriched the clay soil, and turned the hayfield surrounding the pond into an impressionist's canvas. "This garden is meant to be seen as a painting, not stroke by stroke, but from a distance," Miral says. For that she depends on large beds of roses, astilbes, and wildflowers to supply great swaths of color, unifying the effect with a border of plants such as *Sedum spectabile* 'Brilliant'.

Montreal's northern latitude means long growing days from May to September and gardens that are remarkably lush. But "we don't really have spring," explains Miral. "The last frost is at the end of May, and then it's 80 degrees F." However, the deep snow cover and the several hundred trees she has planted mitigate some of the effect of the cold.

LEFT Bobbing at the water's edge, a retired sailboat finds new life as a planter filled with pink geraniums, while arrowhead (*Sagittaria sagittifolia* 'Flore Pleno') and papyrus thrive along the marshy shoreline. Miral overwinters the tender papyrus in a bucket in her greenhouse.

ABOVE An arched wooden bridge, its reflection in the pond broken by water lilies, leads to an island and gazebo. The former hayfield surrounding the pond is now home to roses—including medium pink 'Morden Centennial' and apricot pink 'Leander'—feathery pink astilbe, rough yellow heliopsis (*Heliopsis scabra*), and marguerites (*Anthemis tinctoria*).

ABOVE LEFT The complementary colors of blue great bellflowers (*Campanula lactiflora* 'Prichard's Variety') and yellow marguerites *(Anthemis tinctoria)* seem to vibrate in proximity to each other. During Canada's short but hot, dry summers, they bloom profusely with little attention.

LEFT The showy white flowers of a 12-foot-wide *Hydrangea arborescens* 'Annabelle' crowd the edge of a stream flowing near a corner of Henriette Miral's house. The light purple globes of star-of-Persia *(Allium christophii)* and the red blossoms of the peony 'Sarah Bernhardt' grow along the other shore, which is lined with a stone retaining wall. Miral built the wall to prevent the stream sides from washing out during the spring thaw.

LEFT Bellflowers and marguerites grow on the far bank of the pond, in the field below the barn that once housed Miral's horses. In the foreground, the pink rose 'John Davis', one of the cold-hardy Explorer roses developed in Canada, blooms well in the partial shade of a willow tree. Nearby is the 3-foot salmon pink *Astilbe* 'Erica'.

BELOW The airy white blooms of goat's beard *(Aruncus dioicus)* frame a wooden bench overlooking the pond, their feather-duster shape echoed by similarly flowered pink 'Rheinland' astilbes. Aromatic white thyme and fragrant valerian *(Valeriana officinalis)* at right perfume the air.

A RUSTIC GARDEN
Hewn from stone

Big native rocks and a collection of plants "that don't call undue attention by being rare" make this garden look right at home, according to landscape designer Gordon Hayward. Formerly a weekend "country camp" near Putney, Vermont, this garden is a collaboration between Hayward and his clients, sculptor Gerry Prozzo and his wife, children's book illustrator Cyndy Szekeras. Pathways and low walls of native bluestone, and focal points of massive eye-catching pieces of bedrock and mica schist mark its framework.

Using stones of such large scale did not come naturally to Hayward. "But Gerry got into the larger shapes and the use of stone in the garden. He and I and a backhoe operator found them in the woods and dragged them back, arranging them in groups of three or five."

But rocks alone do not make a garden. Three dump-truck loads of topsoil were brought in to create a large curved berm, enclosing a sitting area looking out toward the woods. White birches create dappled shade for a host of ferns, hostas, and mosses.

FACING PAGE Large bluestone slabs lead to Gerry Prozzo's sculpture studio; lavender-flowering catmint (*Nepeta* 'Six Hills Giant') and yellow-blooming stonecrop line the path.

TOP LEFT A split-rail fence stands amid daisies, blue cornflowers, and silvery lamb's ear (*Stachys byzantina*). In the distance, graceful trunks of whitespire birch rise above an understory of *Hosta sieboldiana* 'Elegans'.

TOP RIGHT Maroon-leafed barberry billows over a massive rock at the entrance to the driveway. Blue-green creeping juniper (*Juniperus horizontalis* 'Hughes') contrasts with yellow-flowering stonecrop.

LEFT These stepping-stones have been carefully grouted with moss gathered in clumps from the woods and with mosslike Corsican pearlwort (*Sagina subulata),* which bears tiny translucent white flowers in spring.

LIVING THE GOOD LIFE
On a Maine farm

When Scott and Helen Nearing published their book *Living the Good Life* in 1954, they inspired generations of "back-to-the-landers" intent on giving up the rat race and becoming self-sustaining farmers. That included photographer Lynn Karlin and her filmmaker husband Stanley Joseph, who in June 1980 bought the Nearings' old farm on Penobscot Bay in Harborside, Maine.

True to their goal of self-sufficiency, the couple grew what they needed on the property, or collected it nearby. Thus the garden's sturdy beauty came of practicality and utility. For instance, a row of willows that had been severely pruned to generate long flexible twigs for baskets would develop a hazy halo of yellow twigs in early spring. The 5-foot-high stone wall around the vegetable garden—a legacy of the Nearings that took them 14 years to build—is a backdrop for a long perennial border and a solid anchor for the froth of white apple blossoms that covers the orchard in spring. Flowers for drying, such as artemisia, nigella, celosia, larkspur, and salvia, are grown in a separate, quarter-acre upper garden. Lynn and Stanley also repaired the barn and the house, expanded the pond, and added a sod-roofed sauna for warming their bones during Maine's 7-month-long winter.

TOP LEFT Foxgloves *(Digitalis purpurea)* rise above the 5-foot-high wall surrounding the vegetable garden. In Maine, foxgloves are hardy biennials that do best in moist, acid soil, where they can reach impressive heights.

ABOVE A long, deep perennial border runs the length of the garden wall, its bloom period peaking in mid-July. The pink dahlias and phlox, purple salvias and delphiniums, and orange and yellow daisylike rudbeckias will eventually find their way into flower arrangements or dried wreaths.

RIGHT A garden cart loaded with buckets of sunflowers from the garden and Queen Anne's lace from a lower field stands ready for delivery to local businesses. By mid-July, the pink, purple, and white petunias in the window boxes reach a height of 2 feet, creating a fragrant curtain that wafts scent into the house through open windows.

HOT COLORS
For the cool Northeast

At first, Elizabeth Sheldon planted her perennial garden in Lansing, New York, "in muted, fancy, refined colors"—blues and yellows, lavender, lime green, rose, white, and silver. Such colors glow more brightly under the gray and filtered skies of the north; brighter hues, she believed, would look garish.

But then, "I ran amok and decided I wanted something stronger," she says. So as not to disturb the serenity of the rest of the garden, Sheldon sequestered her exercise in tropical tints within a small, square formal garden enclosed by a 5-foot-high cedar fence. A visitor entering through the gate of this garden is unprepared for its exhilarating brilliance.

Sheldon believes that relentless exposure to hot colors can be wearying. And so she developed a system to keep the effect from becoming overwhelming: she chose colors that are closely related on the color wheel. Yellows, oranges, and reds, for example, harmonize because they appear next to each other on the wheel. Green or blue serve to cool the combination down. Foliage plants in silver add a bright note; in dark maroon they add depth.

ABOVE The yellow centers of crimson 'Red Riding Hood' dahlias visually connect with the calendula growing in the foreground. Contrasting blue *Salvia* 'Victoria' complements the yellow, while the dahlias' dark foliage anchors the composition.

RIGHT A brick path bisects Elizabeth Sheldon's small enclosed "secret garden" of hotly hued plants. Composed mostly of annuals such as yellow calendulas and 'Disco Orange' marigolds, the mix is punctuated with tubers such as red 'Japanese Bishop' dahlias, perennials that include red and yellow daylilies and 'Red Plume' gaillardia, and foliage plants such as the nearly black, velvety-leaved purple perilla (*Perilla frutescens*).

THE COASTAL NORTHEAST

Gardening by the sea is a world of extremes. Plants exposed to strong winds must be chosen with great care. Turn the corner, and plants protected by buildings or hedges are in a special world—milder climate, longer growing season—which produces amazing growth.
— Nancy DuBrule, Northford, Connecticut

From the rocky shoreline of northern Maine south to the sandy Virginia beaches, the northeast coastline is a beautiful and varied slice of the region. With the many bays, wide river mouths, inlets, and islands—and, of course, the Atlantic Ocean—there are thousands of miles of shore, some of it wild and rugged with towering cliffs, and other spots that seem comparatively tame—but all of it shaped by the dominant elements of wind and water.

Tempered by the ocean, seaside temperatures stay relatively mild. Spring comes later along the coast than inland, but there is less risk of flowers being damaged by late frosts. And because it takes time for the huge water mass to turn cold, the coastal growing season stretches late into autumn.

Despite the temperate climate, natural beauty, and spectacular water views, gardening along the coast can be a challenge. Unless the property is in a protected site, gardeners face salt-laden air, near-constant breezes, and the possibility of damaging storms.

The wind is a natural sculptor, pruning trees and shaping their growth; it is not uncommon to see a tree with a wedged crown angled in the direction of the prevailing wind. As a result of constant buffeting, seacoast plants tend to be shorter and stockier than their inland counterparts.

Within a coastal garden there are three main planting zones, determined by proximity to the sea. The first zone is immediately next to the shore, where wind and salt spray are dominant features and the soil itself is salty. Here gardeners choose trees and shrubs that can that tolerate the rigorous conditions and that also work as screens and windbreaks—scrub oaks, sycamore maples, rugosa roses, black locust, Norway spruce, cotoneaster, and English yew, to name a few. Some flowers, including lupine, evening primrose, Russian sage, sedum, and rock cress *(Arabis)*, also do well in the wind and salt.

The sturdy plants in the first zone act as a buffer, creating a more protected microclimate for plants growing in the second zone. In this intermediate territory, lupines, nasturtiums, and annual geraniums *(Pelargonium)* thrive in the sandy soil and cool night temperatures typical of the northeastern coast. Roses also enjoy these conditions, although they do best with an annual autumn application of well-rotted manure or compost to boost soil fertility.

Zone three is well back from the water and relatively free of the harsh shorefront conditions. Here gardeners can grow anything suitable to the local climate zone. Here also, skillful gardeners often create protected microclimates where they enjoy the challenge of pushing the limits on plant hardiness, growing something that is considered too tender for the typical winter temperatures.

Many coastal gardeners use ornamental grasses extensively in their designs. This diverse family of plants, ranging from tidy, low-growing specimens that are suitable for edging to monumental grasses that grow in large clumps 6 feet high or taller, is ideal for merging a cultivated garden near the house with the native flora. Ornamental grasses provide interest for most of the year, beginning with the fresh new growth in spring that matures into the full forms of summer, followed by the flower panicles in autumn that persist through most of the winter. Sea breezes—as well as gusty winds—add life to the grasses, making them sway and rustle as if in a choreographed dance.

A SEASIDE COTTAGE GARDEN
Summer paradise

E namored of English cottage gardens, the owners of this seaside property wanted a similar look for their weekend residence on Long Island Sound in Connecticut. They also wanted the garden to be low maintenance so they could look after it on evenings and weekends without extra help.

They enlisted the help of garden designer Nancy DuBrule. In keeping with the cottage-garden tradition, DuBrule designed a white arched arbor set in a picket fence to give the garden structure and a focal point. She filled the beds with salt-tolerant perennial plants such as hydrangea, climbing vines, 'New Dawn', 'Rhonda', and 'Viking Queen' roses, *Centranthus*, *Perovskia*, bellflowers, and phlox, keeping to a pink, lavender, blue, and white color theme. In the early years, annuals and quick-growing perennials ably filled the gaps to create an instant effect.

To protect the garden from the ravages of offshore wind and to screen the property from a nearby house, DuBrule also designed a berm. This she planted with ornamental grasses and 'The Fairy' roses.

LEFT Standing like a stately sentinel on the berm, *Miscanthus sinensis* 'Gracillimus' is comfortable in salty breezes, as is the delicate-looking 'The Fairy' rose. This vigorous polyantha rose flowers from early summer until autumn.

ABOVE Framing the view of the garden and sea beyond, the rose-covered arbor is a classic feature in a traditional cottage garden. Pink 'New Dawn' and 'Rhonda' roses add to the lush floral planting.

RIGHT Digging in copious amounts of organic amendments created the rich soil that supports this dense plant population. Here purple sweet rocket *(Hesperis matronalis)*, blue flax *(Linum perenne)*, and pink foxglove *(Digitalis purpurea)*, backed by 'New Dawn' roses, share close quarters.

A DISPLAY GARDEN
Mixing home and work

Carol Mercer, a flower arranger and garden designer by trade, has created a personal haven and a professional laboratory in her East Hampton, New York, garden. The garden is open to clients and tours, and is a testing ground for the hardiness of plants raised from the seeds she imports from Germany, England, and Ireland.

Just two blocks from the sea, the garden has to surmount three obstacles: salt-laden air, wind, and sandy soil. The soil problem is solved with annual spring applications of cow manure and an autumn mulch of washed seaweed. This healthy mix keeps the fenced cutting garden and perennial border alongside the swimming pool growing happily.

The moist soil near the freshwater pond is ideal for the iris Mercer cultivates in abundance, as well as many of the large-leafed tropicals that are currently so popular. Each fall, the canna and calla lily bulbs are dug up and overwintered. Of her vision for the garden Mercer explains, "There is a rhythm and pattern of shades of green achieved by how I planted around the pond."

ABOVE Planted with a host of annuals and perennials, including artemisia for its silver foliage, the cutting garden is an essential source of supplies for Mercer's flower-arranging business.

LEFT Backed by a deep green hedge of arborvitae, the perennial border spills over onto the swimming-pool decking, blurring the lines between garden and hardscape. Clematis chosen for their different bloom times scramble up the arborvitae.

FAR LEFT Fringing the freshwater pond is Mercer's large iris collection, which includes Japanese iris *(Iris ensata)* and Siberian iris *(I. sibirica)*. Tender *Gunnera* is protected by building a shelter around it in winter.

RIGHT Bark paths crisscross the cutting garden, giving easy access to the flowers for maintenance or to cut them. The picket fence sets the garden apart, signaling that it has a special function.

AN ACCIDENTAL GARDEN
Extends the house

Constance Umberger's Nantucket garden is a series of rooms that radiate out from the house, each created to fill a need. "I never had a plan," admitted Umberger. "It grew topsy-turvy."

The first major project began as a shelter from the wind and sun. Umberger enclosed an area near the house with a fence, put in an arbor, and covered it with grape and honeysuckle. Today, the Green Garden, as she calls it, is a medley of boxwood and other foliage plants.

LEFT The "Green Garden" is a sheltered place to sit, protected from the wind and burning sun. Woolly thyme creeps among the paving bricks, and honeysuckle and grapes clamber over the arbor.

LEFT The double perennial border grew out of a need for somewhere to put the excess plants from other parts of the garden. Twelve feet deep, it is planted with hot colors near the house and cool colors on the opposite side.

INSET OPPOSITE PAGE 'Enchantment' lilies and yarrow—both vigorous growers—share space in the hot-colored side of the long perennial border, which runs down the slope below the house.

BELOW The arched gateway in the hedge marks the entrance to the house and garden, framing an enticing view of flowers and shrubs. The path of old bricks leads to several garden rooms beyond.

Next she built a pergola near the house to provide a place to eat outdoors. A gift of old bricks became a plant-lined path linking the Green Garden and the pergola. As Umberger began dividing and propagating plants, she needed to place the leftovers. The result: a double perennial border, each side 12 feet deep and 90 feet long.

And so the garden evolved. "I think people like this garden," reflected Umberger, "because it's controlled chaos. It represents what a person can do who knows a little about gardening and doesn't have a lot of money."

Natural Forms
Using local materials

W hen the Geyelins bought their house, "the property was a moonscape," says Sherry Geyelin of her coastal Maine home. "It was an exposed, windy site, and you could barely see the water because of all the trees." She and her husband, Philip, called in designer Gwen Dolliver to help, and gave her a free hand except for one request: Philip wanted at least a little lawn.

Dead and dying trees along the shore were removed, and the remaining trees were limbed up to reveal the spectacular sea view. Dolliver used local stones to create a terraced rockery, which she planted with hardy perennials and shrubs that could withstand the storms that howl off the coast. "It was trial and error," remembers Sherry. "Some plants didn't last."

The result was a garden with a wild, natural feel to it, with the oval lawn at the bottom of the sloping garden representing a mild concession to traditional landscaping. With its irregular edge marked with local stone, it is an emerald pool echoing the sea beyond.

ABOVE Limbed-up spruces growing amidst wild rugosa roses frame the water view. As it would in the wild, the native ground cover mountain cranberry grows on the protected, leeward side of the pine tree to the left in the lawn.

ABOVE RIGHT Discarded floats from lobster pots, collected off the shore by the grandchildren, hang from one of the spruce trees— becoming both garden art and a tribute to Maine's trade in the delicious crustaceans.

LEFT A meadow of lilies and naturalized red fescue *(Festuca rubra)* transitions into the mixed forest of spruce and fir. The setting sun lights up the fescue, which is planted to resemble a flowing stream.

RIGHT Indigenous stones arranged in natural drifts provide the structure to the sloping rock garden, which is planted with sturdy plants such as heather, aster, perennial poppy, catmint, sedum, cotoneaster, and winterberry.

NATURE AND NURTURE
Blending with the native landscape

Set at the tip of a point reaching out into the sea in Little Compton, Rhode Island, the Brayton home is surrounded by fields and groves of native cedar and spruce trees. With the exception of a few formal areas near the house, the garden is designed to blend seamlessly with the surrounding countryside, successfully merging the nurtured garden with the native vegetation.

Ornamental grasses, daylilies, heaths, and heathers are the cultivated plants, chosen for their willing acceptance of the seaside growing conditions as well as their ability to marry with the native flora. Trees and shrubs such as

oakleaf hydrangea and blue spruce add a sense of mass and structure to the design.

From the house and garden there are views of the sea, as well as of a brackish pond surrounded by native grasses, flowers, and shrubs, including rugosa roses, Queen Anne's lace, tansy, thistle, and tiger lily. "We mow some of the native area for the grandchildren because they were getting ticks," explains Ellen Brayton, "but we leave the rest natural. We can look out and for more than a mile see nothing but green and water."

FAR LEFT Leading the eye to the pond and sea, the bluestone path is bordered on the left by a collection of heathers, heaths, germander, lavender, and an edge of golden thyme. On the right are grasses, daylilies, and a sedum planted there by birds dropping seeds.

LEFT Looking like a friendly hedgehog or porcupine nestled among the foliage of other perennials, this mounding lavender plant is a feature in the perennial border along the drive.

BELOW Old curbstones set on their sides serve as steps leading from a lower patio to the swimming pool. By late summer the *Pennisetum* grass at the bottom of the steps and the *Miscanthus* at the top arch over the steps.

BAY-FRONT GARDEN
A room with a view

Set on a ridge high above Penobscot Bay in Maine, the Keller garden offers a panoramic water view. To maximize the enjoyment of the setting, Marie Keller has created a series of patios and decks around the house. These are furnished with comfortable chairs so that it is always possible to find a sunny spot to sit and relax. "We migrate to the warmest area," she says.

The garden offers more than just places to sit. Stone steps lead down to a terrace overlooking the bay. Here, in the sheltered microclimate, Keller has a cutting garden, a shade border, and a rose garden. "I support my garden habit by doing gardens for other people," explains Keller, "so I try things out here first. When I find something that grows well, I can use it in my designs for others." Her recent plant successes include *Rodgersia* and the dramatic, 4-foot tall *Verbena bonariensis,* a tender perennial in Maine that Keller grows as an annual.

TOP FAR LEFT A retaining wall of railroad ties encloses the brick patio. Low plantings of heather, cotoneaster, juniper, and other small shrubs add greenery without blocking the water view. Offshore breezes keep the wind sculpture, called Sails, alive with movement.

BOTTOM FAR LEFT A large birdhouse and potted plants make a focal point of a corner of the brick patio.

LEFT In the one shady part of the garden, Keller planted a border of *Rhododendron* 'Roseum Elegans' fronted by azaleas. The Adirondack chair is a comfortable perch from which to enjoy the dramatic spring display.

BELOW Facing the water, the deck is a fine place to enjoy the view while dining alfresco. Patios and decks wrap around the house so there is always a warm spot to sit outside, whatever the time of day or year.

OPPOSITES ATTRACT
Combining garden styles

Built into a slope that meets the water's edge in a protected cove of Spa Creek, the Pensky garden in Annapolis, Maryland, satisfies the owners' desire for a romantic English garden adapted to the Annapolis waterfront.

The property was a blank slate, and the goal of the Penskys and their designer, Gay Crowther, was to make the house and garden look as if they had always been there. The added challenge was to create a smooth transition from the traditional garden plants and designs near the house to a naturalistic garden area at the waterfront.

Crowther planted beds surrounding the house with a lush profusion of roses and perennials, choosing varieties that would create a soft, English look and perform well in the hot, humid summers. The climbing 'New Dawn' rose was a prime choice, as were asters and sedum. Closer to the water, the garden becomes wilder, with plantings of ornamental grasses, *Caryopteris,* and Joe-Pye weed. But a sense of design is still evident: the border of grasses, for example, leads the eye to the view of sailboats bobbing on the water in the distance.

LEFT Long panicles of Japanese wisteria *(Wisteria floribunda)* blossoms drop down through the arbor, creating a fragrant bower for alfresco meals. For convenience, this patio is located near the kitchen.

OPPOSITE PAGE Tightly planted together, the lavender-flowered *Aster × frikartii, Sedum* 'Autumn Joy' (not yet with its autumn blush), and profusely blooming roses combine harmoniously near the house.

RIGHT As the garden moves further from the house and toward the cove, *Caryopteris* and ornamental grasses, including *Miscanthus* and *Pennisetum*, merge well with the waterfront.

NATURE'S ABUNDANCE
A glorious excess

Lucie Carlin hated to pull out any plant, and she was always fitting more flowers into the beds of her quarter-acre garden overlooking a bay on Long Island Sound. The result is an exuberant cottage garden rich with floral interest from early spring until late autumn. Carlin planted with a painterly eye, creating a blue, pale pink, and white color scheme with occasional sparks of yellow, orange, or red flowers to accent the soft tones.

'Simplicity' roses are the signature flower in the garden, but mixed democratically with the "Queen of Flowers" are "weeds" with pretty blooms, including yarrow, Queen Anne's lace, celandine poppy, and red campion *(Silene dioica)*. Other cottage-garden plants that are aggressive enough to compete in the tight spaces allowed them include Japanese anemone, Oriental poppies, daylilies, lamb's ears, and perennial sunflower *(Helianthus)*.

Applying a top dressing of composted manure each spring keeps the crowded beds well fed. Although the garden is near the water, a buffer of lilacs and spirea protects the plants from the brunt of the salty spray.

LEFT This showstopper border facing the road screens the view of the house for a little privacy and attracts appreciative attention from passers-by. In June it is bright with 'Simplicity' roses, iris, and violas.

OPPOSITE PAGE One of more than 50 roses growing in the quarter-acre cottage garden, this ancient floribunda produces profuse sprays of flowers next to the house that was once an 18th-century fisherman's shack.

LEFT The prolific Oriental poppies give a magnificent 2- to 3-week floral display in June. Each year these tenacious plants have to be thinned to make room for other, later-blooming perennials.

RIGHT Garden designer Nancy DuBrule named this 50-year-old chrysanthemum growing in the Carlin garden 'Lucie's Pink Daisy' after Lucie Carlin. It is now being propagated commercially.

HUMOROUS INTENT
Having fun with color

When asked about the unexpected, bold colors he uses in his garden, artist Robert Dash explains, "Around here, salt and damp will spoil white paint almost immediately. I had lots of almost-empty cans of colored paint. One day I decided to use them in the garden. I love strong color."

The 2-acre garden is planted in the rich Bridgehampton loam found on the alluvial outwash plains of Sagaponack, New York. Since Dash acquired the property in 1967, he has created a series of distinct garden rooms, all linked by the unexpected use of color. Quoting the painter Manet—"The very color of the air is violet"—Dash explains his color choices. "I use a lot of mauve in the garden," he says. "The yellow paint echoes the foliage in spring and autumn, and keeps the garden vibrant in winter."

Paradoxically, dividing the space makes the garden feel bigger than it is. Paths loop back on themselves, and trees and shrubs screen parts of the garden so there is constant delight and surprise as new vistas and scenes open to the visitor. "Each garden room," says Dash, "is an idea point for a small garden."

FAR LEFT Inspired by the Tudor knot gardens of the 16th century, this intricate design is composed of two kinds of boxwood: 'Suffruticosa' and 'Vardar Valley'. Crushed white marble and broken white dishes fill the center knots; broken clay pots, bricks, and reddish setts provide the contrasting color.

LEFT Even on the grayest winter days this garden has sunny yellow moments. The constrained shape of the pruned Alberta spruce near the door is in amusing contrast to the unclipped 'Dortmund' rose and the shrublike *Clematis heracleifolia* at the right.

ABOVE "Such a lovely plant doesn't deserve a name like *Schizophragma hydrangeoides*," says Dash of the vine that scrambles over the old barn. Its common name, Japanese hydrangea vine, is easier to remember. A native woodland fern has worked its way through the ramp slats.

ABOVE A golden arch punctuates this paved walkway, drawing the eye further into the garden. The arch repeats the color and shape of the doorway pictured on pages 88–89, which is at the opposite end of the path.

TOP RIGHT Cantilevered over the pond, this Japanese-style shelter provides a close-up view of the native American water lilies. The red footstool centered on the red ovals was made of Lloyd Loom—a distinctive, durable wicker—in the latter part of the 19th-century.

BOTTOM RIGHT The classic Chippendale-style gazebo is given an unexpected tweak. The bluish green foliage of the three Irish junipers (*Juniperus communis* 'Hibernica') complements the lavender paint.

ABOVE A study in opposites, the tall, narrow trunks of fastigiate ginkgo trees are in humorous juxtaposition to the boxwood balls planted at their feet. A hedge of *Rhododendron catawbiense* 'Album' frames the scene.

CITIES AND SUBURBS

Perhaps there is no place where having a connection with nature is more important than in the urban environment. There, any patch of green becomes a verdant oasis and stepping into your own garden feels like a trip to the country.

—Ken Druse, Brooklyn, New York

One of the unlikeliest places for a garden is in an urban center of the Northeast. But it is exactly in a big city like New York, Washington, or Philadelphia where the serenity and plush greenery of a garden is most needed. The cramped spaces, large buildings that deprive a garden of sunlight and air circulation, and the task of moving soil, mulch, plants, and refuse in and out of a city yard all challenge a gardener's most determined efforts.

In addition to making use of planters and containers of all shapes and sizes, urban gardeners have perfected the technique of going vertical. Tall fences and walls that enclose a plot behind a townhouse readily support vines and climbers. Shade-loving Dutchman's-pipe and *Akebia* receive a royal welcome in gardens cast in the shadows of nearby homes and office buildings, as do all the varieties and cultivars of ivy. Clematis, which loves to have its roots in shaded, moist soil, flourishes once it rises above the shadow line into the sunlight.

The latitude of an urban garden also governs what is planted and how it is planted, although any in-town garden will benefit in winter from the tempering influences an urban heat island provides. The *Magnolia grandiflora* that forms the center-

piece of a Charlottesville back-yard may grow as far north as Philadelphia and Boston, provided it is espaliered against a heat-radiating wall. The blue spruce that grows statelier each year in Portland, Maine, can do equally well much farther south if the smaller bird's-nest cultivar is planted in the shade of a house or wall.

Just outside the city, suburbanites value their increased green space. Gardeners north of the Mason-Dixon Line are generally blessed with spring and fall so consistently cool and damp that turf grass flourishes. Nowhere in the United States do lawns play such a dominant role in the suburban landscape. From Brookline, Massachusetts, to Main Line Philadelphia, one of the most common sights in well-heeled suburbia is a center-hall colonial sitting smack-dab in the middle of a well-tended lawn that backs up onto an equally manicured golf course. Despite the derision—deserved or un-deserved—heaped on lawns by environmentalists, they remain the preeminent landscape feature of the suburban Northeast.

Flowers are not to be ignored, however: the close proximity to lavish garden centers stocking every-thing from peonies to primulas to hellebores makes it possible to keep northeastern gardens in bloom throughout most of the year. Over the past 20 years

suburban gardeners have been intro-duced to those herbaceous perennials and woody shrubs that before were the sole province of estate gardens and arboretums. Even more modest subur-ban homes boast one or more beds or borders brimming with a Latinate pantheon of *Heliopsis, Coreopsis, Liatris, Hemerocallis,* and *Centranthus,* with *Skimmia, Kerria, Hamamelis,* and *Mahonia* tucked between leafy hedges of yew, boxwood, and privet.

With the sheer abundance of plants that thrive in northeastern climates, it's no wonder there is no one garden style pecular to suburban gardens. The gardens around a fieldstone house may rely more on foliage than on bloom, a clapboard

structure may share the landscape with an intensely planted cottage garden, and a sleek modern resi-dence with glass walls may look out over a small fishpond and waterfall. Wherever you may find yourself in the suburbs of the Northeast—Fairfield County, Connecticut, or Fairfax County, Virginia—you'll find gardens as unusual and breathtaking as the thought and labor that went into making them.

A GARDEN FOR ALL SEASONS
In Washington, D.C.

Spring, says landscape architect Florence Everts about her Northwest Washington home, "is the time for color in my garden." Relying on tulips and scilla in pastel tints, Everts paints a springtime portrait of cool beauty in her partly shady front yard. A small patch of lawn sets off the scene with a pool of bright green.

The narrow sun pocket on the side of her house enables Everts to indulge in even more springtime splendor with bright pink roses and stunning white oriental lilies. Her shady backyard is planted for all seasons, relying on *Saxifraga stolonifera*, Algerian ivy, epimedium, and liriope for variety of foliage color and texture, and on low-pruned azaleas and hollies for structural year-round interest. Hellebores are another favorite of Everts, and she has had great luck with them self-seeding and multiplying. In February and March, she removes the bedraggled evergreen leaves to expose the cup-shaped flowers. Occasionally some bloom earlier, including the white Christmas rose *(Helleborus niger)*, which blooms as early as December.

FACING PAGE The front yard of this Washington, D.C., residence lights up in spring with double pink 'Angelique', single late 'Queen of the Bartigons', and double white 'Mt. Tacoma' tulips, pale lilac scilla, and two 15-year-old dogwood trees on either side of the steps.

LEFT Pink and white dogwoods bloom in the shady backyard garden with rosy pink tulips, light purple *Phlox stolonifera,* and forget-me-nots. The leaves of Algerian ivy (right foreground) and the Himalayan box alongside the path add foliage color and texture.

BELOW The side garden sports sun-loving white 'Casablanca' Oriental lilies, deep pink 'Carefree Beauty' roses, and pink coneflowers. The flagstone path interspersed with rounded Delaware River stones is edged on the left with *Begonia grandis,* which blooms in September.

MIRACLE IN MANHATTAN
A rooftop community garden

In 1976, neighborhood gardeners took over an empty lot on Manhattan's Upper West Side, planting an array of flowers to add color to a drab expanse of Broadway. The lot didn't remain empty for long. The prized site gave way to development, including a parking garage for the residents of a new condominium building. Community activists worked with and eventually persuaded the real estate developer that a green amenity would enhance the new building's charm and value. Thus was born the Lotus Garden on the roof of the condominium's garage.

The obliging developer built stairs to the roof from a gate on the street; a cherry picker lifted tons of topsoil onto the garage roof. Winding paths were laid out through 27 garden plots made available to neighborhood gardeners. The perimeter and pathways of the 75-by-95-foot rooftop area were planted with fruit trees, such as quince, crabapple, mulberry, and dwarf peach and cherry; grape vines and wisteria; and handsome shrubs including many different witch hazels, hydrangeas, rhododendrons, and viburnums.

More than 600 community members pay a small fee to hold keys to the garden, allowing them access during daylight hours. On Sundays between 1 p.m. and 4 p.m. the garden is open to the public.

BELOW In late summer, large frosty white conical blooms of oakleaf hydrangea vie for attention with the blue-violet flowerheads of its more cultivated cousin, *Hydrangea aspera,* 'Villosa'.

LEFT A small pond ringed with irises and ornamental grasses reflects a neighboring apartment building in this Manhattan rooftop garden.

ABOVE Hosta and ferns grow beneath a red-fruiting cherry tree at the junction of two winding paths surfaced with shredded bark.

A QUIET RETREAT
For mother and child

A mother and her young child share not only this 50-year-old brick colonial home in Bethesda, Maryland, but the garden designed by landscape architect Yunghi Epstein as well. Each can claim her own special place in the enclosed, mazelike space of their backyard world.

The organizing design technique is paving, beginning with the redwood deck situated at grade off the screened-in back porch. A fieldstone wall low enough for a child to sit on, and a combination of granite setts and quarry flagstones define the compact lawn area, shaped to repeat the diagonal

lines of the deck. The paving also functions as a path and provides spaces for low-growing plants and a flat surface for a freestanding water garden (inset).

An existing oakleaf hydrangea *(Hydrangea quercifolia),* thornless honey locust, Burford holly, and oak tree were incorporated into the new design; these also serve to screen small areas that accommodate a child's play equipment. Hidden behind a massive hydrangea, a dependable bloomer for shade, and a tulip magnolia is a 13-foot cedar tower for climbing, jumping, and hiding, with a sandbox below.

ABOVE A small freestanding water feature sits at the juncture where the decking yields to stone. Golden-edged yucca and an *Allium giganteum* are to the right; in the background are an oak-leaf hydrangea and clematis hybrids growing up a pole.

FACING PAGE A thornless honey locust stands in a bed planted with an assortment of sweet woodruff, culinary herbs, and epimedium, all contained by a low fieldstone wall. In the right foreground, a fountain sends forth a jet of water through the granite setts.

FORMAL PLACES, INTIMATE SPACES
A mansion of outdoor rooms

Designed and installed more than 50 years ago by horticulturist J. Liddon Pennock Jr., the gardens surrounding Meadowbrook Farm, his fieldstone home just north of Philadelphia, were made to be lived in. Forming "a mansion of intimate outdoor rooms," according to Pennock, each interconnected garden reveals a fondness for straight lines, taut angles, and garden ornament.

Low stone and masonry walls separate each enclosure, and steps link the varying levels. Gazebos— "I have been asked whether it is overgazeboed," jokes Pennock— swimming pools, fountains, and

statuary adorn each garden. The plants in the gardens share the architectural discipline of the stone furnishings.

"Some men walk around with watches in their pockets," remarks Pennock. "I'm far more apt to carry pruning shears and a ruler." In his gardens, precisely trimmed standards, topiaries, and espaliers abound, including a magnificent espaliered *Magnolia grandiflora* and a white-flowering camellia against the wall of the house. The abundance of trained foliage in hanging baskets and planters gives way now and then to a spot of color, mostly white, provided by a climbing hydrangea, azaleas, or a viburnum.

FACING PAGE, TOP A flagstone terrace at the rear of the fieldstone house at Meadowbrook Farm, built in 1931, flows into the first of more than a dozen distinct and formal garden areas surrounding the main residence. The Glass Room at left, a greenhouselike sitting area, smooths the transition between indoors and out.

FACING PAGE, BOTTOM The Eagle Garden, named for the statue flanked by severely pruned hemlock trees at the oval turf area's focal point, is framed by four quadrants of trimmed boxwood and pink New Guinea impatiens.

LEFT An English belvedere with limestone pillars and a wrought-iron dome crowns an alley of turf grass and 'Old Gold' euonymus. The lute-playing cherub is surrounded by an outer ring of *Chamaecyparis pisifera* 'Golden Mop' and an inner circle of feathery red celosia.

BELOW The formal herb garden with beds delineated by low-growing junipers contains a grand ivy topiary at its center, two ivy swans in the foreground, and two ornamental circles of bay in the background. Crushed Brazilian red shale from Scranton, Pennsylvania, lines the patio.

ABOVE This small lath house holds a tinted, full length mirror, creating the impression that there is yet another garden beyond. A gate in the center adds to the illusion.

LEFT An ogee curve and a copper roof with standing seams add interest to this small garden pavilion constructed of latticework. Hybrid cannas grow to the right of the doorway enveloped in Virginia creeper. A tall 'Perfecta' juniper stands at the left.

RIGHT Granite setts and bluestone pavers form a path around the intensely planted center bed of phlox, daylilies, ferns, and cannas. Junipers form a privacy screen to the right; beneath the fence on the left are hosta, a garden hydrangea, and more cannas.

A GEMLIKE SPACE
In a townhouse setting

Garden structures add a dash of architectural whimsy to Calder Loth's Richmond, Virginia, townhouse garden. Based on an 18th-century design of a primitive Doric temple, the lath house (left), constructed of telephone poles and latticework, boasts open metopes with terra-cotta pots placed in each opening for added interest. A tinted mirror in the center of the structure produces a deception that seems to expand the garden's depth, suggesting the presence of another garden through the opening.

A small latticework pavilion anchors the inner corner of the garden (facing page, bottom). Featuring an ogee arch, the faintly Gothic composition is based on a drawing of a similar building by Thomas Jefferson. The two buildings impart grandeur to the confined space of the small garden.

Loth's philosophy on selecting plants consists of the pragmatic "whatever grows well." He plants ferns, daylilies, liriope, and hosta chock-a-block with an assortment of hybrid cannas, all set so close together that the bed and border don't require mulch. The cannas overwinter in the garden with little damage.

RESPITE FROM THE CONCRETE JUNGLE
A Brooklyn backyard

The Brooklyn backyard of garden photographer and author Ken Druse serves as a lush oasis of escape from the black-topped urban environment of New York City. The permanent plantings of honeysuckle, ferns, weigela, ivy, roses, and hosta share garden space during the summer with Druse's pampered potted exotics, which he sets outside to enjoy the salutary benefits of the open air. Many of them double in size during their vacation out of the house.

A favorite feature of the garden is the small koi pond, which, Druse says, repays him amply for the labor it requires. The original PVC liner degraded, sprung a leak, and had to be replaced with a rubber one. Druse doesn't feed the fish when the temperature is lower than 40 degrees Fahrenheit, and he makes sure to float a stock tank electric heater over the water when it threatens to ice over. "Fish don't die from freezing," says Druse. "They die from suffocation." The heater keeps an opening in the ice to prevent a buildup of gases.

FAR LEFT An aerial view of Druse's garden reveals a verdant oasis of bloom and foliage. Summering outdoors beneath a pink-blooming *Weigela florida* is the palmlike foliage of the potted cycad *Zamia florida.* In the foreground, *Lonicera × heckrottii* 'Goldflame' wends it way across a support, and in the background, a thornless honey locust forms a canopy over the entrance to a sitting area.

ABOVE An orange-and-pink koi investigates the plantings of 'Burgundy Glow' ajuga with maroon and dark green leaves, *Iris pseudacorus* with swordlike leaves, a tall sedum, and trailing moneywort at the edge of the small pond.

LEFT Housebound over the winter, the many pots of xerophytic exotics share the outdoors with pink impatiens and magenta petunias, where the fresh air and summer rainfall rejuvenate them.

ABOVE The 2,500-gallon koi pond and miniature waterfall can be seen from the large kitchen window of the Stewart home. The northern exposure and two sweet gums provide shade for the umbrella-like foliage of *Darmera peltata* (left), an arborvitae pruned back hard so as not to spoil the view of the pond from the window, and a fanciful gray-painted crane.

FAR RIGHT A narrow, copper-roofed butterfly house stands in front of a thicket of sheared white pine. Before it are a hedge of boxleaf euonymus and a container of white alyssum, purple petunias, and pink geranium 'Americana'.

RIGHT A flagstone terrace covers what was originally a basketball court. A flower border edged with pink and white impatiens alternating with 30-year-old miniature boxwood and abloom with begonias, roses, and salvia leads the way to the terrace.

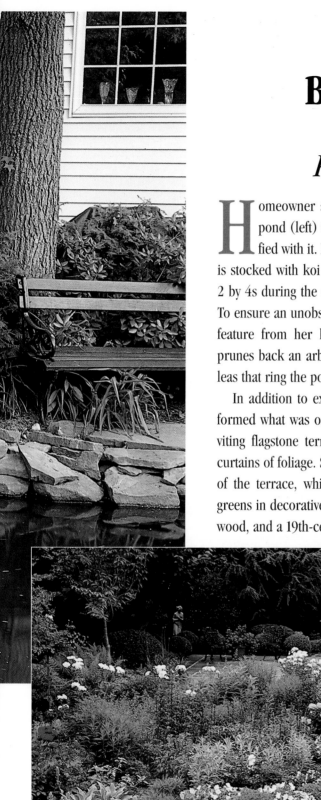

BEAUTY BY DINT OF HARD WORK
Remodeling a garden

Homeowner and garden designer Marilyn Coombe Stewart dug her backyard pond (left) three times and expanded it to 2,500 gallons before she was satisfied with it. Lined with rubber and connected to a recycling waterfall, the pond is stocked with koi that benefit from an electric heater suspended over the pond on 2 by 4s during the cold southern New Jersey winters. To ensure an unobstructed view of the stunning water feature from her kitchen window, Stewart severely prunes back an arborvitae, rhododendrons, and azaleas that ring the pond near the house.

In addition to excavating the pond, Stewart transformed what was once a basketball court into an inviting flagstone terrace, enclosed on three sides by curtains of foliage. Shrubs and trees border the edges of the terrace, which gracefully hosts shaped evergreens in decorative planters, elegant spheres of boxwood, and a 19th-century statue of a demure maiden.

A GARDEN SPLIT IN TWO
Unifying the whole

In 1947, Joanna Reed's half-dozen or so acres in Malvern stood dead center in the path of the planned route for a new highway-—the Pennsylvania Turnpike. Today, her gardens, christened Longview Farm, stand roughly bisected by the turnpike.

"It changed life radically," remarks Reed, understating the problems she encountered once the highway engineers bid farewell in 1950. Construction altered the terrain, leaving the main house resituated at the base of a hillock where surface water collected. Dismayed but not willing to call it quits, Reed had a dam built and dug a retention pond to drain the runoff and provide a source for gravity-feed watering. A cistern eight feet in diameter began a new life as a fishpond.

For years, the Reeds grew enough vegetables and harvested enough fruit from their trees to feed themselves nine months out of the year. Today, much of the surrounding property has undergone the transformation from rural to suburban, and the deer, voles, and rabbits that once competed for her edible plants now content themselves with browsing among her stupendous collection of ornamentals.

LEFT *Canna* × *generalis* 'Stricta' with variegated foliage and a salmon-colored flower shares the entranceway to a large garden area with white-flowering *Cleome* 'Helen Campbell'.

ABOVE A fertile plot of soil in front of the well house on Longview Farm gives rise to a massed planting of *Santolina chamaecyparissus* in the foreground, yellow *Achillea filipendulina,* pink Gallica roses, and the tall white blooms of *Chrysanthemum leucanthemum.*

RIGHT Interspersed among the clumps of yellow achillea in this pointed bed are santolina, *Salvia* × *superba* 'Lubecka', and Gallica roses. The small shrub at the bed's tip is *Hypericum frondosum.*

ABOVE The rose 'Alchymist' with fully double apricot blooms is underplanted with 'Morgenrot' Maltese cross, whose blooms share the same delicate tints. The colorful border against the house and latticework is filled with nepeta, lavender, salvia, bellflower, and valerian.

RIGHT The planting alongside the lower deck repeats the house border with deep tones of *Heuchera* 'Palace Purple' and *Berberis thunbergii* 'Atropurpurea' added for emphasis. Purple-violet 'Veilchenblau' and pale pink 'New Dawn' roses grow on either side of the arbor.

JUNE BLOOMS
On Boston's South Shore

Hectic travel schedules play havoc with the care and maintenance needed in the lavishly colorful gardens of the Pixley home on Boston's suburban South Shore. Planned for an explosion of color in June, the beds and borders were planted extensively with pink and apricot roses, accented by other flowers of pale yellow and blue-violet. An occasional hot-toned magenta and strong yellow add contrast.

Sandy soil and a windy seaside exposure in this suburban garden make many demands on plant hardiness. Not surprisingly, gray foliage plants like achillea, lamb's ear, and rue perform well. But so do many roses such as 'Constance Spry', 'New Dawn', 'Alchymist', 'Veilchenblau', and 'Leverkusen', although one or more may occasionally succumb to the hot, muggy summers and cold, windy winters.

Additional drama is supplied by climbing and trailing plants that seem to drape the tall deck at the rear of the house. Goldflame honeysuckle and a climbing 'Cécile Brunner' rose frame the colorful vista from the elevated deck.

SUBURBAN SPLENDOR
And low maintenance

The half-acre suburban Baltimore residence and gardens of Pauline Vollmer have undergone a tremendous transformation since she moved there in 1962. Working with landscape designer Wolfgang Oehme, Vollmer eliminated the lawn in front of the house, replacing it with two enormous lacebark pines, a hedge of Foster hollies to shield the house from the street, and ground covers of epimedium and liriope.

To the rear of the house, Vollmer's objective was to create "a garden pleasant to live with and in." She had a large pond dug and surfaced the surrounding deck with bluestone pavers. The pond is home to goldfish, 10 or so green frogs, and a northern water snake, which Vollmer credits with keeping the rapidly expanding goldfish population in check.

The garage that adjoined the house was converted into a glass-enclosed garden room with superb views of the pond and a courtyard area gated with wrought iron. With no lawn to mow and plantings requiring little or no additional water, the primary garden chore is pruning. In the autumn, perhaps the garden's most visually striking season, fallen leaves are mechanically shredded and immediately put to good use as mulch.

ABOVE The shallow end of the Vollmer goldfish pond hosts water lilies and cattails, along with 'Indian Chief' sedum with pink flowers that turn ruby red in September.

A seating area and the corner of an enclosed sunporch are glimpsed through the multiple trunks of *Photinia villosa,* with apricot-colored fall foliage and an underplanting of St.-John's-wort. To the left of the tree is *Miscanthus sinensis* 'Purpurascens', which turns reddish pink in the fall, and to the right is a sturdy stand of Mexican bamboo *(Polygonum japonicum),* with stems 2 inches in diameter.

THE PIEDMONT

*Gardening is a great experiment in what
will and what won't grow here.*
—Pat Alliger, Afton, Virginia

In children's books the seasons are always described as benign and predictable. March is windy; the children pictured in the books wear sweaters and fly kites. In April it rains; they wear galoshes and carry umbrellas. Summer is always hot enough to go swimming, but there are never any tornadoes. In fall, the trees turn glorious shades of red and orange; the raked piles are just right for jumping in. In winter, the children sled down snowy hills and don't have to check each others' noses for frostbite.

While the archetypical seasons of books are nothing like the weather people experience in most parts of the country, that schoolbook climate actually exists in the Piedmont region of the Northeast. It is a place of four proverbial seasons. Spring is a gentle warming that blows in with March and stretches into three glorious months. Summer is hot, but it lasts only three months. Fall is the reverse of spring— a leisurely, gradual cooling that gives you plenty of time to put the garden to bed. Winter is cold, but not too cold, and often snowy.

Of course, there are exceptions—ice storms, blizzards, hurricanes, droughts, periods of intense heat and cold. But they are always the exceptions, never the norm.

Geographically, the Northeast owes its moderate climate not merely to latitude but to its location in the Piedmont Plateau. Located between the Appalachian Mountains and the coastal plain, the Piedmont Plateau is a broad band of elevated, undulating land with a name that comes from the Italian for "foot of the mountains." In Italy, a region of the same name is noted for fruit growing because of its moderate climate.

The Piedmont's weather, though influenced by the Atlantic Ocean, is cooler than that of the coastal plain. While subject to the effects of latitude, the plateau's central position mitigates extremes of temperature. Stretching from New York to Alabama, the Piedmont is hilly at its western edge where it rises into the foothills of the Appalachian Mountain chain. It flattens gradually into rolling land as it moves eastward. On its eastern edge, called the fall line, it falls to the softer soils and flat topography of the coastal plain. Rivers that traverse the Piedmont race through rapids as they flow to the sea.

Cities have developed along the fall line, a number of them along rivers. Philadelphia is located on the Delaware River; Washington, D.C., on the Potomac; and Richmond, Virginia, on the James. West of the cities, the Piedmont rolls toward the ancient Appalachians. It is a gentle land of misty hills, horse and fruit farms, rich forests, beautiful vistas, and bountiful gardens.

In addition to at least six months of mild weather in which to work in the garden, Piedmont gardeners are fortunate in an exceptionally broad plant palette from which to choose. The climate is both cold enough to support plants that need chilling—tulips, daffodils, fruit trees, and lilacs—and warm enough for magnolias, azaleas, stewartias, and many broadleaf evergreens. In summer, heat lovers like tomatoes thrive.

The number of ornamental natives that abound in this region is astonishing. Among these are vines, including climbing aster and cross vine *(Anisostichus capreolatus)*, shrubs such as *Fothergilla*, and a dozen species of native azaleas including the pinkshell azalea *(Rhododendron Vaseyi)*, the rose azalea *(Rhododendron prinophyllum)*, and the southern pinxter *(Rhododendron canescens)*. Springtime in the Piedmont means flowering trees such as dogwoods and redbuds lining the waysides. The woods and fields brim with showy wildflowers—*Trillium*, bloodroot *(Sanguinaria canadensis)*, cardinal flower *(Lobelia cardinalis)*, and perennial sunflowers.

Piedmont gardens are as blessed with a rich flora as they are gifted with a gentle climate. And, whether they acknowledge it or not, Piedmont gardeners live in gardening heaven.

FOLLOWING NATURE'S PLAN
Marries natives and friends

Sheela and François Lampietti personally landscaped and now maintain the 10-acre garden that surrounds their 18th-century house in Purcellville, Virginia. Their secret is a well-thought-out plan that allows the garden to become more natural the farther it is from the house.

Close to the house and the 4-acre pond, the plantings—including a perennial border near the front door—have a cottage-garden feel. Maintenance in this area is high and the scale is small. As one moves away from the house, the scale of the plantings grows and chores diminish. "Planting in large volumes cuts down on maintenance," explains Sheela, who is a professional landscaper.

Another reason the garden stays trim without endless hours of labor is that the Lampiettis have chosen plants that are well suited to the site and climate. "When something thrives," Sheela says, "I tend to leave it. Maybe I'll divide it and experiment." As a result of the Lampiettis' laissez-faire attitude toward the garden's inhabitants, it has a relaxed, country feel. Of its style, Sheela says, "I would put it in the category of the natural garden."

TOP LEFT Yellow flag irises *(Iris pseudacorus)* were allowed to naturalize into a large mass around the pond. This sturdy iris has stiff, straplike leaves and bright yellow flowers in spring.

ABOVE Nearer the house, the plantings—which include a perennial border, tree peonies, wormwood, and dwarf forms of nandina and mugo pine—are on a smaller, more intimate scale.

RIGHT Daylilies *(Hemerocallis),* pinkish purple *Phlox paniculata,* and *Picea pungens* 'Glauca Prostrata' (background, left), flank a rustic footbridge in the Lampiettis' garden. The bridge leads into a shady glade that was the setting for their daughter's wedding.

A SERIES OF GARDENS
To suit every sensibility

Taking advantage of the immense variety of plants that can be grown in their area, Ellen and Gordon Penick developed a series of gardens on their three acres in rural Ruther Glen, Virginia. Each garden has a separate focus. In addition to perennial borders, there is a patio garden, a garden with gazebo, and a mixed border of perennials, shrubs, and trees. There's also a dwarf conifer collection, a bog garden, and the latest addition, which Ellen calls the "camper's garden." This one commemorates her childhood camping experiences (see page 280).

Ellen appreciates the wide range of plants that can be grown in Virginia, but at times she finds the heat daunting. When it's too hot to step outside into the gardens that surround her home, she and her husband enjoy them from the inside. From their bedroom, they can gaze at their plantings and beyond to the 45-acre Reedy Mill Lake, which borders

LEFT Orange geum, 'Crater Lake Blue' salvia, pink peonies, variegated stonecrop *(Sedum albomarginatum)*, and bluestar *(Amsonia tabernaemontana)* bloom in concert in a lakeside perennial border.

their property. From the kitchen, the dwarf conifer garden is handsome throughout the year. And from the dining room, the view of the double borders is truly splendid.

"I wanted to achieve something that's harmonious and beautiful," says Ellen Penick. She is especially proud of her perennial borders. "There is nothing as beautiful as a perennial border at its peak. It requires so many things to come together."

ABOVE Blooms of a 'Betty Prior' rose stand out against the mist coming off the lake on the Penick property. Bluestar *(Amsonia tabernaemontana)*, valerian *(Valeriana officinalis)*, and, in the foreground, variegated stonecrop *(Sedum albomarginatum)* contribute a variety of flower color and leaf shape to the border.

RIGHT Stepping-stones lead from the driveway through a bed of bridal wreath *(Spiraea)*, junipers, and variegated yucca. A large arborvitae serves as a focal point, while the mounding habit of the plants is echoed in the round stones and the curve of the bed.

RIGHT Gordon Penick built this waterfall to drop over several layers of rock and flow 50 feet to the lake. Contrasting with evergreen junipers and mugo pine are mounds of variegated ornamental grasses, a sedge *(Carex morrowii),* and two clumps of miscanthus—*Miscanthus sinensis* 'Variegatus' and *Miscanthus* 'Morning Light'.

BELOW In late spring, a fragrant fringe tree *(Chionanthus virginicus)* and bearded irises *(Iris germanica)* light up a bed adjacent to the driveway.

BOTTOM The patio garden offers a restful oasis bordered by pink phlox, punctuated by a spruce *(Picea orientalis),* and shaded by a brilliantly hued honey locust.

THE ALLEGHENY PLATEAU AND GREAT LAKES REGION

Designing a landscape is like solving a puzzle.
—Leslie Scott, Cleveland Heights, Ohio

Between the Great Lakes and the Appalachian Mountains is a region dominated by the rounded hills and deep valleys of the Allegheny Plateau. Open to cold air masses from Canada and the central plains and to moisture-laden air from the Gulf of Mexico, its geography renders the climate continental, unpredictable, and challenging.

Usually wet, spring can be short one year and long the next with late frosts arriving in late May. Summers are humid and warm to hot—but never overlong. By late August or early September, bracing fall breezes herald the Allegheny's spectacular autumn, brilliant with the colors of turning leaves. Winter follows quickly. Usually long with subzero temperatures, winter can also produce 60-degree days in January—followed by snow. At higher elevations and especially along the lakes, snow is a given.

Blizzards that would break all records in other parts of the Northeast occur routinely on the lee shores of Lake Erie and Lake Ontario in Pennsylvania, Ohio, and New York. Their accumulations and duration are remarkable. In 1977, for example, Buffalo recorded 199.4 inches of snow for the season, with one period of 53 consecutive days of precipitation. In the same year, 60-mile-per-hour winds over Lake Huron dropped 39 inches of snow around London, Ontario, in just three days.

Arising from a phenomenon known as the lake effect, these snowstorms occur when very cold air, flowing over the relatively warm waters of a large lake, picks up moisture and heat, forming low clouds just above the water. The clouds are blown to the downwind shore where they reach land, and, having nowhere else to go, rise and converge with the cold air above them, triggering snowfall.

Abundant snow and rainfall, great rivers—the Ohio, the Monongahela, and the Allegheny—and a thousand tributaries, lakes, and streams irrigate the region and support rich and varied vegetation. Flowing down from the higher elevations, forests of sturdy natives—mixed hardwoods, rhododendron, mountain laurel *(Kalmia)*, and hemlock *(Tsuga)*— cast long shadows over patchworks of trillium, foamflower *(Tiarella)*, bloodroot *(Sanguinaria)*, wild columbine *(Aquilegia)*, hepatica, and jack-in-the-pulpit *(Arisaema)*.

At low elevations near the Great Lakes, the expanse of water moderates temperatures throughout the year, creating uniquely salubrious growing conditions. Summers are a few degrees cooler on the lakeshore than inland. In winter, snow insulates against extremes and fluctuations of winter temperature. Since the earliest European settlement, this area has supported vineyards and orchards of apples and peaches.

It was no accident that, in the mid-1800s, astute Shakers chose what is now known as Shaker Heights on the Lake Erie shore to undertake forward-thinking, organic farming methods. They selected seeds of superior vegetables. They perfected fruit-tree culture. Their carefully harvested, pure herbs supported a thriving mail-order business.

Their methods for improving the area's predominantly clay soil are valid today. While the Shakers applied plentiful manure to their soil, gardeners now can substitute compost to improve tilth in stiff clay soils. Gardeners can also choose landscape plants that tolerate clay, such as river birch *(Betula nigra)*, dogwood *(Cornus)*, witch hazel *(Hamamelis)*, juniper, daylilies *(Hemerocallis)*, ornamental grasses, bayberry *(Myrica)*, cut-leaf sumac *(Rhus)*, and viburnum.

On the Allegheny Plateau and along the Great Lakes, despite the challenges of an unpredictable climate, there is a long tradition of gardening excellence. It endures in the region's outstanding horticultural institutions, in its nursery industry, and in its varied private gardens.

GARDEN ROOMS
Designed with winter in mind

A stunning series of garden rooms is the hallmark of Bill and Susie Johnson's garden in the hills above the Ohio River just a few miles northeast of Pittsburgh. Easily viewed from the house, the outdoor rooms include a long border, a secret garden, and a courtyard garden.

The sunny terrace that runs the length of the house overlooks the border of lavender, santolina, mugo pine *(Pinus mugo mugo)*, and, in summer, annuals. The border is at its best in mid-June, when 80 feet of lavender are in bloom.

Farther from the house, the secret garden is enclosed by walls of Pleached Rivers purple beech (*Fagus sylvatica* 'Riversii'); tall yews; false cypress and arborvitae; and an assortment of woody plants. Within the living walls, stone paths wind past collections of purple-leafed plants, deciduous azaleas, and dwarf conifers—all underplanted with ferns and wildflowers.

From the kitchen and sunroom, the view is of the courtyard garden, defined by limestone-topped stucco walls and a curving pergola edged with dwarf conifers and annuals. Designed to be "serene, beautiful, and orderly," the courtyard's strong bones provide a beautiful focus throughout Pittsburgh's long, gray winters.

LEFT In the tradition of medieval courtyard gardens, these fruit trees—dwarf apples, pears, and an apricot—have been espaliered, trained to grow flat against the stucco wall. At their feet are mounds of mugo pine, santolina, and a ribbon of bright annual impatiens.

ABOVE Designed by Pittsburgh landscape architect Edward Werley, this gracefully curved pergola creates an all-season vista in the courtyard garden. The wood was stained white, rather than painted, to eliminate the need for scraping. In summer, the pergola serves as a spa for houseplants, a palm, figs *(Ficus)*, and hanging geraniums *(Pelargonium)*. Variegated hostas and impatiens add summer interest.

RIGHT Wisteria standards rise above a low mixed hedge of lavender and mugo pine. At 80 feet long, the hedge runs the full length of the sunny terrace.

FORM FOLLOWS FUNCTION
A garden for pets and people

Landscape designer Leslie Scott put many of her trademark touches to work when she planned and designed her own extensive Cleveland Heights garden—the bold use of lines, especially diagonals; love of structures; asymmetry; use of recycled materials; and a deliberate imperfection that adds a feeling of spontaneity and also cuts down on chore time. But her garden has one other, unusual feature: she designed it with Kelly and Dick, her two Gordon setters, in mind.

Saying she can't imagine life without dogs, Scott created an environment in which pooches and plants enjoy a peaceful coexistence. By strategically placing woody, thorned shrubs, such as roses, she effectively steers the dogs away from delicate perennials. And after observing

the dogs' running patterns—they kept to the sides of the yard—she put in paths that bordered a large raised bed.

In the second of her two garden rooms, entered via an arbor entwined with climbing roses and clematis, Scott cleverly recycled her children's outgrown swing set and used the poles as the base for a pergola: wisteria covers the frame and provides shelter for a table and chairs.

FACING PAGE In response to Cleveland's iffy weather, Scott makes good use of containers. Here a *Mandevilla* vine climbs a trellis backed by pots of annual blue salvia, *Centaurea* (annual blue bachelor's buttons), and white Boston daisies.

ABOVE Gordon setters Kelly and Dick rest on a wide walkway of brick, surrounded by lush borders that include *Nicotiana sylvestris, Hydrangea quercifolia,* and a climbing 'New Dawn' rose. Container plantings include yellow and purple petunias, red sweet peas, marigolds, and dusty miller. Because the dogs like to dig, Scott kept the lawn to a minimum.

LANDSCAPING WITH STRUCTURES

Structures give your garden its shape and dimension. By paying attention to the materials you use to build them, you can enrich your outdoor space with subtle texture and color.

Garden structures also play strong architectural roles. Fences and trellises can create separate "rooms," while low, wide walls provide seating as well. Gazebos and arbors add shelter, privacy, and support for plants. Spas, decks, and patios can recreate the ambience and convenience of an indoor room for enjoyment outdoors.

Structures are the costliest part of the garden, so plan them with care and learn your local building codes before you start. The design should blend well with the architecture of your house and its setting. Finally, choose the most durable and suitable materials you can afford to ensure that your structures are long-lasting as well as pleasing.

ARBORS AND TRELLISES

Arbors and trellises—along with other such vertical garden elements as pergolas, lath houses, and gazebos—can be among the most interesting structures in your garden. They provide a visual change of pace by leading the eye upward. And along with fences and walls, they contribute to the skeleton of the garden, strengthening its composition.

Two of the simplest vertical structures, arbors and trellises, have both decorative and practical functions. They can support climbing plants, tie together garden areas, define zones of use, direct foot traffic, and mask a plain or unsightly feature such as a garage or toolshed.

Arbors tend to be sizable structures—albeit not as large or imposing as pergolas, which traditionally function as covered walkways—that afford a quiet place to relax and reflect.

Generally rendered less imposing by simple design and graceful arches, arbors can be partly attached to a house wall or roof, or built freestanding, colonnade-style. The frame of most arbors is similar in construction to that of many overheads and some gazebos, but arbors are generally less enclosed.

Trellises serve primarily as plant supports; they may be freestanding or mounted to a wall, a fence, or the side of a house, or to a deck to serve as a windbreak or privacy screen. You can make your own trellis or buy a commercial model at a garden center or through a mail-order supplier. Some types are made of wooden strips or lattice, others of natural vines or sturdier wrought iron. Whatever the material, the trellis must be strong enough to support the weight of mature plants and durable enough to stand up to the rigors of your climate.

Tucked into a corner of the garden, this simple arbor provides a quiet place to sit and watch birds drawn to the feeder, and to enjoy the surrounding plantings in privacy.

A. This weathered trellis serves as a focal point in the garden, breaking the horizontal plane of plantings and sending the eye up to take in the roses and flowering clematis 'General Sikorski' cloaking the frame.

B. A simple, rustic overhead combines sturdy 6-by-6 posts with spare roof framing. Vines snake up the posts and out across plain galvanized pipes. A raised, casual tub fountain provides soothing sounds of water.

C. The curving features and sinuous lines of this arbor and bench swing create a sense of movement. The lumber was cut from 8-by-8 and 12-by-12 redwood beams salvaged from a demolished barn.

Beams bridge posts; local codes specify sizes and spans

A BASIC ARBOR

Lattice screen adds privacy and shade; doubles as a trellis

Piers of cast concrete are embedded in poured concrete footings

A. Part of a boundary fence, just the top of this graceful, arched white trellis peers from behind its blanket of *Clematis × jackmanii*. Not only does the trellis provide a beautiful focal point in the garden, it acts as a privacy screen as well.

B. Natural vines woven together create this rustic trellis, which bridges the gravel path and highlights a gentle curve. The structure is built from two stick frames with overarching branches. Make one yourself or look for a prefabricated version.

Designing an arbor

The key to arbor construction is to think of a crisscross or stacking principle, with each new layer placed perpendicular to the one below it. Keep in mind that although you build an overhead from the ground up, you should design it from the top down. First choose the kind of roof you want. That decision will influence the size and spacing of the support members below.

Whether freestanding or attached to a building, the structure is held up by a series of posts or columns. These support horizontal beams, which in turn support rafters. In a house-attached overhead a ledger takes the place of a beam and the rafters are laid directly on the ledger. The rafters can be left uncovered or covered with lath, lattice, poles, or grape stakes.

Rafters sit atop beams and are spaced for plant support or shade. Orientation determines the extent of shade cast below

Posts are 4-by-4 lumber or larger; post-to-beam connections may need bracing. Metal anchors secure posts to piers or to a concrete slab

Concrete footings extend below the frost line, supporting posts and the weight of arbor and plants

In most cases arbors are built from standard-dimension lumber. To increase the life of an arbor, use only pressure-treated or naturally decay-resistant materials such as redwood or cedar heartwood. Open arbors don't collect much rain or snow, so they need only support the weight of the materials themselves, plus the weight of any plants growing on them. For added strength, brace the structure where the posts meet the beams.

As you plan, check with your local building department to find out about the regulations affecting the size, design, and construction of your project. In most communities, you'll have to meet building codes and obtain a building permit before you begin work. For do-it-yourself details, see Overheads, pages 370–371.

Shopping for a Trellis

An easy and attractive way to support twining and vining plants is with handcrafted trellises, available from garden retailers and mail-order suppliers.

Some sources carry an impressive array of trellises, ranging from hand-forged metal to woven willow, that can serve as decorative elements as well as plant supports. Woven wooden or vine trellises bring a casual or rustic touch to the garden, while the architectural wooden and metal ones generally look more formal.

These trellises are extremely simple to use. Most come ready to install: just push the posts into the soil next to a wall or in a planter box, plant a vine nearby, and wrap the stems around the supports. A few need minor assembly, and some wooden ones with "feet" must be anchored to a wall.

For the creative do-it-yourselfer, hardware stores and home centers also stock lath, lattice, galvanized wire, plastic clothesline, copper plumbing pipe, and assorted fasteners that can be fashioned into a trellis. Simply mount redwood strips, copper pipe, or prefabricated lattice panels to fence posts or a wall. Use lag screws or galvanized nails for fastening to wood and expanding anchors for stucco or masonry. Whenever possible, leave some room between trellis and wall.

Both of the trellises shown here are simply constructed. At top, four arched, prefabricated trellises were lined up, anchored in concrete, and fastened to the walls with barbed nails. The trellises were joined with overhead 2 by 2s. The trellis at right, cloaked with clematis 'General Sikorski', is constructed of gray-stained cedar strips fastened to the brick wall.

DECKS

A deck sets the stage for outdoor activity and expands the total living space of a house. A properly planned deck forms a focal point in the landscape, redefines grade, and provides new views of the garden and its surroundings. Built to accommodate seating, tables, or a hot tub, a deck can function as an outdoor room.

Decks can abut the house or tuck into a remote corner of the garden. The classic attached deck is typically accessed from the house through French or sliding doors from a living room, kitchen, or master bedroom—or all three. So when planning your deck, keep in mind interior traffic patterns as well as outdoor ones.

Why build a deck rather than a patio? Your site or the style of your house can be determining factors. A deck can bridge bumps and slopes or "float" over swampy low spots that might sink a brick patio. Decking lumber is resilient underfoot, and it doesn't store heat the way masonry can, making a deck cooler in hot areas.

A low-level deck can link house and garden at flower height, offering a new perspective on garden beds. Such a deck makes a good replacement for an existing concrete slab—you can often use the slab as a base for the deck. A low-level wraparound deck links interior spaces with a series of boardwalks or landings. You can follow your home's shape or play off it with angular extensions or soft curves.

If you're faced with a hilly, poorly drained site, try cantilevering a deck over the steep slope, or plan on a step-down, multiplatform arrangement like the one shown at right.

Detached decks form quiet retreats, whether tucked behind lush plantings or elevated to catch afternoon sun or shade. The route to such a deck can be direct or circuitous. You can enhance the feeling of a hideaway with the addition of an overhead, a fountain, or a spa or hot tub.

Design options include decking patterns (see page 367) and railing styles. The ultimate feel of a deck is determined by the details, and safety is the only limit.

Pressure-treated lumber (see page 363) is the most affordable material for building a deck. The wood, typically southern pine, has been treated with chemical preservatives that guard against rot, insects, and other sources of decay. Other options include redwood or cedar heartwood, which are more pleasing visually and are naturally resistant to decay, but much more expensive.

Coat any deck periodically with a wood preservative or stain (see page 365) to prevent water absorption and reduce the swelling and contracting that lead to cracking, splintering, and warping.

A

A. **This multilevel deck** of pressure-treated lumber runs the full length of the house, linking the interior with the outdoors. Steel railings, built-in benches, and deck-level planters give the structure continuity and an open, contemporary feel.

B. **The warm, rich tones** of redwood heartwood are elegantly showcased here. Overlapping angles and changes in decking direction signal steps, highlight benches and planters, and turn a potentially plain deck into an architectural statement.

C. **To maximize the view** from this seaside deck, railings are steel and kept to a minimum. Lighting and a tableside grill provide all the amenities needed for dining by the sea.

Deck-building guidelines

Lumber grades vary greatly in appearance and price. One cost-saving trick is to determine the least expensive lumber for decking and trim that's acceptable to you (see pages 362–363). Whatever the species and grade of visible wood, it makes sense to use pressure-treated lumber for the substructure. It stands up to weather and in-ground conditions, and is less expensive, too.

A deck can be freestanding or, as shown here, attached to the house with a horizontal ledger. Concrete footings secure precast piers or poured tubular pads, which in turn support vertical wooden posts. One or more horizontal beams span the posts; smaller joists bridge ledger and beams. The decking itself, typically 5/4-by-6 or 2-by-6 lumber, is nailed or screwed to the joists. The design shown, while standard, is but one of many options.

Overheads, benches, railings, and steps are often integral to a deck's framing. While it may be feasible to add these extras later, it's simplest to design and build the whole structure at once. While you're planning, think about whether you'll need to install plumbing pipes for running water or wiring for electric outlets and outdoor light fixtures. And if you need extra storage space or planters, build them into the deck as permanent features.

One advantage of building a deck as a do-it-yourself project is that much of the engineering work has probably been done for you. Standard span tables (listing safe working spans by dimension for each of the common lumber species) are widely available—most lumberyards have them. Remember that these are minimum guidelines; for firmer footing, choose beefier members or reduce the spacing between them.

Posts taller than 3 feet may require bracing, especially in areas prone to high winds. Elevated decks must be surrounded with railings for safety, with slats no more than 4 to 6 inches apart (again, check local code). Fascia boards, skirts, and other trim details can dress up the basic structure.

A low-level deck is the simplest kind to build, but a simple raised deck like the one shown at right can also be constructed by a homeowner. Generally, decks that are cantilevered out from an upper story or over water or a promontory must be designed by a qualified structural engineer and installed by a professional. Decks on steep hillsides or unstable soil or those more than a story high should receive the same professional attention.

A BASIC DECK

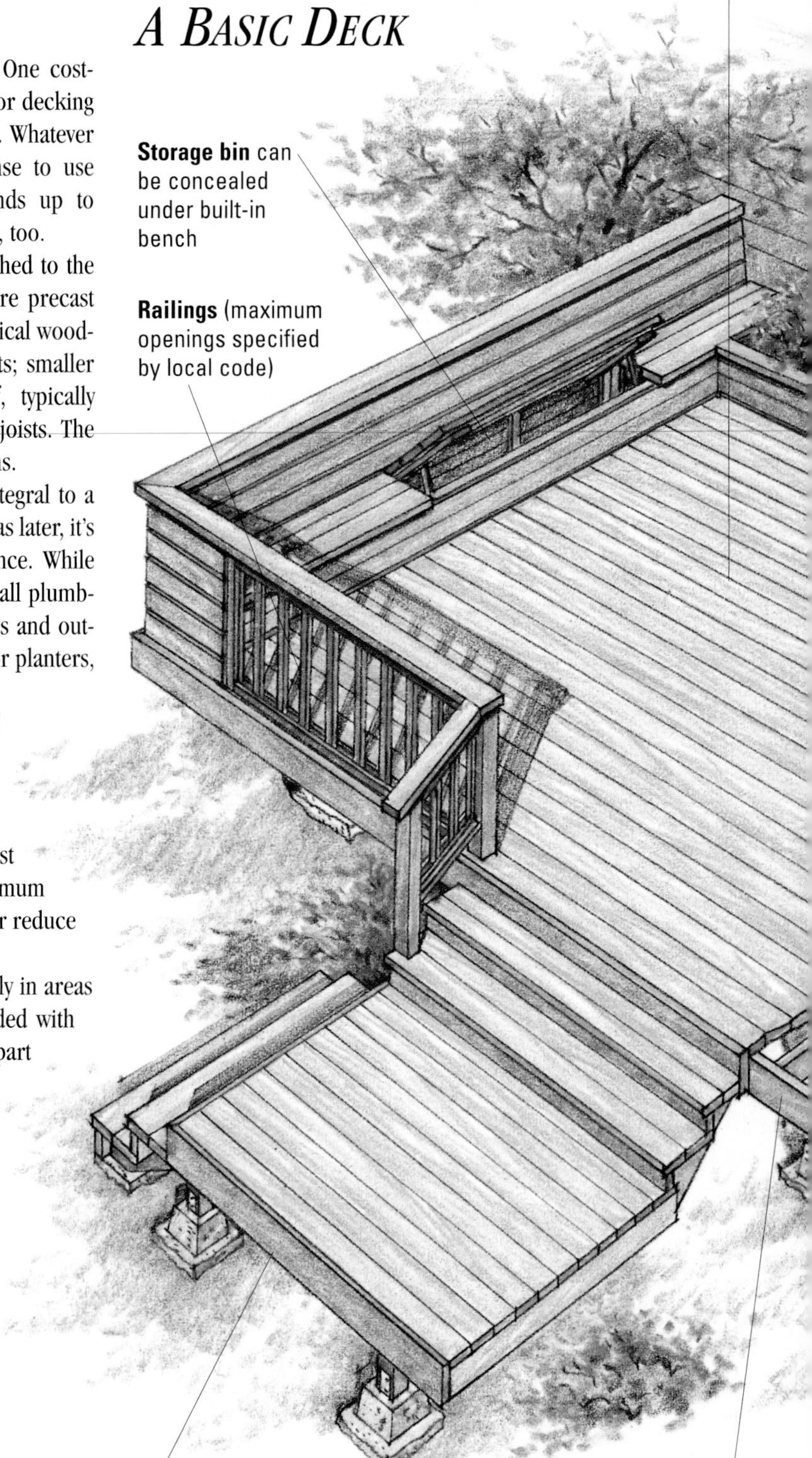

Decking boards are nailed or screwed perpendicular to joists; they are typically 5/4-by-6 or 2-by-6 lumber

Storage bin can be concealed under built-in bench

Railings (maximum openings specified by local code)

Fascia (trim)

Rim joist secures joist ends

Planters on deck require adequate drainage; deck must support weight of soil and plants

Doors to deck lead from dining or living room, kitchen, or bedrooms. French or sliding doors are best choices

Electric lighting and outlets may be 120 volt or 12 volt and may require permit to install

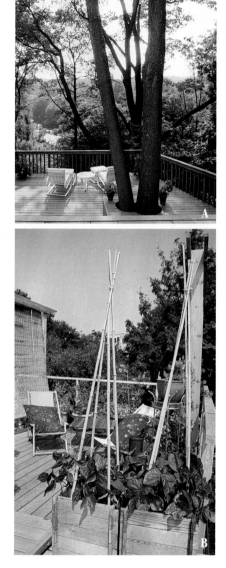

Ledger secures deck to house framing. Flashing guards against moisture

Beams bridge posts; they may be single timbers or twin 2-by members that "sandwich" posts as shown

Joists are typically spaced 16 or 24 inches center-to-center, and secured to ledger with joist hangers

Posts are secured to piers with post anchors. Minimum post sizes and spacings are set by local codes

Poured concrete footings extend below the frost line

Piers are made of precast concrete and embedded in poured footings

A. **Built out over a steep hillside,** this deck takes on the feel of a tree house: holes were cut in the decking to accommodate the mature trees that provide shade and breezes.

B. **This tiny rooftop deck** functions as resting place and container garden. While in the process of adding the requisite railings, the designer—who specializes in rooftop architecture—hung woven screens for privacy and to enhance the cozy feeling of the space.

FENCES AND GATES

Fences and outdoor screens can transform a garden into a secure, attractive retreat from the outside world. When well designed, they filter the sun's glare, turn a biting wind into a pleasant breeze, and help to muffle the cacophony of street traffic, noisy neighbors, and barking dogs. As partitions, they divide the yard into separate areas for recreation, relaxation, gardening, and storage. Fences serve many of the same purposes as walls, but are generally less formal in appearance, easier to construct, and, when you calculate labor costs, less expensive.

Most fences are built partly or entirely of wood. The versatility of wood as a fencing material is reflected in the wide variety of its forms—split rails, grape stakes, dimension lumber, poles, and manufactured wood products such as plywood and tempered hardboard. Though the design possibilities are endless, wooden fences fall into one of three basic types: post-and-rail, picket, and solid board. The one you choose may depend on the function the fence is to serve; a board fence may be the best choice for a full privacy screen, for example. Fences can also be designed to "edit" views with the inclusion of louvers, slats, lattice, or see-through trellises that provide a glimpse of what lies beyond.

Alternative materials beyond boards, slats, and timbers include vinyl, galvanized wire, plastic mesh, and ornamental iron. Vinyl fences are readily available, easy to maintain, and simple to install. If you don't like the look of wire or mesh fencing, plant annual vines such as morning glories or climbing nasturtiums for quick cover, or install plantings for permanent cover (see pages 218–219).

Whatever your choice of fencing, coordinate the fence with the style and materials of your house. A picket fence that would be too dainty for a contemporary stone-and-glass house might look fine

Spare post-and-rail zigzags mark boundaries. Poppies and roses dress up the fence with scarlet blooms.

with a colonial brick or clapboard structure. Louvered or board fences, however, can complement a variety of house styles.

Most communities have regulations restricting fence height. In many places the maximum allowable height is 42 inches for front-yard fences and 6 feet for backyard fences. Tall fences are also more difficult to build and require more materials. An alternative way to gain more height is to train a plant to clothe the top of a fence.

Normally a boundary fence is commonly owned and maintained by both neighbors. Make every effort to come to a friendly agreement with your neighbor on the location, design, and construction of the fence. (One option is a "good-neighbor" fence with cross-pieces mounted in alternating directions.) If you can't come to an agreement, you can circumvent the problem by building the fence entirely on your land, just a few inches inside your boundary.

Choosing a gate

Place a gate for access, to frame a view, or to make a design statement in tandem with the fence. You may want to build the gate in a style and material that match the fence, but you can also choose a contrasting material or design, such as a wooden or wrought-iron gate within flanking brick pilasters. A low picket gate or one made of airy lath invites people in with its open, friendly appearance; a high, solid gate guards the privacy and safety of those within.

The minimum width for a gate is usually 3 feet, but an extra foot creates a more gracious feeling. If you anticipate moving gardening or other equipment through the gate, make the opening wider. For an extra-wide space, consider a two-part gate or even a gate on rollers designed for a driveway.

A. This tall, vertical board fence affords the homeowners a sense of privacy that is enhanced by the plants—including 'Magic Carpet' rose—that grow behind it and spill over the shorter section. The slim openings between the boards allow air to circulate through the garden.

B. Its unique herringbone pattern sets this split-rail fence apart from the crowd. Open fences such as this one have the effect of merging the property with the surrounding landscape, and serve more as psychological barriers against intrusion than as true privacy fences.

C. This traditional picket fence is a perfect partner to the white clapboard house and the rustic stone wall that fronts it. For variation, the space between pickets can be either wide or narrow, and tops can be pointed, rounded, spearheaded, or double- or triple-saw-toothed.

Building a fence

Most wooden fences have three parts: vertical posts, horizontal rails or stringers, and siding. Posts are usually 4-by-4 timbers; rails are usually 2 by 4s. Fence siding can range from rough grape stakes to ready-cut pickets, from finished boards to plywood panels. Posts should be made of pressure-treated or decay-resistant redwood or cedar heartwood. Redwood can be left to weather naturally, but fir or pine should be painted or stained.

If your fence will be on or near the boundary line between your property and your neighbor's, make certain you have the property line clearly established. If there's any doubt, call in a surveyor to review it.

Few lots are perfectly smooth, flat, and obstruction free. If your fence line runs up a hill, build the fence so that it follows the contours of the land, or construct stepped panels that will maintain horizontal lines (see pages 368–369).

Building a gate

A basic gate consists of a rectangular frame of 2 by 4s with a diagonal 2-by-4 brace running from the bottom corner of the hinge side to the top corner of the latch side. Siding fastened to the frame completes the gate.

Choose strong hinges and latches. It's better to select hardware that's too hefty than too flimsy. Plan to attach both hinges and latches with long galvanized screws that won't pull out, and be sure to use galvanized hardware.

A. This classic wooden gate welcomes visitors with its low, widely spaced rails and cheerful yellow paint.

B. A traditional picket gate creates a pleasing contrast with the dense stone wall surrounding this seaside garden, beckoning visitors to pass through and wander down the pathway.

C. The decorative carving and handsome hardware on this wooden gate transform it into garden art.

D. Bamboo sets the theme in this garden: the gate's frame and rails echo the living bamboo lining the pathway.

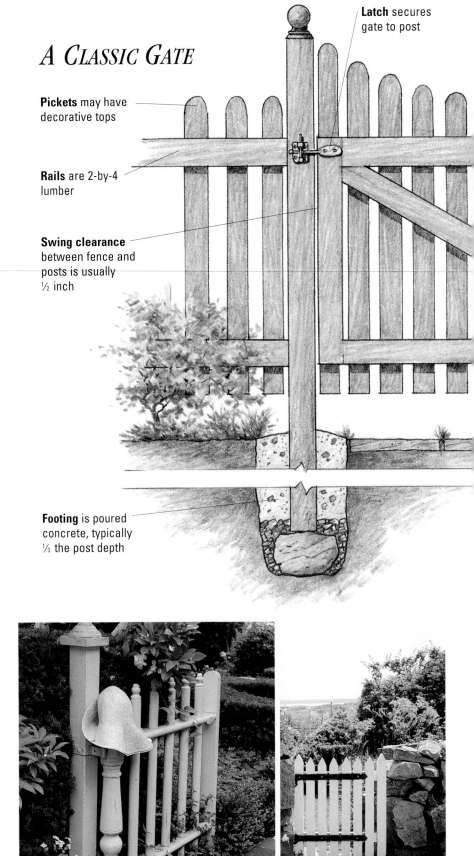

A CLASSIC GATE

Latch secures gate to post

Pickets may have decorative tops

Rails are 2-by-4 lumber

Swing clearance between fence and posts is usually ½ inch

Footing is poured concrete, typically ⅓ the post depth

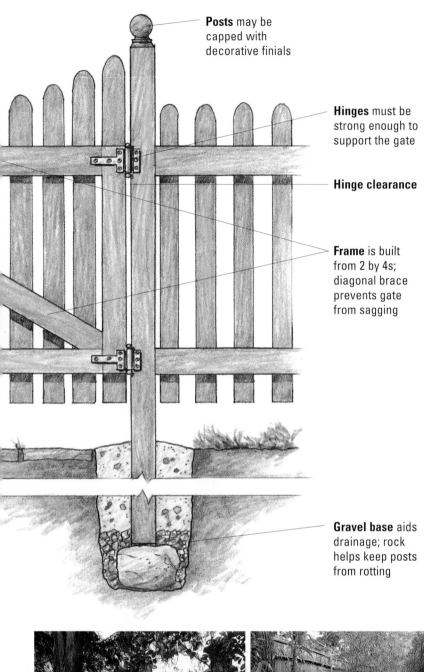

Posts may be capped with decorative finials

Hinges must be strong enough to support the gate

Hinge clearance

Frame is built from 2 by 4s; diagonal brace prevents gate from sagging

Gravel base aids drainage; rock helps keep posts from rotting

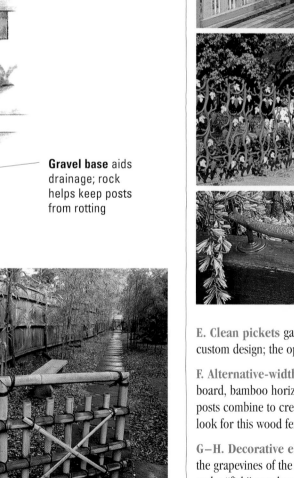

E. **Clean pickets** gain appeal from this custom design; the options are endless.

F. **Alternative-width boards,** a kick-board, bamboo horizontals, and detailed posts combine to create a contemporary look for this wood fence.

G–H. **Decorative elements** such as the grapevines of the cast-iron fence (**G**) and a "fish" gate handle above (**H**) lend personality to the practical.

GREENHOUSES AND LATH HOUSES

In a climate where killing cold is a reality of winter, a greenhouse broadens the scope of gardening, making it possible to overwinter tender perennials—and even tropical plants—and to get a head start in spring with seedlings and cuttings.

If designed to do so, a greenhouse can double as a conservatory. The heated greenhouse shown opposite, top, is furnished with a table and chairs in summer. Most of the plants are taken outside when the weather warms, so there is plenty of room to sit, and the family has a glassed-in space with a broad view of the garden.

There are three kinds of greenhouses: cold, cool, and warm. A cold greenhouse is heated only by the sun. While unsuitable for tropical plants, it

Constructed with old windows so that it resembles a pretty summerhouse rather than a utilitarian workspace, this greenhouse is an attractive garden feature.

provides protection for plants that are borderline hardy, and also extends the growing season in spring and autumn. A cool greenhouse is heated, keeping the ambient temperature above 45°F—warm enough to overwinter frost-tender plants. A hothouse, used for growing tropicals, must be kept above 55°F.

Even in very cold climates you can keep the temperature in an unheated greenhouse above freezing. The unheated greenhouse shown above is located in Norfolk, nicknamed "the icebox of Connecticut." Owner Penny Michels manages to keep the temperatures inside above freezing throughout the winter. The greenhouse is located on the south side of the property to catch as much sun as possible. A

long mirror mounted inside on the north-facing wall catches the sun and reflects it back, and the black gravel floor absorbs the heat. In winter, 11 water-filled barrels covered with black plastic are positioned under the benches. The water heats up during the day, and radiates that warmth at night.

Accessories available for greenhouses include heaters ranging from small electric units to large natural gas heaters; thermostatically controlled fans to circulate the air, keeping the temperature even throughout the space and helping to prevent mildew and condensation; vents, including automatic models that open and close on their own as the temperature inside fluctuates; water-misting systems; benches and shelves, also known as staging; and lights.

Depending on your budget, you can have anything from a basic, unheated greenhouse, either freestanding or attached to the house, for relatively little money, or a state-of-the-art marvel outfitted with all the bells and whistles of modern computer technology.

A. Because this greenhouse was built as an extension of the house, heat is shared between the two spaces, saving on energy. The shade cloth cools the greenhouse in summer.

B. During the hot months, the deciduous trees nearby help cool this greenhouse; in winter, the sun shines on the glass for full-strength heat.

C. Akin to a small greenhouse and easy to build, a cold frame is an inexpensive way of extending the growing season in spring and autumn.

Lath houses

A lath house is a multifunction space. With its filtered light, a lath house is an ideal place to start seeds and cuttings in warm weather; it is also an excellent space for potting because it screens the work area from view. You can also use a lath house as a plant hospital and as storage space for out-of-season plants.

Locate a lath house in full sun with the lath strips running north and south; this way, the shade will shift evenly as the sun moves from east to west. For durability, build it of naturally rot-resistant wood, such as red cedar, or out of pressure-treated lumber. While the floor under the workbenches can be left as bare soil, pave the areas where you walk and stand with gravel, stepping-stones, or concrete to keep your feet dry. Adding an automatic mister or drip watering system will save hours of watering, but at the very least have a hose and faucet nearby so you don't have to carry in water.

A. The filtered shade and protected environment provided by a lath house are ideal for seedlings and young plants.

B. With its trellislike pattern, a lath house is an attractive as well as useful feature in the garden.

GARDEN SHEDS

For anyone who loves to garden—as opposed to simply maintaining a given landscape—a garden shed is a necessary luxury. Where else do you store all the tools and equipment necessary to do the job?

Older properties often have outbuildings that lend themselves admirably to storage. Add a few hooks to the wall for hanging rakes, shovels, and hoes, install some shelves, and you have an excellent place to keep your gardening supplies.

Prefabricated sheds, which come in sections ready to assemble, are relatively inexpensive. Or you can custom-build a storage room that blends with the architectural style of your home. If you are putting up a new structure on your property, even a prefabricated kit, check with your local building authorities. Some communities require permits.

Choose the site for a storage shed carefully. Unless the shed exterior is designed to be a special garden feature, you will probably want to tuck it into an obscure corner of the property. At the same time, it needs to be situated where it is convenient for getting the tools and supplies you need. Choose a level site, and one that is easily accessible by wheelbarrow or cart. It's much easier to wheel supplies about the garden than to make several trips with armloads of tools.

If a plain shed strikes you as an eyesore, dress it up with a false window, as shown top left, or cover it with trelliswork painted a pretty, contrasting color. Plant a vine to mask the structure, at the same time adding a pleasing vertical element to your garden design. With little work, a utilitarian shed can be transformed into a charming asset.

A. A faux window made of mirror and decorated with a window box transforms this shed from a utilitarian box to a pretty garden structure.

B. Known as "necessaries" in colonial times, today old outhouses are useful as storage space for garden tools and equipment.

C. Draped in vinca and scarlet runner bean, this gray, weathered shed has a rustic charm enhanced by the decorative wood pattern built into the door.

D. Painted the classic red of American barns, this storage shed echoes the architecture of the nearby house and picks up the color of the terra-cotta pots sitting nearby.

GAZEBOS

An enclosed garden structure is a refuge away from household bustle, a place to sit quietly or to host a party on a warm evening. It provides shade during the day and shelter during cool evenings, yet is open to breezes, the scent of flowers, and—if near a pool or fountain—the sight or sound of water.

When most of us say we're going to sit outside, we walk out our back door directly onto a patio or deck. But putting a structure away from the house changes how you perceive and use the outdoor space. To find the best site for the structure, walk around your property, glancing back at the house. Look for a vantage point that provides long, diagonal views across the garden; avoid unsightly areas such as the toolshed or garage in favor of a striking bed or a grape arbor. Consider which exposure you want—if your main deck or patio is in full sun, you may prefer to find a shady corner, for example. Then start to think about the design of the structure itself.

Choosing a gazebo

Reminiscent of country bandstands in small-town parks, gazebos can be romantic garden hideaways. The traditional gazebo is a freestanding version of an overhead, with either six or eight sides and sloping rafters joined in a central hub at the roof peak. Often the hexagonal or octagonal sides are partly enclosed with lath, lattice, or even metal grillwork.

Gazebos have come a long way from the old-fashioned Victorian-style version. Construction can either be substantial, with hefty corner columns and stacked beams, or light, with little more than four posts connected by pairs of 2 by 6s. The design may be enhanced by features such as path lighting or downlights, built-in benches or swings, window boxes, fountains, or spas.

A

The ramada idea

Traditional ramadas are simple structures, often rustic, that originally provided shelter from the sun during harvest time. Derived from the Spanish word *ramaje* (which means arbor), they were built of mesquite or cottonwood poles and ocotillo stems, and were open on at least three sides to take advantage of breezes.

Though southwestern in origin, the ramada or pavilion idea translates well to the Northeast. Modern versions are permanent structures, which may be freestanding or attached to houses. Roofs can be solid or partly open. Materials vary according to the design of the house and garden. If you're using wood in a hot climate, it should be thick enough to withstand the sun of many summers; thin wood such as lath tends to dry out and crack.

Canvas or split bamboo shades offer protection from wind and low-angled sun. A fan increases air circulation and cools the structure. For evening use, some lighting—either electric or perhaps just lanterns or luminarias—is essential.

Add a table and chairs to turn a ramada into an outdoor dining room; or add a low perimeter wall for extra seating.

A. Late-afternoon sun warms this traditional gazebo, which was assembled from a kit. Rocking chairs that match the framing offer a comfortable spot for the homeowners to enjoy their garden.

B. An Asian flavor produces a variation on the ramada concept. This open-sided pavilion offers shelter for outdoor dining, rafters for hanging plants, and a prime spot for enjoying both swimming pool and burbling stream.

C. Atop a raised platform, a simple frame becomes a Japanese "engawa" overlooking a large, serene pond.

D. Pennsylvania Dutch design influences this gazebo, situated to take in views of the garden and the multilevel pool.

PATHS

Although it's true that the shortest distance between two points is a straight line, garden walkways often work best when this idea is ignored.

In fact, a path is most interesting when it provides a series of experiences along the way. It can alternately reveal and conceal special plantings, a piece of sculpture, a small bench, or a pleasing view. On a small lot, space expands when you obscure the pathway's end or use "forced perspective," gradually diminishing the width of the path to make it appear longer.

Tailor your choice of materials to the task at hand. Major access walks should be made of brick, pavers, concrete, unglazed tile, or uniform stone slabs for easy traffic flow and an even, nonskid surface. Leave space between pavers for low-growing plants such as rupturewort *(Herniaria glabra)* or moss rose.

On the other hand, a rustic path of gravel or bark chips can meander through the garden, its serpentine form leading you around each bend until the path ahead disappears, its uneven texture and natural colors blending into the surroundings.

Fieldstone, rough cobbles, wood rounds, and other casual stepping-stones also make appealing paths, especially when embedded in a less expensive, contrasting filler material, such as river rock or wood chips.

Another choice is lumber—redwood or cedar decking atop a pressure-treated base, or pressure-treated timbers or railroad ties laid side by side.

Well-defined, broad edgings of brick, bender boards, landscape timbers, or concrete arranged at right angles set a formal tone, which can be further emphasized with a low edging of clipped boxwood.

Unless you've chosen a highly porous material like gravel, plan to pitch the path slightly to one side for drainage, or build it with a slight crown in the center. Runoff needs about ¼ inch of slope per foot.

At night, shielded path lights (see pages 284–285) provide plenty of illumination but little glare. Their low-voltage wires can be snaked through garden plantings, adjacent to planting beds, or along edgings.

How wide should your path be? It depends on how you'll use it. If it will wind discreetly through a garden and serve only as a walking surface, 2 feet is adequate. To allow room for lawn mowers and wheelbarrows, make it 3 feet wide. For two people to walk abreast, as on an entry path, it should be 5 feet wide.

Finally, if your terrain is a little too steep for comfortable walking, plan for one or more broadly spaced steps.

A. Cherry blossoms drift across this grassy path, which gently curves past evergreen plantings of conifers and heathers. The vertical elements not only lend a more formal look to the border but also allow easy maintenance: the grass path can be mowed without damaging the plants.

B. Stones decorated with brightly hued mosaic tiles form a vivid pathway through this New York City garden, where waves of variegated euonymus and pinpoints of color from impatiens brighten a shady spot. Such unusual stones create a beautiful short walkway, or a lovely focal point in a longer path.

C. The same mulch that protects the plants in this woodland garden in Maine creates a trail for visitors to follow. The informality of the path is underscored by the choice of plants that spill out onto the trail, at times obscuring the view of what lies around the next bend.

D. The straight lines of this cut bluestone walkway, flanked by colorful clumps of zinnia, marigold, vinca, and black-eyed Susan, direct visitors quickly to their destination. Durable materials such as stone, brick, or unglazed tile are ideal for heavily trafficked areas, such as those leading to the house from the front sidewalk or the driveway. For safety's sake, make sure they have nonslick surfaces.

Patio-building pointers

Most patios are constructed either as a poured concrete slab or as a surface atop a bed of clean, packed sand.

A concrete slab suits heavy-use areas and formal designs. The slab should be at least 4 inches thick and underlaid with 2 to 8 inches of gravel. Wooden forms define the slab's shape. A thinner concrete pad, typically 3 inches thick, can serve as a base for masonry units such as ceramic tile or flagstones set in mortar.

For casual brick, paver, and cobblestone patios and walks, use a sand bed. A layer of gravel provides drainage and stability; damp sand is then carefully leveled—or "screeded"—on top. Paving units, either spaced or tightly butted, are prevented by edgings from shifting.

In general, patios laid in sand are good do-it-yourself projects. Concrete work is more demanding because there's little room for error; the trick is to pace your formwork and to limit the "pour" to small sections at a time.

If you're thinking of adding an overhead to your patio, you'll find building instructions on pages 370–371. Posts can straddle the paving area atop concrete piers and footings, or be affixed directly to the patio surface with post anchors.

A. Striking on its own for the fieldstone and concrete design, this terrace takes on a new dimension with its water view and faux temple-ruin detail.

B. This inviting flagstone patio, open to the garden yet made cozy by the wisteria-covered arbor, offers a relaxing spot for dining.

C. Reflecting the facade of the house, this brick patio is set in sand for an informal look. Despite the expansiveness of the patio—which means no grass to mow—the herringbone brick pattern lends a sense of containment.

D. White patches in these once-used bricks unify the house and patio. The color and size of the brick and the pattern all contribute to the feeling it imparts. The brick "run" in the inset, for example, imparts a contemporary, geometric feel.

Renovating Concrete

If you have a deteriorating patio or driveway, you can either demolish it and build anew or, in some cases, install a replacement surface. Asphalt is usually best removed, but an existing concrete slab, unless heavily damaged, can serve admirably as a base for brick, pavers, tile, or stone. Another possibility is to construct a low-level deck over the slab. Or you can break up damaged areas of concrete and let casual plantings grow in the resulting gaps.

Professional solutions include the treatment of concrete with one of three methods: bonding, staining, or topcoating. In bonding, a mix of colored cement and a binder is sprayed over the entire surface. Then cracks are blended into a network of faux grout lines created by stenciled patterns or by a special tape that's later removed. The cost, depending on the complexity of the design, ranges from one-quarter to one-third that of total replacement.

Several companies also offer chemical stains in a variety of colors that can be applied directly to the surface of an existing slab to give it a camouflaging patina. Contractors will often score a cracked concrete slab into shapes and apply different colors of stain to them to draw the eye away from the cracks.

A topcoating that completely covers a cracked concrete surface can make a dramatic change. One innovative covering is made of ground-up bits of colored recycled rubber bonded together with a clear epoxy. Other contractors specialize in adding aggregate topcoats or floating on a new colored mix, which can then be stamped or textured.

PLAY YARDS

Kids love the outdoors and need a place to expend their energy. Yet young children (and some older ones) have little sense of danger, so play areas must be both fun and safe. The first decision to make when planning a play yard is where to place it. Preschoolers feel safer—and can be more easily watched—if the play area is close to the house. You may prefer to corral older, noisier children within view, but farther away.

Also take into account sun, wind, and shade. Hot sun increases the risk of sunburn and can make metal slides or bars, as well as concrete walks, burning hot, so install slide surfaces facing north. If your property is in the path of strong winds, locate the play yard inside a windbreak of fencing or dense trees. Dappled shade is ideal. If you have no spreading foliage, position the play yard on the north side of your house, construct a simple canopy of lath or canvas, or plan a play structure that includes a shaded portion.

Many public playgrounds feature metal play structures rather than timber, because wood may eventually rot and break. Still, wood is a warmer and friendlier material—and a good-quality wooden structure will last as long as your children will be using it.

Some timbers used in play structures are pressure-treated with a chemical preservative, especially if they'll be buried underground. Though the Environmental Protection Agency considers these chemicals safe in regulated amounts, check the kind of preservative used before purchasing or building a play structure, and consider alternatives, such as rot-resistant cedar or redwood.

Perhaps you'll want a play structure scaled beyond your youngster's present abilities. Some structures allow you to add or change components as your child grows. Many mail-order companies offer structures that you can assemble yourself. Before you buy, try to view an assembled structure and talk with the owners to evaluate its safety and design. Look through the instructions beforehand to be sure you can carry out the assembly.

Allow at least 6 feet of space around all sides of swings, slides, and climbing structures for a fall zone, then cushion it well. A 3-inch layer of wood chips is one choice; increase the depth to 6 inches under a swing. Shredded bark holds up well, even in windy areas or on slopes. Use ¼- to 1-inch particles of Douglas or white fir bark. Sand provides another safe landing for falls. For children, the more sand the better—even a depth of 121 inches is not too much. Building a low wall around a play yard will help to contain loose materials, keeping the cushion thick and reducing the cost of replenishing.

Turf grass also makes a functional play surface. (But avoid mixtures that contain clover, as its flowers attract bees.) Keep grass about 2 inches high for maximum cushioning.

If your little one will be pedaling a riding toy or tricycle, plan a smooth concrete path at least 24 inches wide, preferably as wide as 4 feet. Gravel paths are frustrating for kids on wheels and for very young walkers.

The need for fencing along property boundaries is obvious. Also securely fence the play area from the driveway, as well as from the pool, spa, or other body of water. You may need to fence off sharp or heavy tools, garden supplies, and garbage cans, too.

A. Gangplanks, turrets, and ramparts, all coated in electric colors, ensure plenty of fun. Forgiving wood chips and ground cover link the structure with the garden.

B. The lucky owner of this rustic child-size cabin has a minigarden out front—a tiny window box, a trellis, and a friendly nasturtium-covered scarecrow.

C. Stained pine presents a quiet facade, but this structure packs playhouse, ladder, observation deck, slide, swing, and storage bins into one dynamic design.

PONDS AND FOUNTAINS

It doesn't take much water to soothe the soul—even the smallest pond can have a cooling effect on a garden. The size of your pond will be restricted by the space available, but its shape and style are limited only by your imagination. If you wish to start small, consider the portable decorative pools available at garden centers and statuary stores, or create your own tub version (see page 299).

Large traditional ponds of brick, concrete, fitted stone, or tile can blend as easily into contemporary gardens as formal ones. They present the opportunity to introduce color and texture to the garden with aquatic plants like water lilies and water hyacinths. A raised pond with brick walls provides a classic home for goldfish and koi.

Water features fall into one of three categories: spray fountains, waterfalls, and spill fountains. Spray fountains are most suitable for formal ponds and are made versatile by assorted heads that shoot water in massive columns or lacy mists. Waterfalls send a cascade toward the pond from a simple outlet pipe. Spill or wall fountains flow from the outlet into a pool or series of tiered pans or shelves. They're good choices for smaller gardens and can even stand alone, independent of ponds (see pages 296–299).

Placing the pond

The obvious spot for a pond is where everyone can enjoy it. But because children find ponds irresistible, the safest locations are in fenced backyards. Check with your local building department about any requirements for fencing with self-latching gates, as well as setbacks from property lines, electric circuits for pumps and lights, and pond depth. Generally, ponds less than 24 inches deep do not need a building permit.

Water trickles from a rustic spout into this rock-edged pond set with log stepping-stones.

If you are planning to add plants or fish to your pond, first consider the climate in your garden. The pond must be protected from wind and situated away from deciduous trees that shed a steady supply of leaves and twigs into the water. Proper drainage is also important: *don't* choose a low-lying (or "bottom") area that will constantly overflow in wet weather. And remember that the backyard needn't be the only place for a pond. The addition of moving water to a front patio or entryway both cools the air and blocks the noise of passing traffic.

Often it's the border that harmonizes the pond with the surrounding landscape. The choices are many: a grass lawn; an adjoining bog garden or rock garden (often piled against a partly raised pond or used at one end of a sloping site); native stones and boulders; flagstones laid in mortar; a wide concrete lip (especially useful as a mowing strip if grass adjoins the area); brick laid in sand or mortar; redwood or other rot-resistant wood laid as rounds or upright columns; terra-cotta tiles; or railroad ties.

You can find flexible pond liners at home-and-garden centers or through mail-order catalogs. Although PVC plastic is the standard material, it becomes brittle with exposure to the sun. More UV resistant—but twice the price—are industrial-grade PVC and butyl-rubber liners. Some pool builders prefer EPDM, a roofing material, available in 10- to 40-foot-wide rolls. Most liners can be cut and solvent-welded to fit odd-shaped water features.

Another option is a preformed fiberglass pool shell. A number of shapes and sizes are available, but many are too shallow to accommodate fish. Although these cost more than PVC-lined pools, they can be expected to last longer—up to 20 years.

A. Rock is the theme of this pond: stepping-stones lead up to the pond and a bridge of stone slabs leads across to the rock garden. A spray fountain tucked behind the juniper shoots water into the pond.

B. Lush ferns, *Phlox divaricata,* and Japanese primrose marry this pond with its woodland surroundings. Well-placed rocks enhance the illusion that it is a natural water feature, not man-made.

C. The clean lines of this square pond are preserved by the water lilies floating on its surface; only the burbling fountain breaks the vertical plane. The pond's dark liner intensifies reflections and produces a mirrorlike effect.

STREAMS AND WATER RUNNELS

I f your property is without a natural stream that can be incorporated into your garden design, you might consider creating one. The style of your garden and home will guide your choice, but whether your property is in the country or the suburbs, formal or informal in character, you can still fulfill your wish for running water.

For a garden that is more orderly and formal, consider building a straight, shallow channel of water called a runnel. Runnels are more geometric in form than streams and do not necessarily reflect the landscape's natural contours. Often constructed of man-made materials such as brick and tile, runnels should be set on an axis to guide the eye through the garden. This type of watercourse marries well with uniformly clipped shrubbery and mass plantings of a single annual or perennial.

Informal streams have irregular features that follow what appears to be nature's own design. Of course, the beauty of creating your own stream is that you can enhance what nature offers. Locate it in an area with a change of grade from high to low. Ideally, the water will follow a course marked by obstacles—rocks, ledges, or weirs (a notch through which water flows)—to change the pace and direction of the flow of water. You can bring in and position local rocks as needed to help the water cascade and fall in a pleasing manner over ledges and boulders, and to create areas for it to pool along its descent. At the sides of the stream, well-placed naturalistic plantings will enhance the scene. The water will eventually collect in a pool at the foot of the stream, to be pumped back to the source through PVC piping camouflaged by plants or buried underground.

A. An informal, natural-looking stream meanders past a well-placed bench in this garden in Beltsville, Maryland. Edged in local shale, the shallows along the shore give visiting wildlife access to the water. Vertical accents in yellow and orange include red-hot pokers *(Kniphofia),* zebra rush, and daylilies. Golden barberry *(Berberis thunbergii* 'Aurea'), pink hardy geraniums, and thyme billow over the rocks.

B. A small, arched bridge spans a rocky stream in this hilly garden in Bedford, New York. Its clean lines, like those of the fence beyond, provide elements of order in the informal landscape. Yellow-blooming daylilies, grasses, ferns, and astilbes flourish among the rocks, backed by evergreen cotoneasters and rhododendrons.

C. A long formal runnel gives the perception of extra depth to this narrow Georgetown garden in Washington, D.C.; a transverse pool would have made the garden look shorter and wider. An allee of river birches enhances the illusion, implying a boulevard leading from the elegant Federal-style house and inviting a stroll along its length. A bed of pachysandra surrounding the runnel disguises its downward slope; a rough piece of stone conceals the water's source.

Pool Safety

For pool owners with children—or with young visitors or neighbors—accidents remain a constant threat. That's why all swimming pools require protective barriers.

Although height requirements vary, most communities insist that properties with pools have a fence that completely encloses the yard (or the fence might surround three sides of the garden and connect to the house). The fence should have self-closing gates with self-latching mechanisms that are beyond the reach of young children.

Another fence, at least 5 feet tall, should enclose the pool or separate it from the house. If it has vertical bars, they should be no more than 4 inches apart, and the fence should have no horizontal pieces that could provide toeholds for climbing. The pool should be clearly visible from the house; panels of safety glass, clear acrylic, or see-through mesh can enhance the view.

All gates to the pool should be child resistant, self-closing, and self-locking. Areas immediately outside the pool fence should not have chairs or other objects that can be easily moved or climbed.

Doors and windows that lead from the house to the pool can be made more secure with additional locking mechanisms installed at least 5 feet above the floor. Options for sliding glass doors include locks for the top of the moving panel and its frame, automatic sliding door closers, or removable bars that mount to the frame.

A properly installed and approved safety cover is also critical. The safest types either have tracks mounted to the decking or fastening devices set in the pool deck (this type is especially good for odd-shaped pools). Never *allow swimming in a partially covered pool; completely remove the cover before entering the pool.*

---

beach" pool, which helps swimmers, especially children, to enter the water gradually.

Pool equipment includes the pump, heater, and filter. You'll need to provide a concrete slab to support them, ideally hidden from sight and sound by a screen, shrubs, or a lushly planted trellis. Place the slab between 25 and 50 feet from the pool; any closer and the noise may be overwhelming; any farther away and you'll need larger equipment to pump water the extra distance.

Before building a swimming pool, look into the legal requirements set forth in deed restrictions, zoning laws, and building, health, and safety codes. Also familiarize yourself with the building codes that apply to associated structures such as decks, fences, and overheads.

Constructing a pool

Pools can be built above ground or completely or partly in-ground. Fully in-ground pools are accessible from patio areas and fit best into most landscapes, but both aboveground and partly in-ground pools can be integrated into your garden's design.

For the structure, concrete (usually sprayed as gunite or shot-crete and reinforced with steel) combines workability, strength, permanence, and flexibility of design. Interior finishes include paint, plaster, and tile, in ascending order of cost. To keep the price down, save tile for details—edgings, step markers, and around the waterline.

Vinyl-lined pools are usually much less expensive than concrete, because the liner is prefabricated and because the pool can be installed in as little as a few days. The liner generally rests on a bed of sand and is supported by walls made of aluminum, steel, plaster, concrete block, or wood. These walls can extend above grade, making them especially economical for sloping sites. Vinyl is not as durable as concrete, but leaks can be repaired.

Fiberglass pools consist of a one-piece rigid fiberglass shell supported by beds of sand. These pools are also fairly quick to install, but the choice of pool shapes and sizes is limited.

Some homeowners choose to start out with aboveground pools, such as the familiar vinyl-lined pool. Since no excavation is required, an aboveground pool can be easy to install and certainly costs less than an in-ground type. These installations, whether temporary or permanent, are most successfully integrated into a garden's design when recessed at least partly below grade and built with a surrounding deck or raised platform.

If you are inheriting an older pool with your new home, there are ways to update it. New edging (called coping) or a deck surround can dramatically improve the look of an old pool. Surrounding a pool with a new selection of plants can also transform its appearance and help merge the pool with the landscape. The addition of a spa or a waterfall is another way to give a pool new appeal.

SPAS AND HOT TUBS

Whether the focal point of a garden or a private retreat, a hot tub or spa has understandable appeal: an invigorating bath alfresco, enlivened by jets of water, in a vessel large enough to accommodate both social and solitary soaks.

Hot tubs differ from spas in materials and form, not function. Both use virtually identical support equipment to massage bathers with hot, bubbling water, but hot tubs—large, straight sided, and barrel shaped—are made of wood.

Proponents of hot tubs appreciate wood—the way it feels, its aroma, and its natural appearance. They also prefer the generally deeper soak of tubs composed of redwood, cedar, teak, or other woods. These materials require careful maintenance, however. Too much chlorine or bromine can degrade wood; too little allows bacteria to grow. And wooden hot tubs must not be allowed to dry out or leaks can develop as the staves shrink.

Spas depart from the rustic simplicity of hot tubs, running the gamut of design choices from boxy portable models to installations of pool-size proportions. The portable, or self-contained, spa is more like a home appliance: it doesn't have to be permanently installed and comes as a complete unit, ready to be plugged into a 120-volt outlet (or wired to a 240-volt circuit). Its support equipment is part of the package. A "skirt," typically of redwood, surrounds the shell.

In-ground types can be set into a hole dug into the ground or into an above-grade surface such as a deck. Shopping for an in-ground spa means choosing between a factory-molded shell made of acrylic reinforced with fiberglass or high-impact thermoplastics, or a more expensive, longer-lasting shell made of concrete.

Concrete spas can be custom-designed, allowing for a virtually limitless range of shapes and sizes. They are also the most durable. Often adjuncts to swimming pools, concrete spas enjoy a longer season of use than swimming pools. After the pool has been closed for the cold season, the spa's hot bubbling water keeps bathers comfortable while the leaves fall and the snow flies.

An offshoot of the spa industry is the "swim spa"—an elongated version of an in-ground spa. Strong hydrojets in swim spas create currents that allow bathers to swim for miles—without moving forward an inch.

Strictly symmetrical, the alignment of this circular spa, pool, and paving establishes a formal mood. A round brass bowl, transferring water from spa to pool, adds a finishing touch to the circular theme.

Wall-building basics

Regardless of the type of wall you plan to raise, you will have to support it with a solid foundation, or footing. Poured concrete is about the best footing you can provide because it can be smoothed and leveled better than other materials. Usually, footings are twice the width of the wall and at least as deep as the frost line. But consult local codes for exceptions.

For very low walls (no more than 12 inches high) or for low raised beds, you can lay the base of the wall directly on tamped soil or in a leveled trench.

In most cases, a freestanding wall more than 2 or 3 feet high should have some kind of reinforcement to tie portions of the wall together and prevent it from collapsing. Steel reinforcing bars, laid with the mortar along the length of a wall, provide horizontal stiffening. Placed upright (for example, between double rows of brick or within the hollow cores of concrete blocks), reinforcing adds vertical strength that can keep a wall from toppling under its own weight.

Special steel ties of various patterns are made for reinforcing unit masonry and attaching veneers to substructures. An example is shown on the facing page.

Vertical columns of masonry, called pilasters, can be tied into a wall to provide additional vertical support. Many building departments require that they be used at least every 12 feet. Also consider placing pilasters on either side of an entrance gate and at the ends of freestanding walls. When you're building the foundation of your wall, the footing will have to be twice the width of the pilasters.

A. This dry stone wall—meaning there is no mortar between the stones—supports a moderate slope. The stones tie in with the facade of the house to give the property a visual unity.

B. The pleasing texture of this mortared stone wall, set into a gentle slope, blends well with the surroundings and provides a perfect stage for the low mounding plants growing above it.

A BRICK WALL

Reinforcing bars strengthen structure (check local codes)

Poured footing is typically twice wall's width and 12 inches deep (or as deep as frost line)

Gravel base ensures good drainage

Header course (every fifth, sixth, or seventh course) spans front to back, helps lock the wall together

Corners overlap with ¾- and ¼- inch "closure" bricks

Common-bond wall has staggered joints from course to course. Double-thickness ("double wythe") wall is much stronger than a single row of bricks

A CONCRETE BLOCK WALL

Bond-beam block adds strength at top

Concrete block core is set with ⅜-inch mortar joints

Stone veneer set in mortar covers block core

Grout

Wall ties help connect veneer to block core

Poured footing is typically twice wall's width and 12 inches deep (or as deep as frost line)

Reinforcing bars strengthen structure (check local codes)

LANDSCAPING WITH PLANTS

Each plant in the garden has its purpose. Trees, vines, and tall shrubs provide shade, privacy, and protection from wind. Perennials brighten beds and borders. Ground covers blanket the soil. Some plants attract wildlife; others prevent erosion or perfume the air.

The challenge is to place plants where their unique qualities are shown to advantage and can play off one another. Silvery foliage defines borders in moonlight and soothes strong color combinations. Wispy grasses shiver in the slightest breeze and capture the golden light of late afternoon in their feathery seed heads. A graceful eastern redbud brings dappled shade to a patio and a burst of vibrant color in spring.

Understanding how the plants combine will help you create the ambience you seek in your garden—whether it's serene and filled with white flowers or dramatic and shot through with vivid hues.

PLANTING FOR FOUR SEASONS OF INTEREST

A gardener's rewards are most often realized in spring and summer, when most plants are in active growth. Although the spectacular show wanes as the weather turns colder, fall and winter need not be forlorn seasons. With a judicious selection of plants, it is possible to plan a landscape with interest throughout the year.

Evergreens are the mainstay of most fall and winter landscapes, but there are also herbaceous plants to take up the standard. If you thought you could never have blooms in winter, hellebores will change your mind. *Helleborus niger*—the Christmas rose—blooms earliest, with showy flowers that open white, then turn pink. The vein-leafed Corsican hellebore *(Helleborus argutifolius)* has showy foliage and bears clusters of nodding apple green flowers. But it is the so-called Lenten rose—*Helleborus orientalis*—that is the most reliable of the group. Appearing in late winter or early spring, the blooms—ranging from pale green to white, maroon, and pink on 18-inch plants—last for weeks.

If the hellebores usher in the blooming season, the ornamental grasses see it out. Many grasses don't begin growth until late spring. They make great partners for displays of spring bulbs, and when the bulbs go dormant, the grasses take over; their growth is rapid and vigorous. By midsummer, they are voluptuous, the very metaphor for summer's fullness.

A host of ornamental grasses bloom late, often in October. Then, with the first few frosts, the grasses fade from summer greens to shades of tan and almond.

A. In early spring, dormant ornamental grasses in this garden are self-effacing partners to displays of spring bulbs, including daffodils and tulips.

B. As grasses mature, they add great volume. Here, maiden grass (*Miscanthus sinensis* 'Gracillimus') and three striped zebra grasses (*Miscanthus sinensis* 'Zebrinus') form a backdrop to gardener's garters (*Phalaris arundinacea* 'Picta').

C. Fall brings plume flowers and a gradual fading from summer's vibrant colors.

D. Like tireless sentinels, ornamental grasses stand throughout the frigid weather. Their winter hues bring warmth to this snowy landscape.

Plants for the Winter Garden

WINTER BLOOMS

Helleborus argutifolius
CORSICAN HELLEBORE

H. foetidus
STINKING HELLEBORE

H. niger
CHRISTMAS ROSE

H. orientalis
LENTEN ROSE

WINTER FOLIAGE

Ajuga reptans
BUGLEWEED CULTIVARS

Arum italicum
ITALIAN ARUM

Asarum europaeum
ASARABACCA

Bergenia cordifolia
HEART-LEAF BERGENIA

Dianthus spp.
PINKS

Festuca ovina 'Glauca'
SHEEP'S FESCUE

Heuchera micrantha 'Palace Purple'
ALUMROOT

Iberis sempervirens
CANDYTUFT

Lavandula augustifolia
ENGLISH LAVENDER

Polystichum acrostichoides
CHRISTMAS FERN

ORNAMENTAL GRASSES

Miscanthus 'Giganteus'
GIANT MISCANTHUS

M. sinensis 'Gracillimus'
MAIDEN GRASS

Pennisetum alopecuroides
FOUNTAIN GRASS

Saccharum ravennae
RAVENNA GRASS

TREES

Whether they are sugar maples coloring New England's mountain slopes in fall or dogwoods adding pastel splashes to Pennsylvania's woods in spring, trees help define the general character of a landscape. In a garden setting, trees serve so many purposes—both aesthetic and practical—that few gardeners would consider doing without them. Trees offer cooling shade, provide shelter, and establish perspective. Trees can frame special vistas and block out unattractive views. They can also make dramatic statements, enhance the garden with sculptural effects, or form the dominant focal point of a landscape.

Although trees may be the most expensive individual plants to buy, they can be relied on to give permanence to any landscape. Not surprisingly, they are particularly valued in new

Trees dominate this simple, Japanese-inspired stream garden. The graceful form and delicate texture of the Japanese maples offer yearlong visual interest; during the growing season, their feathery leaves cast dappled shade on the azaleas and other moisture-loving plants below. The contrast of dark evergreen trees provides a beautiful backdrop.

housing developments. Often overlooked is the role trees play in a house's energy conservation. For example, a tree-shaded house will require less air conditioning in summer than one that is exposed. And if deciduous trees, which lose their leaves in winter, are planted around the south side of a house, the warmth of winter sunshine will be able to penetrate to the interior of the house, helping to reduce heating and lighting costs.

Your choice of trees will be determined largely by their purpose in the landscape. To block the sun, for example, select only trees that develop sizable canopies. If you need a screen, look for trees that produce branches on their lower trunks, or combine trees that have bare lower trunks with shrubs or walls. For a focal point, choose a tree that displays flowers or fruits, or one with attractive foliage, bark, or a striking bare silhouette in winter.

Tree characteristics

Trees usually live for decades, if not for centuries. Each year new growth springs from a framework of last year's branches to form a gradually enlarging structure. Tree silhouettes vary greatly from one species to another (see above right), and a tree's ultimate shape may not be obvious in young nursery specimens.

Though the range of shapes is enormous, all trees are classified as either *deciduous* or *evergreen*. Most *deciduous* types produce new leaves in spring and retain them throughout the summer. In the fall, leaf color may change from green to warm autumnal tones, and the trees then drop their foliage for the winter, revealing bare limbs. *Broad-leafed evergreens,* such as hollies, have wide leaves similar to many deciduous trees, but these cover the plant year-round. (Older leaves may drop, however.) *Needle-leafed evergreens* include trees with needlelike foliage—firs, spruces, and pines, for example—and those whose leaves are actually tiny scales, such as cypresses and junipers. Because they keep their foliage in winter, conifers retain their appearance throughout the year, though their colors may change slightly during cold months.

TREE SILHOUETTES

Columnar   Narrowly oval   Cone shaped   Globular   Horizontally spreading   Weeping

Selecting trees

To avoid disappointment, choose plants that will flourish in your garden's conditions. What are your summers like? Are they hot, cool, dry, or humid? Does your region experience summer drought? If trees are not perfectly suited to your environment, consider placing them where the conditions can be moderated, such as in irrigable or sheltered positions close to the house. Young trees can easily succumb to frost, so purchase only those plants that can easily survive the lowest temperatures normally found in your area.

Take into account the ultimate height and growth rate of a tree *before* you buy it. A desire for shade or privacy may tempt you to purchase a fast-growing plant, but a tree that soon overpowers its space will prove a poor choice, forcing you to prune heavily, remove the tree, or live with your mistake.

Trees known to have aggressive root systems or those that drop masses of leaves or fruits should be planted in a background location, not near pools or patios. Likewise, avoid siting trees with brittle wood in wind- or storm-swept areas; instead, use them as specimen trees in protected locations and position them away from a house or roadway. Some trees are susceptible to pests or diseases prevalent in particular regions. The European white birch *(Betula pendula),* for example, succumbs to a borer in the East, but the hardy river birch *(Betula nigra* 'Heritage') is totally resistant.

Depending on the species of tree, foliage color can vary from greens and pale yellows to almost-black reds. Numerous trees—including crabapple, dogwood, and flowering cherry—provide spectacular color with spring or summer blooms or late-season berries. And in autumn, many trees produce brilliantly colored leaves: sugar maples, for example, turn yellow, orange, and red, while white oaks show burgundy and crimson. After leaves fall, some trees exhibit dramatic gnarled, twisted, or knotted trunks or branches. The salmon-white bark of 'Heritage' river birch peels away in papery strips; the cascading branches of cutleaf Japanese maple *(Acer palmatum dissectum)* are supported by a twisted trunk; and *Corylus avellana* 'Contorta' (Harry Lauder's walking stick) grows strikingly twisted branches.

In addition to the visual appeal of trees, many easterners live in climates perfect for decorative and delicious fruit- and nut-bearing trees, including crabapples, persimmons, mulberries, northern pecans, pawpaws, and serviceberries.

PLANTING TREES

HOUSE

◀ NORTH

A. **Mature deciduous trees** lend an established look, and shade the front of the house in summer.

B. **Flowering crabapple** adds color to the front walk.

C. **Needle-leafed evergreens** screen the driveway year-round.

D. **Semidwarf** and standard fruit trees thrive when placed along south- and west-facing walls.

E. **Flowering specimen tree** offers privacy and shade.

Height is under 40 feet when tree reaches maturity.

Species is free of pests and diseases, particularly any that could quickly destroy or disfigure a small tree.

Canopy is tall enough to walk under and wide enough for at least two people to sit under.

Roots won't lift up paving, form sprouts, or invade lawns or nearby planting beds.

Litter is minimal, as leaves, fruits, flowers, and seedpods fall only once a year and are easily cleared up.

SMALL PATIO TREES

A good tree for patios and decks is well mannered. Its roots remain under the ground, rather than prying up paving or invading nearby flower beds. In addition, it does not produce pollen to plague allergy sufferers or continuously drop leaves or messy fruits. Even when fully grown, a patio tree should not be too tall, yet its canopy must be high and wide enough to cast shade.

Small deciduous trees work well, as long as you don't mind sweeping up their autumn leaves. Consider a graceful Japanese maple or an eastern redbud to bring dappled shade and a touch of elegance to a patio. Evergreens are not recommended; their rangy growth habits require frequent pruning, they often drop spiky needles, and the shade they cast is extremely dense.

In general the best patio trees are small and relatively slow growing; to quickly achieve your desired effect, purchase an older

tree. Although few retail nurseries stock trees larger than 10-feet tall, you can often find larger trees through wholesale suppliers. A landscape architect, contractor, or garden designer will also be able to help with such a purchase, as well as provide necessary planting assistance.

October, when temperatures are cool and rains are on the way, is the best month to plant most ornamental trees. Planting during dormancy permits all of the tree's energy to go toward developing additional roots. Above ground, young tree trunks are vulnerable to animal pests such as rabbits and deer nibbling on the bark. To protect the trunk, surround it with a collar of hardware cloth buried a few inches into the ground and extending as high as the anticipated snowfall level. Be sure to remove the collar as the tree grows, however: a tight collar can also damage the trunk.

Acer palmatum

Great Choices for Patios

FOR ALL AREAS

Acer palmatum
JAPANESE MAPLE

Cercis canadensis
EASTERN REDBUD

Crataegus 'Winter King'
HAWTHORN

Magnolia virginiana
SWEET BAY

Malus 'Prince Georges'
NON-FRUITING CRABAPPLE

**Prunus blireiana,
P. cerasifera 'Purple Pony'**
FLOWERING PLUM

P. sargentii
SARGENT CHERRY

Ulmus parvifolia
CHINESE ELM

FOR HIGHER ALTITUDES

Amelanchier canadensis
SERVICEBERRY

Syringa amurensis japonica
JAPANESE LILAC

FOR WARMER AREAS

Lagerstroemia 'Natchez'
CRAPE MYRTLE

Ligustrum lucidum
GLOSSY PRIVET

Caring for Landscape Trees

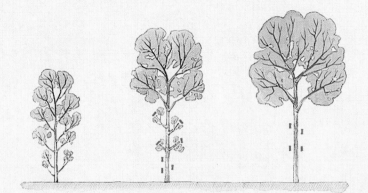

Forming a strong trunk. *A young tree develops a strong trunk faster if its lower branches are removed gradually. At first, allow the branches on the trunk to acquire thickness. As the tree matures, shorten the lower branches so that growth will be directed upward to increase the tree's height. Eventually, you may remove all the lower branches.*

Preserving the roots. *Healthy roots are vital to a tree's well-being. If you install paving underneath an established tree, avoid solid materials such as poured concrete—they will totally prevent air and water from reaching the roots. Instead, leave as much open soil as possible around the trunk, and select a paving design that allows water to penetrate. Set bricks or paving stones in sand, rather than cement, or use loose materials.*

Any major soil removal around a tree (for construction of a retaining wall, for example) will take with it some of the roots that sustain and anchor the tree. Try to preserve the existing grade beneath the tree by making elevation changes beyond the branch spread. Seek professional advice for soil-level changes over 2 feet deep.

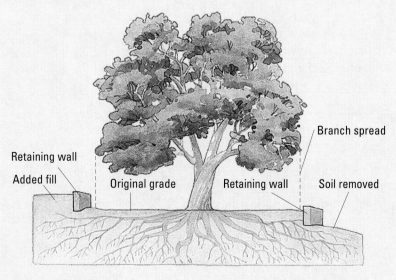

a preliminary cut on the underside of the branch just beyond the collar. This will prevent the falling limb from tearing bark on the trunk. Then cut through the branch from the upper side. Avoid using pruning paints or tree sealant to seal the wound; these products have no effect on a tree's ability to resist infection.

If pruning alone won't open up views, consider having any offending trees removed. Keep some trees on the edges of your outlook, however, as these are the ones that frame the view.

Windowing. Some trees that are close to a house or patio grow so densely that they block views of the surrounding landscape. By selectively removing some of the lateral branches (below), you can open up the tree, creating fully framed views—or windows—of whatever lies beyond. When you window a tree on one side, balance it with some pruning on the opposite side, even if both sides are not obstructing the view.

FRAMING VIEWS

Trees are so valuable to any landscape that they should be incorporated into a view—or used to enhance it—whenever possible. They are wonderful for establishing a sense of perspective for distant vistas, such as a body of water or mountains, thus creating closeness and intimacy within a grand panorama. And city lights become magical and animated when seen through leafy, rustling branches at night.

Occasionally, however, trees interrupt key parts of a view and require selective pruning. As with any tree surgery, pruning to perfect a view must be carried out without endangering the health of the tree. Depending on how you wish to frame the view, several techniques will accomplish this goal: windowing, thinning, skirting up, or crown reduction. If you are not an experienced pruner, don't attempt to prune large trees. Hire a professional arborist who knows how to do the job properly. In many states, arborists must be licensed and must carry their own insurance; you can find an arborist by checking in the Yellow Pages under Trees, by asking for recommendations from friends, or by contacting the American Society of Arborists.

If you are skillful enough to remove a good-size tree limb, look for its branch collar—a raised lip or wrinkle at the junction of the trunk and the limb. Make

An English walnut, skirted up to make way for clusters of bright perennials, is the focus of this garden situated on a ridge near New York's Finger Lakes. Removal of the tree's lower limbs also allows an unobstructed view of the region's green valleys and rolling hills.

Thinning.
Selectively thinning the branches of a midrange tree can open up views, and gives a tree better resistance to the wind. Do not prune the main limbs, but clear out bunches of foliage and the smaller branches that grow between them (left). Remove weak limbs and vertical water sprouts first, and any branches that are rubbing or crossing each other. Then you will have a better view of the overall branch shape and can prune selectively along the main limbs. As you work toward the ends of each main limb, prune less vigorously in order to leave a natural-looking, broad, and bushy top.

 Skirting up. Removing some of the lower limbs (also known as limbing up) of a midrange tree can reveal a view without ruining the lines of the tree (right). As a rule of thumb, don't skirt up more than half of the tree's height, less if possible. If the tree is top-heavy, thin it so that it doesn't look like a lollipop.

Crown reduction. To lower a tree's canopy, use a technique called crown reduction (not shown), which reduces the size of the tree while retaining its natural growth lines. Prune the tallest branches as far down to the trunk as possible, but near small side branches that point in the same upward direction. If there are no such branches, track the tall limb down to one of its own upward-pointing, robust secondary branches. Cut just above this branch.

Trees vs. Power Lines

Keeping trees clear of utility lines can be a never-ending and costly struggle. To make matters worse, inexperienced pruners, with only the clearance of the power lines in mind, will often shear tree tops indiscriminately, reducing limbs to unsightly stumps. Not only will the tree suffer and possibly become unstable, but new growth will inevitably threaten the lines again. There are ways to keep trees healthy and power lines clear, however.

By the method known as thinning, entire lateral branches are removed. Select branches can also be reduced in length by a process known as drop crotching. In these ways, new growth can be directed away from the lines, which can now pass freely among the tree's limbs while the tree retains a more natural shape and appearance. Maintenance costs are reduced, too, since a properly thinned tree will need fewer prunings. Perhaps the best way to avoid interference with power lines is to plant low-growing trees where power lines are a consideration. Some excellent choices include gray birch (Betula populifolia), Franklin tree (Franklinia alatamaha), snowbell (Styrax), many hawthorns (Crataegus), Japanese maples (Acer palmatum cultivars), Japanese flowering dogwood (Cornus kousa), Magnolia × soulangiana cultivars, Laburnum, and most crabapples.

PLANTING UNDER TREES

Trees in the garden naturally result in shady areas. And as trees grow, the amount of shade they cast increases — sometimes beyond the limits that many plants can tolerate. When selecting plants, keep in mind that all shade is not created equal. Although most trees cast the dappled light usually referred to as partial shade, some tree canopies are so dense they allow no light to penetrate. Planting to create shade — and landscaping in its presence — calls for extra diligence in the planning stages. Choices of colorful plants for shade are more limited than those for the sun. But you can create interesting effects by combining plants for foliage texture and color.

A. In the dappled sunlight of this Pennsylvania garden, an area of moss thrives in a moist spot. Mounding azaleas and leggy rhododendrons, along with the weighty boulders, contrast with the delicate moss in size, color, and texture.

B. In a shady corner of this Philadelphia terrace, rose and red impatiens and red tuberous begonias pop against a background of foliage in various shades of green. The silvery cutleaf Japanese maple and the ferns at the base of the tree add variety in foliage texture as well as color.

C. Set off by swaths of low-growing juniper and euonymus, clumps of *Hosta undulata*, with stark white centers in medium green leaves, thrive in the shade of this Virginia garden. Hostas range in color from variegated leaves combining yellow, gold, or creamy white to the entire spectrum of greens and blues.

Plantings beneath trees need not be confined to ground covers. Here a profusion of shade-loving plants flourishes in the dappled light beneath a dogwood and a golden locust. Both trees burst into white bloom in spring; the foliage plants below feature soft hues that prevail throughout the growing season.

A Shade Garden

The Plants

PERENNIALS

A. Alchemilla mollis
LADY'S-MANTLE **(2)**

B. Anemone hybrida 'Honorine Jobert'
JAPANESE ANEMONE **(5)**

C. Arrhenatherum elatius bulbosum 'Variegatum'
BULBOUS OAT GRASS **(1)**

D. Berberis thunbergii 'Atropurpurea'
RED-LEAF JAPANESE BARBERRY **(2)**

E. Digitalis purpurea
COMMON FOXGLOVE **(4)**

F. Helleborus argutifolius var. corsicus
CORSICAN HELLEBORE **(3)**

G. H. orientalis
LENTEN ROSE **(3)**

H. Hosta 'Gold Standard' (4)

I. H. sieboldiana 'Elegans' (1)

J. Lamium maculatum 'White Nancy'
DEAD NETTLE **(3)**

K. Liriope muscari
BIG BLUE LILY TURF **(3)**

L. L. m. 'Variegata'
BIG STRIPED LILY TURF **(4)**

M. Thalictrum aquilegifolium
MEADOW RUE **(3)**

N. T. rochebrunianum
LAVENDER MIST **(3)**

TREES

O. Cornus × rutgersensis 'Aurora'
STELLAR DOGWOOD **(1)**

P. Robinia pseudoacacia 'Frisia'
GOLDEN LOCUST **(1)**

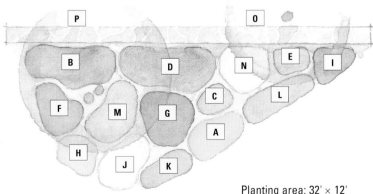

Planting area: 32' × 12'

TREES AND SHRUBS FOR THE WINTER GARDEN

The Northeast's bracing winter months need not signal a time-out from gardening, nor should snow and ice necessarily diminish your garden's glory. With the right mix of trees and shrubs to provide texture and color, winter's sparkling snows and frosts can transform an otherwise dormant garden into an enchanted landscape.

Against the neutral background of a winter sky, snow-encrusted evergreens or the frosted limbs of a Japanese maple can provide plenty of contrast and texture. And for color, shrubs such as hollies, nandinas, cotoneasters, and firethorns, with their brilliant orange and red berries, make striking seasonal standouts.

Among trees and shrubs best suited to the winter garden there are several excellent choices, plus a few practical hints to bear in mind. Hardy conifers, gorgeous in the winter garden in their green needles and white snow, can also double as windbreaks. Plant them along your garden's northeast corner to protect more delicate plants against winter's fiercest blasts. Some good choices include false cypress, juniper, spruce, pine, arborvitae, and hemlock. Conversely, your garden's southern exposure is the perfect spot for tall, deciduous trees such as the river birch or the sugar maple. Once they've shed their brilliant autumn leaves, winter's warmth and sunlight can freely enter the garden.

To take full advantage of your garden's winter features, be sure to site outstanding trees and shrubs within the view line of windows whenever possible. That way, you can enjoy your winter garden even more from the warmth of indoors. And by all means, don't forget the birds. Feathers and song can go a long way to cheer even the bleakest winter day. Keep feeders full, and choose such winter-hardy specimens as arborvitae, hemlock, holly, fir, cotoneaster, firethorn, juniper, and pine, which provide food and shelter.

Achieving success in the winter garden is easy. The secret is not to resist the season, but instead to stay open to all of nature's intriguing possibilities.

A. A generous mix of deciduous and evergreen trees and shrubs of varying densities and heights gives this snow-covered garden plenty of shape and visual interest.

B. Noted for its showy fruit clusters that appear in fall and last all winter, firethorn is available in several species to add brilliance in the winter garden.

C. The crackling reddish brown bark of a paperbark maple (*Acer griseum*) continually peels, adding color, texture, and drama to a winter garden.

D. A Japanese maple's wide-spreading and twisting branches catch and hold winter's glistening snows.

A

B

Great Choices for the Winter Garden

EVERGREEN TREES

Abies concolor
WHITE FIR

Chamaecyparis nootkatensis 'Pendula'
NOOTKA FALSE CYPRESS

Picea omorika
SERBIAN SPRUCE

Pinus bungeana
LACE-BARK PINE

Pinus thunbergii
JAPANESE BLACK PINE

Pinus wallichiana 'Zebrina'
HIMALAYAN OR BHUTAN PINE

DECIDUOUS TREES

Acer griseum
PAPERBARK MAPLE

Acer palmatum cultivars
JAPANESE MAPLE

Betula nigra 'Heritage'
RIVER BIRCH

Crataegus viridis 'Winter King'
WINTER KING GREEN HAWTHORN

Fagus sylvatica 'Pendula'
EUROPEAN BEECH

Stewartia koreana
KOREAN STEWARTIA

Syringa amurensis japonica
JAPANESE LILAC TREE

Ulmus parvifolia
CHINESE ELM

SHRUBS

Chamaecyparis obtusa 'Crippsii'
HINOKI FALSE CYPRESS

Cornus alba 'Sibirica'
RED TWIG DOGWOOD

Cotoneaster apiculatus
CRANBERRY COTONEASTER

Hamamelis × intermedia cultivars
WITCH HAZEL

Ilex verticillata
COMMON WINTERBERRY

Ilex × 'Sparkleberry'
HOLLY

Juniperus horizontalis 'Douglasii'
CREEPING JUNIPER

Nandina domestica
HEAVENLY BAMBOO

Pieris japonica cultivars
JAPANESE PIERIS

Pyracantha cultivars
FIRETHORN

Tsuga canadensis 'Pendula'
CANADIAN HEMLOCK

SHRUBS

If you try to visualize your property without shrubs, you'll quickly grasp the importance of these plants in landscape design. Without them, there would be no hedges to keep children and pets safely in bounds, no lilacs or roses to gather for bouquets. House lines would be stark and angular without the softening effect of feathery evergreens or bushy hydrangeas.

Just as a large sofa or a bulky upholstered chair can help fill a room, shrubs can add form, weight, and substance to a landscape. They become permanent

fixtures, altering traffic flow and framing views. Planted near a wall, they create attractive backdrops; set close together, they form a living fence. For example, clipped boxwood, just a few feet high, helps define a formal garden, while a staggered row of loose, flowery lilacs *(Syringa)* works well as a summer privacy screen. And a hedge of thorny, dense shrubs, such as barberry and clipped hawthorn *(Crataegus)*, makes an effective barrier against unwelcome intruders.

Judiciously placed, a single flowering shrub can punctuate

Northeastern favorites, azaleas and rhododendrons transform a simple staircase into a hidden entryway.

the landscape as a focal point; short or dwarf shrubs, when grouped together, can add heft and structure to a flower border or create a smooth transition from tree canopy to ground level. In tiny gardens, consider pruning a shrub into a standard—a topiary form that resembles a small tree.

Like trees, shrubs are either deciduous or evergreen. They grow in a variety of rounded, tapered, or fountainlike shapes. With their showy flowers, fruits, or autumn foliage, shrubs offer seasonal appeal. Some, however, have decorative foliage throughout the growing season. Others, such as daphnes, lilacs, and viburnums, are primarily valued for their fragrance.

With hundreds of shrubs available, one key to successful landscaping is to select bushes that suit your garden's site—its soil conditions, available sunlight, and water resources. Certain favorites such as azaleas and rhododendrons, for example, thrive in the semishade of overhead trees and acid soil that is both moisture retentive and fast draining. Rosebushes, on the other hand, prefer bright light and a nearly neutral soil.

To ensure low maintenance, choose shrubs with similar cultural requirements. Remember, too, that for shrubs to look their best, they must be given adequate space to grow into their natural shapes.

'Cécile Brunner,' a polyantha rose, bears its fragrant, exquisitely shaped blooms in clusters on a low shrub that fits nicely into flower and shrub borders.

Considering size

It's important to keep a shrub's ultimate size in mind when siting it and not succumb to the urge to put it too close to another shrub, walk, or doorway. Unlike perennials, with their shorter life spans and smaller, infinitely transplantable sizes, shrubs will become large, permanent additions to a landscape.

It's hard to imagine their potential growth when you buy small, compact shrubs from a nursery. Newly installed, they almost always look too small for their spaces. Remember that the yew now blotting out your neighbor's window was once a tiny 2-foot mound, and that the forsythia overgrowing a walkway was once a few wispy sprays. To fill the gaps around newly planted shrubs, plant annual or perennial flowers for color and volume.

Regular pruning is one way to contain shrubs, but for fast growers, it can become a tedious chore. Slow-growing dwarf forms require less maintenance.

Pruning Needs

Most shrubs require some kind of pruning to control size, keep them in shape, and—in the case of some flowering shrubs—increase flower production. Many summer- and fall-blooming shrubs, such as the hydrangea shown above and the butterfly bush (Buddleia) pictured below, produce flowers on the current year's growth. If allowed to grow unchecked, the quality and quantity of flowers may deteriorate, and the new growth on which the flower buds form may be too high on the plant for you to see and enjoy.

A hard pruning in early spring results in vigorous new shoots that will flower in summer or early fall. It's a good idea to feed the shrub when it is cut back and to apply a top dressing of compost or manure to support and encourage the new growth. Other shrubs that benefit from this maintenance include polyantha roses, such as the 'Cécile Brunner' pictured at left, spirea, and Perovskia.

In those cases in which large shrubs have grown unpruned for many years, the most prudent treatment may be simply to trim the shrub into tree form by cutting out the lower branches. Often the only difference between a large shrub and a small tree is its shape.

SHRUBS IN BORDERS

Borders filled with several plant types display shrubs to their greatest advantage. All shrubs, but especially evergreen ones, lend permanence to flowering borders that change with the seasons; in winter, shrubs may be the only source of visual interest. They can be focal points and accents or, conversely, serve as backgrounds for showier plants. Shrubs that reflect the color or texture of nearby trees link the planting scheme to the surrounding landscape. The weight and substance of many shrubs contrast with more delicate herbaceous plants. Flowering shrubs furnish color and fragrance, as well as attract birds and butterflies.

Select shrubs with a variety of foliage colors and blooms to keep the garden colorful in all seasons. The border at right contains shrubs, subshrubs, and shrubby perennials that exhibit blooms from early spring (magnolia) into fall (abelia, butterfly bush, and roses).

The border is also filled with color, including purple-leafed barberry; the gray or gray green foliage of lavender, lavender cotton, sage, and wallflower; and the yellowish leaves of blue mist and spirea. Greens vary from bright green broom to dark green germander to apple green *Kerria.* Bronze-purple tints infuse the foliage of abelia and heavenly bamboo. In fall, deciduous barberry, plumbago, and spirea, and evergreen heavenly bamboo present good color.

A. This shady corner is brightened with shrubs such as golden-leafed box honeysuckle (*Lonicera nitida* 'Baggesen's Gold'). Its color is complemented by the rosy lavender of flowering onion (*Allium*) and is echoed by the chartreuse bracts of euphorbia in the foreground. Various hostas add bold foliage contrasts.

B. Along the path perennials grow. Shrub roses dominate borders on both sides of the walkway. The bluish green leaves of sea kale (*Crambe maritima*) and *Sedum spectabile,* each displaying masses of flowers in season, combine well with the silvery grasses (*Festuca* and *Miscanthus*) and the teal garden shelter.

C. Spring-blooming bulbs, including daffodils (*Narcissus*) and wood hyacinths (*Scilla*), combine with riveting red azaleas to create a dazzling spring show. Long after the bulbs disappear into dormancy, the evergreen azaleas will remain, a quiet but constant presence.

A MIXED PLANTING

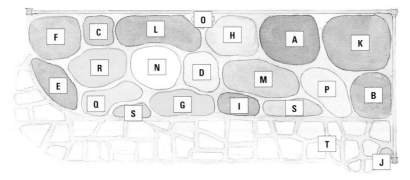

Planting area: 24' × 12'

The Plants

A. Abelia grandiflora 'Sherwoodii'
GLOSSY ABELIA (**1**)

B. Berberis thunbergii 'Cherry Bomb'
JAPANESE BARBERRY (**1**)

C. Buddleia davidii 'Black Knight'
BUTTERFLY BUSH (**1**)

D. Caryopteris clandonensis 'Worcester Gold'
BLUE MIST (**1**)

E. Ceratostigma plumbaginoides
DWARF PLUMBAGO (**3**)

F. Erysimum 'Bowles' Mauve'
WALLFLOWER (**1**)

G. Genista lydia
BROOM (**2**)

H. Lavandula angustifolia
ENGLISH LAVENDER (**3**)

I. L. a. 'Munstead'
ENGLISH LAVENDER (**2**)

J. Lonicera heckrottii
GOLD FLAME HONEYSUCKLE (**1**)

K. Magnolia 'Randy'
HYBRID MAGNOLIA (1)

L. Nandina domestica 'Woods Dwarf'
HEAVENLY BAMBOO (**3**)

M. Potentilla 'Katherine Dykes'
CINQUEFOIL (**2**)

N. Rosa 'Fair Bianca'
ROSE (**1**)

O. Rosa 'New Dawn'
ROSE (**1**)

P. Salvia officinalis 'Berggarten'
COMMON SAGE (**2**)

Q. Santolina chamaecyparissus 'Nana'
LAVENDER COTTON (**3**)

R. Spiraea bumalda 'Limemound' (**2**)

S. Teucrium chamaedrys 'Prostratum'
GERMANDER (**5**)

T. Thymus pseudolanuginosus
WOOLLY THYME

GARDEN-FRIENDLY ROSES

'Mary Rose'

Be bold with roses and you can create a spectacularly colorful landscape. But first, you may have to change the way you think about these familiar plants. Many gardeners grew up in the heyday of hybrid teas—long-stemmed beauties with perfectly formed buds that make wonderful cut flowers but so-so landscape plants. But lately, eastern gardeners are trying floribundas, grandifloras, and English roses, as well as rediscovering old roses for hedges and borders.

The best roses for landscape use are repeat bloomers—attractive, compact plants with clean-looking foliage and strong resistance to pests. While many roses meet these criteria, some stand out for particular uses.

SMALL HEDGES, BORDERS. As a group, floribundas are probably the finest landscape roses. They bear large clusters of flowers atop compact 2- to 5-foot-tall plants that are covered with glossy green leaves. Spaced 18 to 24 inches apart, they make excellent hedges, borders, or edgings along garden paths. Dependable varieties include white 'Iceberg', pink 'Simplicity', yellow 'Sun Flare', and red 'Europeana'. The polyantha rose, a parent of many modern floribundas, carries abundant small flowers in big clusters, making it, too, an excellent hedge. Particularly attractive are 'The Fairy' and 'Nearly Wild'.

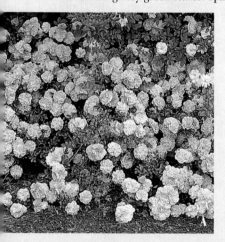

GROUND COVERS. For low raised beds and banks, roses that grow no taller than 2 feet and spread their canes widely are perfect. Choose vigorous, disease-resistant growers such as 'Alberic Barbier', with creamy white flowers with a yellow blush.

FENCE DRAPES. Some climbers (leaners, really, that do not cling to surfaces on their own) are particularly beautiful against weathered split-rail fences. Easy-care types include red 'Blaze', pink 'Cl. The Fairy', and the deep pink shrub rose 'William Baffin'.

MIXED BORDERS. Some roses combine handsomely with perennials in mixed borders. 'Graham Thomas' (a yellow English rose), 'Sally Holmes' (a pale pink to white shrub rose), and 'Dainty Bess' (a rose pink hybrid tea) pair well with perennials like catmint, cranesbill, lavender, and *Salvia superba* 'East Friesland'.

TRELLISES, ARBORS. Some climbing roses are quite vigorous and are at their best when supported on sturdy trellises or arches. Two climbers to consider are 'Cl. Cécile Brunner', a polyantha with pale pink flowers that has a romantic old-fashioned look (especially when trained against white lattice), and the large-flowered climber 'Silver Moon', with 4-inch creamy white flowers that are stunning against a sun-splashed wall.

A. 'Pink Bells' repeats its profuse bloom to make it a colorful and low-maintenance ground cover. Its compact dimensions (2½ by 4 feet) are ideal for a small, sunny spot.

B. Full bloom in spring. A cream-colored rose and a purple clematis entwine above brilliant pink peonies. With proper pruning of the rose and the clematis, the show repeats yearly.

Choosing roses

Of course, the best roses for you are the ones that will do best in your particular climate and conditions. If winter temperatures in your area regularly drop below 10°F, your choices are limited to species, old garden, and modern shrubs bred for cold climates. If cold winters contrast with hot summers, try a hardy modern shrub rose. Some floribundas, grandifloras, and hybrid teas will also do well as long as they have some winter protection. You may also want to purchase roses that are growing on their own roots instead of on grafted ones—own-root roses have a better chance of surviving harsh winters.

And finally, some of the best advice you can get about growing roses is local advice. Visit nearby public gardens to see what grows well in your area, and talk to your neighbors who cultivate roses. Also, contact the American Rose Society (ARS). Composed of hundreds of local rose societies around the United States, the ARS provides information to anyone who wants to grow roses. In addition, it grades all roses currently in commerce, rating them on a scale of 1 to 10 in terms of quality, with any rose rated 9 and above considered "outstanding" and any rose rated below 6 "of questionable value."

The large blooms of Rosa rugosa (inset), nestled among foliage that turns bonfire shades in autumn, are followed by plump orange-red hips, such as those of the alba cultivar above. Rugosas are extremely hardy and adapt to a wide range of soils and conditions, including seaside locations.

DISPLAYING VINES

Lightweight wooden or metal trellises of different sizes can hold only lightweight climbers such as clematis. More sturdy are the types that have posts that can be anchored in the ground or in a large pot.

Freestanding trellises and arbors support permanent vines with hard, woody stems, such as grape or wisteria. The stems twirl up the posts, and the spreading foliage provides shade.

A sturdy wall bears the weight of heavy, vigorous growers such as trumpet vine or climbing hydrangea. Prune and tie to prevent the plants from sprawling.

VINES

Whether framing an entry, draping a pillar, or just rambling along the ground, vines can bring dazzling color to the garden. The fast growth of many vines makes them ideal plants for temporary screens and permanent structures alike. They can cover a large area such as a fence, or weave a delicate tracery on a wall in a small garden. Trailing vines can be planted in hanging containers on a small deck or balcony to shield the space from view. And because many vines are evergreen or feature variegated foliage and decorative fruits, they can provide year-round interest.

Not only do vines have a softening effect on walls, they also greatly improve the appearance of other garden structures, such as lattice screens, gazebos, and spa surrounds. Keep in mind that plants climbing on vertical supports need less frequent clipping and training than those that are trained horizontally. The latter tend to bloom more heavily, however, because their stems are more exposed to sunlight.

Wisteria, which looks equally at home in an Oriental setting or a cottage garden, can be grown as a tree, a shrub, or a vine. In this garden, its exceptionally abundant flower clusters embellish an arbor.

VINES CAN DO MANY THINGS

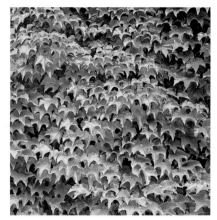

Soften a fence. Encourage vigorous growers such as clematis (above), ivy, or honeysuckle to weave through an open-work fence to hide unsightly chain link or disguise old or sagging wood.

Another option is to plant vines beside the fence and allow them to grow and dangle over the top in lavish sprays. Danglers with showy flowers include rambler roses, trumpet honeysuckle, and clematis.

Brighten an entry. Train woody vines such as wisteria, climbing roses, or honeysuckle (above) to frame entryways, gables, and balconies. Their flowers can dress up walls or soften an angular deck. Wires fastened to eye screws will hold main branches to the wall, or the vine may be run up porch or deck posts. Do not allow them to cling to wood clapboards or shingles, however.

Screens and boundaries. Quick climbers such as morning glory or more permanent perennials such as Boston ivy (above) or Virginia creeper can cover plain fences and walls with color. Vines covering a boundary fence increase the feeling of enclosure on the garden side, while the thick cover of greenery also serves as an attractive windbreak or privacy screen.

Shade and fragrance. A sturdy arbor becomes a haven when used as a support for vines that cast cooling summer shade. Fragrant vines suitable for arbors include sweet autumn clematis, honeysuckle, roses, and wisteria. Tie the growing vines to the structure with tree tape or strips of soft cloth until the plant has established good contact with the frame. To shade porches during hot summers, train annual vines such as moonflower or morning glory up lengths of twine or garden netting.

LAWNS

The lawn is generally the simplest—and usually the most conspicuous—feature of a home landscape. But it need not be large to enhance the overall beauty of a property. A compact and well-designed lawn area can be just as functional and handsome as an extensive expanse of turf grass. And a small lawn requires much less work.

A well-tended lawn offers many assets to a home landscape. Pleasing to the eye and soft underfoot, durable enough to withstand foot traffic and an exemplary surface for entertaining, relaxation, and recreation, a lawn also serves as a velvety buffer between the more public reaches of a property and the privacy of a house. Moreover, lawns throughout the suburbs and countryside of the northeastern United States have become an integral part of the landscape picture that frames a house, making the surrounding neighborhood more habitable and attractive to all.

Turf grass offers environmental benefits as well. It absorbs carbon dioxide and chemical pollutants such as sulfur dioxide and ground-level ozone from the atmosphere and releases oxygen. A lawn also stabilizes dust and pollen, muffles sound levels, and absorbs glare, and a chemical-free lawn acts as a sponge, collecting surface water so that the underlying soil can filter out impurities and replenish underground aquifers with untainted water.

Lawns in the landscape

A lawn area needn't be square or rectangular. A small circle of lawn ringed by trees and flowers, for example, can form the centerpiece of a formal garden; a curved or kidney-shaped lawn can direct the eye to a focal point, such as a specimen tree or a piece of sculpture. A grass path can entice a visitor around a stand of shrubs to a private garden room beyond. And squares of turf alternated with paving can create a striking patterned carpet for a seating area.

When designing or redesigning a lawn area, give serious thought to the amount of care turf grass will require. In a shady spot or on a dry hillock, you may be better off planting a ground cover such as ivy or creeping juniper (see pages 224–225). And if you prefer tending your plants to mowing the lawn, be selective about the type of grass seed to sow or sod (see pages 222–223).

For easier maintenance, install mowing strips around the perimeter of your lawn. A ribbon of concrete, brick, or paving set slightly lower than lawn level will allow you to cut right to the edge of the grass. Lawns with simple, rounded, or geometric shapes and uninterrupted by plantings and decorative obstacles are quicker to mow.

Also, sink edgings of plastic, metal, or wood benderboard to contain your lawn, as well as any plantings on the other side. If you plant a grass that spreads by stolons or rhizomes—such as creeping bent grass, the bluegrasses, and the zoysias—an edging 8 inches deep will keep the turf grass from invading nearby flower beds.

A. A narrow curving lawn
lends graceful sightlines to the
formal shrub borders on either
side and the larger lawn area
in the near distance. On the left,
a lavender-flowering garden
hydrangea and a rhododendron
lead the visitor to a half-hidden
grass path. On the right, a stately
Hinoki false cypress with flattened
sprays of shiny evergreen foliage
backs a bristle of winter heath.
Contained by edging strips and
the deeply mulched plantings,
the lawn is easy to mow.

B. A terrace of turf grass
surrounded by pink impatiens,
variegated hosta, and evergreen
foliage makes this small,
rectangular retreat cool and inviting. The formal entrance of cut
stone steps flanked by rococo
fruited urns stands in vivid contrast to the cozy interior.

C. A neatly trimmed hedge
surrounds the grassy area of an
open-air seating nook. The sense
of containment is enhanced by
tall-growing conifers and roses.
The gap between the plantings
permits viewers to observe
passersby as they stroll along the
curved strip of lawn that permits
passage through the garden.

D. The grass median between
two strips of paving bids a rustic
welcome to this country home.
The turf grass can be easily
mowed, and the pavers form a
barrier, preventing the grass from
spreading into the daylily beds
that edge the driveway.

Northeastern Turf Grasses

Cool-season turf grasses—which grow in spring, fall, and early and late summer when the weather is cool—constitute the major choices for gardeners in the Northeast. Zoysia, a warm-season grass that grows in the heat of late spring and summer, is an alternative for southerly parts of the northeast subject to extreme heat and periods of drought. It turns an unattractive brown and goes dormant from fall frost to spring thaw.

ZONE 1: From southern Pennsylvania north to the Canadian border and west to Ohio, spring and fall are cool and rainy, summers are typically warm with some precipitation, and winters are cold. The soil is generally acid and a mixture of sand and clay, although there are local variations. Good turf grass choices include Kentucky bluegrass—'Challenger', 'Ram I', 'Park', and 'Eclipse'; perennial ryegrasses—'Manhattan II' and 'Yorktown II'; tall fescue—'Falcon', 'Mustang', and 'Rebel'; and the fine fescues.

In the northern tier of the Northeast—which includes New England and upstate New York—where winters are very cold, summers are hot for only a brief period of time, and ample precipitation throughout the year eliminates the potential for extended drought, the bent grasses can be grown.

ZONE 2: From southern Pennsylvania south through Maryland and Virginia, parts of southern West Virginia, and in coastal areas as far north as southern New Jersey, the growing season is long, summers are hot and humid, and winters are generally cool with ample precipitation. The soil is somewhat acid and composed of sand, clay, and loam. In this transition zone between strictly northern and southern climates, Kentucky bluegrass—'Midnight', 'Adelphi', and 'America'; the perennial ryegrasses; the tall fescues; hard fescue—'Aurora' and 'Reliant'; and the zoysias grow well.

CHOOSING THE RIGHT

Gardeners in the Northeast can choose from a wide variety of grasses that are far more disease resistant and possess a vigor and vitality that can withstand drought and stress far better than their predecessors. In addition, most commercially available grass seed is sold as a mixture (two or more species) or a blend (two or more cultivars of the same species). Planting these combinations of seed with their varying resistance to diseases and adaptability to different growing conditions and soils will improve your chances of establishing the lawn of your dreams.

Kentucky bluegrass *is lauded for its deep green appearance, fine texture, ability to form dense sod quickly, long life, and relatively high tolerance of moderate heat, drought, and frigid winters. However, it requires a lot of fertilizer. One of the best all-around cultivars is 'Midnight', low growing, semidwarf, and very dark green; it tolerates heat well. The dense sod produced by 'Adelphi' and 'America' has the added advantages of lower maintenance and good resistance to a wide range of diseases. 'Eclipse' is well regarded for its shade tolerance, vigor, and dense growth.*

Perennial ryegrass, *with its exceptional ruggedness, is a superb complement to Kentucky bluegrass in seed mixtures. The two turf grasses are tolerant of different diseases (perennial ryegrass being far more resistant to insect and fungus damage), ensuring that one will survive a serious assault from biological foes. The widely used medium green, medium fine textured cultivar 'Pennfine' adapts well to a wide range of climates and soils. Darker green 'Palmer' produces a denser turf and tolerates temperature extremes slightly better.*

Tall fescue *was once considered a weed by northern gardeners, but this low-maintenance grass now has finer leaves and a darker green color while retaining its shade tolerance, toughness, and resistance to insect damage. Rugged 'Falcon' is low growing and dense and grows in a wide range of soil types. 'Rebel' can be mowed closely and combines a slow growth rate with medium green color and fine texture. Dark green 'Mustang' will grow well in hotter areas of the Northeast, and its leaves are softer than other*

GRASS FOR YOUR LAWN

cultivars. Dark bluish green 'Apache' tolerates heat, drought, and wear.

Fine fescue grasses include creeping, spreading or red; Chewings; and hard. Rugged, shade tolerant, and winter hardy, the fine fescues require very little fertilizer and water. However, most are not appropriate for the northeastern transition zone. 'Wintergreen' and 'Pennlawn' are two creeping fescues recommended for their density, disease resistance, and growth rate. Look for vigorous, dark green spreading fescue 'Ruby' in seed mixes for cool climates. With very fine leaf texture, dense growth, shade tolerance, dark green 'Agram' and medium green 'Banner' are two highly regarded Chewings fescues.

Bent grass, fine textured and low growing, withstands close mowing and competes well with weedy annual grasses—but it requires much watering, mowing, dethatching, and top-dressing. Two species of bent grass— creeping bent grass and colonial bent grass—can be grown successfully in very cool and humid parts of the Northeast. Creeping bent grass will thrive in moist soils. The cultivar 'Penncross' performs well over the widest range of northeastern climates. Colonial bent grass grows more upright than creeping be flourishes in acid soils. The premium cultiv New England and upstate New York is 'Exet sesses a very fine texture, excellent winter ha rich green color.

Zoysia grows on nearly all soils, forming turf that chokes out weeds—but it remain the first frost in fall to the last frost in spring. in hot and humid parts of the transition zo north as southern Pennsylvania and New offers a wear-resistant, low-maintenance other turf grasses. Slow to establish but dro with few insect and disease problems, recom vars of Zoysia spp. include fast-spreading 'Mi dense-growing, and drought-tolerant 'Meyer'; dark green fine-textured 'Emerald'.

Seed, Sod, Plugs, and Sprigs

Sowing grass seed to establish a lawn may require more patience and skill than laying sod, but it has several distinct advantages. Seed is much less expensive than sod. And with the wide variety of seed lots available, you will be able to choose the grass mixture that will perform best in the soil, sunlight, and moisture conditions of your property. In addition, seeded lawns develop deep roots, making them more durable and more likely to live longer. But it does take several months of care to create a lawn from seed. The seedbed should be covered with straw mulch, watered vigilantly for at least three weeks, and weeded. Fertilize the area during soil preparation and after the grass has become established.

Laying sod means you will have a good-looking lawn instantly. Although sod must be watered daily for as long as three weeks after it is installed to encourage rooting, you do not need to fight weeds, seedling diseases, and seed-eating birds, as you do with seeded lawns. And sod is especially effective on slopes, where seeds may be washed away. But sod is expensive, and your choice ...ses will be ...od is mostly ...y bluegrass. ...ecide on sod, ..., buy it lo- ...here it will ...l of grasses ...n the sod has ...r property. ...s or sprigs. ...e sprigs are ...paced inter- ...ts will fill in

...me to do so ...ough, make ...the soil, if

needed, and by tilling, leveling, weeding, and fertilizing.

Perennial Ryegrass— "Palmer"
Kentucky Bluegrass — "Eclipse"

Left to right: Bent grass, Kentucky bluegrass, perennial ryegrass, Chewings fescue.

LAWN ALTERNATIVES

For many gardeners, traditional turf grass is just one option in an expanding palette of low-growing, ground-covering plants. As both a design and an environmental feature, ground covers serve several important purposes. They frequently lay the foundation of an entire landscape, unifying more-disparate plantings of perennials, shrubs, and trees. As a living mulch, they shelter the soil from extremes of hot and cold, preserve moisture, and can smother weeds. And if your property has slopes or areas where a lawn will be difficult to establish and maintain, a ground cover is your answer.

The big three

Periwinkle, pachysandra, and ivy are the three most popular and widely planted ground covers in northeastern gardens. In difficult-to-mow areas of a garden, periwinkle boasts charming springtime flowers, striking foliage, and vigorous growth. It even stays healthy in deep shade and dry soil, where turf grasses falter. Cultivars that merit attention include 'Bowles' Variety' periwinkle, with dark green foliage and lavender-blue flowers; cream-edged 'Sterling Silver'; and gold-veined 'Aureola'.

Pachysandra shares many of periwinkle's attributes, as well as an easy nature that wards off pests and diseases. Planted in moist, humus-rich soil in partial shade, it demands little upkeep.

Two cultivars of *Pachysandra terminalis* to consider are 'Green Sheen', with shiny leaves; and 'Silver Edge', with narrow silvery margins. Although ivy can't brag about its flowers, which are small and whitish and appear only on very mature plants, the foliage of many *Hedera helix* cultivars is far from plain. Search for 'Baltica', with spectacular white veining; 'Aureo-variegata', with yellow margins; 'Argenteo-variegata', with creamy edges; and 'Gold Heart', with great splotches of yellow.

So many ground covers

There are so many plants suitable for ground covers that limiting your consideration to the big three would be premature. Choose a ground cover from the list on the facing page that is adapted to the soil, sunlight, and moisture conditions on your property.

The lush dark green growth of ivy flourishes alongside a colorful flagstone walk and beneath a stand of trees in this shady front yard. Befitting its nature as a woody vine, the ivy not only covers the ground but climbs upward on the tree trunks.

A rocky and sun-filled side yard, which would be inhospitable to turf grass, hosts creeping junipers, rose pink azaleas, and a carpet of cotoneaster mulched with tan and gray gravel. The gravel must be raked occasionally to remove debris.

GROUND COVERS FOR EVERY LOCATION

NAME	LIGHT	BLOOMS	DESCRIPTION/LANDSCAPE USES
Ajuga reptans 'Bronze Beauty' Bugleweed	Sun or partial shade	Spring to summer	Spreads quickly into a 3- to 6-inch-tall mat of purplish bronze leaves with purple flowers. Foliage of other cultivars is shiny green, gray green, or purplish, most with cream, pink, or yellow splotches and spikes of blue flowers.
Arctostaphylos uva-ursi Bearberry, kinnikinnick	Sun or partial shade	Spring	Handsome evergreen foliage turns bronze in winter on prostrate stems 5 to 6 feet in length. Nodding, bell-shaped, waxy pink flowers are followed by showy, long-lasting red fruit. Does best in sandy or rocky soil.
Asarum europaeum European wild ginger	Partial shade or shade	Insignificant	Hardy, elegant evergreen ground cover with 2- to 3-inch glossy, heart-shaped dark green leaves. Excellent in the shade under trees and evergreen shrubs provided soil is moist and rich with ample humus.
Cotoneaster salicifolius 'Repens' Dwarf willowleaf cotoneaster	Sun or partial shade	Spring to summer	Sturdy, compact shrub with a fanlike branching habit barely reaching 2 feet in height. Lacy leaves; small, whitish pink flowers followed by bright red berries. Can site in hot, dry locations and on slopes exposed to the wind.
Epimedium grandiflorum Longspur epimedium	Partial shade or shade	Spring	Tolerant of shade and dry soil, this long-lived, somewhat woody perennial herb sports rounded leaves tinged with bronze-purple in the fall. Clusters of 1- to 2-inch-wide rose pink ('Rose Queen') or white ('White Queen') flowers dangle above the foliage on wiry stems up to 12 inches tall.
Festuca ovina var. *glauca* Blue fescue	Sun or partial shade	Summer	Thriving best in poor, well-drained soil, this very blue ornamental grass has fine, threadlike leaves up to 10 inches in length forming a bushy mound. Cut back the pale gold flowers to avoid self-seeding of plants not true to type.
Geranium macrorrhizum Bigroot cranesbill	Sun or partial shade	Summer	Spreads quickly to form a close-knit, weed-smothering cover with large, aromatic, deeply lobed leaves and magenta or pink five-petaled flowers on wiry stems. Suitable for any soil conditions; durable and resistant to deer, pests, and diseases.
Hakonechloa macra 'Aureola' Golden variegated hakonechloa	Partial shade or shade	Summer to fall	Long, narrow bright yellow leaves striped with green form a graceful, arching mound that spreads slowly. Clusters of small flower spikelets appear August to October. Distinctive in the high shade of deciduous trees, cascading down a hillside, or draped over rocks and low walls.
Hedera helix 'Baltica' Baltic ivy	Partial shade or shade	Not applicable	Popular and versatile as a ground cover, Baltic ivy has medium-size, triangular, glossy dark green leaves with prominent white veining. Ideal for slopes or level ground where other plants are difficult to establish.
Iberis sempervirens 'Snowflake' Perennial candytuft	Sun or partial shade	Spring	Forms a spreading mound 12 inches in height with dark green leaves and stunning pure white flowers in dense finger-shaped clusters. Prefers full sun. Cut back woody stems after flowering to keep tidy and vigorous.
Juniperus horizontalis 'Bar Harbor' Creeping juniper	Sun	Not applicable	Adaptable, extremely hardy, prostrate needled evergreen with long, ground-hugging steely blue branches turning silvery purple in winter. Forms a dense mat 1 foot high. Excellent for covering slopes to halt erosion and around garden structures and buildings, and to link changes in uneven terrain.
Microbiota decussata Siberian carpet cypress	Sun or partial shade	Not applicable	Lacy, needled conifer stays rich green in summer, turning coppery in winter. Arching branches form an ornamental 2-foot-high mound spreading to 15 feet. Drought tolerant when established.
Pachysandra terminalis Japanese spurge	Partial shade or shade	Spring	Popular low-maintenace spreader rapidly forming a 6-inch-tall carpet of green foliage. Tolerates dry shade. Leaves are toothed, vaguely oval, and 3 to 4 inches long. Choose the cultivars 'Silver Edge', with a silver leaf margin, and 'Green Sheen', with glossy leaves, for added impact.
Phlox subulata Moss pink	Sun or partial shade	Spring to summer	American native moss pink is also called ground pink and mountain pink; the species flowers magenta, cultivars flower rose pink, pale pink, lavender, or white with a red center. The needlelike foliage forms a mat 6 inches high and is superb on rocky or hilly terrain.
Vinca minor Periwinkle	Partial shade or shade	Spring	Refined-looking ground cover popular for large areas under trees, alongside paths, on slopes, and trailing down a wall or raised bed. Best cultivars include 'Bowles' Variety', with dark green foliage and lavender-blue flowers; cream-edged 'Sterling Silver' and gold-veined 'Aureola', with blue flowers; and 'Alba', with white flowers.

BUILDING A BORDER

A successful flower border is largely a matter of good marriages between plants. The best ones combine just the right blend of "bones," "binders," and "bursts."

The easy border pictured at right shows how these three groups of plants work together to ensure a long season of bloom. The "bones" are the sizable perennials around which the composition is built, including delphinium and perennial hibiscus *(Hibiscus moscheutos)*. Other perennials mound and billow around them, their flowers coming and going throughout the summer. A supporting cast for the bones includes plantings of iris, coreopsis, and daylily *(Hemerocallis* cultivars).

Echinacea purpurea

"Binders," planted between the bones, are low-growing, spreading annual bloomers such as impatiens, marigolds, geraniums, and coleus. They ramble around the taller perennials, creating a sea of bloom that binds the border together.

In early spring, spaces left by annuals between the bones allow for glorious "bursts" of spring-flowering bulbs—

such as crocuses, daffodils, and tulips. What makes this border work is the pleasing combination of warm colors and the repetition of plant varieties. Occasional points of interest are tied together by the consistency of the orange marigolds and red geraniums. When combining plants, remember that a limited color palette usually lends a more integrated and visually pleasing look than a cacophony of color.

Perennial borders are best planted in spring or autumn. After choosing your plants, prepare the soil by digging and amending it to a depth of 2 feet. Install a drip irrigation system at this point, if desired (pages 330–331).

During the blooming season, clip off faded flowers and shear back trailing plants to keep a succession of blossoms coming. To help smother weeds, lay 2 to 3 inches of mulch around plants.

A. The border at right, pictured in summer, is orchestrated for bloom over a long season. Spring bloomers such as crocuses, daffodils, tulips, irises, and candytuft *(Iberis sempervirens)* start the show. Summer bloomers include delphinium, perennial hibiscus *(Hibiscus moscheutos),* coreopsis, and daylily *(Hemerocallis* cultivars). Annuals tie it all together; the copious blooms of marigolds and geraniums, and the richly colored foliage of coleus star from the last frost in the spring to the first frost in the fall.

B. This container adds sculptural elements between plantings. By featuring golden creeping Jenny *(Lysimachia nummularia* 'Aurea'), it ties directly into the surrounding plantings.

A

B

LANDSCAPING WITH PERENNIALS

P erennials are long-lived plants prized because they come back to bloom year after year. Although easy to grow, most perennials take a few years to get established and vary in the length of time they can grow in one spot without needing division or replanting to rejuvenate them.

There are perennials suitable for every location and site, for sun or shade, for moist or dry soil. The majority die down to the ground after the first hard frost, then reappear the following spring. A few, such as coral bells (*Heuchera* species), live most of the year as low-key foliage plants, then explode in brilliant color. Dead-heading—the removal of spent flowers—encourages repeat bloom. Becoming familiar with the various characteristics of perennials will help you make wise selections.

A border composed entirely of perennials can provide a spectacular display as well as an engaging challenge for the gardener who wants to orchestrate plantings for color and form. Borders can take just about any shape—kidney, circular, or rectangular. They can be islands, surrounded by paving or lawn; these have the advantage of being viewable from all sides. Or they can take the classic form of a double border that flanks two sides of a walk or lawn.

Many gardeners like to create "mixed" borders, which can include small trees and shrubs, bulbs, roses, ornamental grasses, and annual flowers, in addition to perennials. But the perennials are the mainstays, supplying successive color throughout much of the year, lengthening the borders' period of attraction, and lending it enormous variety in color and form.

This colorful border combines pink perennial verbena (Verbena canadensis) *with blue oat grass* (Helictotrichon sempervirens) *for sharp contrast. Shrub plantings include golden spirea* (Spiraea japonica 'Goldmound') *and crimson pygmy barberry* (Berberis thunbergii 'Crimson Pygmy').

BARGAINS FOR BORDERS

Filling this border with plants from small containers can dramatically cut its cost.

Smart nursery shopping

In the course of buying perennials, you can easily spend more than you expected. But careful planning and selective shopping can help you stay within your budget. For example, you'll get better value from a plant such as coneflower *(Echinacea)* or sky blue aster *(Aster × frikartii* 'Mönch') that has a lengthy flowering period than from one with a brilliant but short-lived display.

For the longest possible period of bloom, buy plants before they flower. This does not mean that you should never buy blooming plants, however; some prized perennials are available at nurseries only during their flowering season. But look for those without bloom or just starting to bud.

Small plants are also a better value. In most cases, when perennials are transplanted from 1-gallon containers, quarts, and 4-inch pots, the plants in the smaller containers will catch up to the growth of the 1-gallon plants within 6 weeks. If plant roots are allowed continued, unimpeded growth, and never experience being root-bound—as do most plants held in larger containers—they will establish and grow swiftly, without transplant setback.

The border shown above contains 14 perennials: 3 hybrid penstemons, 2 dwarf Shasta daisies, 3 coreopsis, 4 'Homestead Purple' verbena, and 2 catmint. If you plant these varieties from 4-inch containers or quarts, you'll spend quite a bit less than if you had bought all plants in 1-gallon containers.

Moreover, it pays to shop around. The cost of the same 4-inch container plant can triple from one nursery to another—a big difference in cost when you want to fill an entire border with flowers. But don't sacrifice quality for price. Starting with a robust plant will pay off for years to come.

Coreopsis verticillata 'Moonbeam'   *Hosta* 'On Stage'   *Echinacea purpurea* 'Magnus'

SAVING WATER

Gardeners in the Northeast can expect a period of summer drought almost every year. If the dry weather also brings on water restrictions, traditional garden borders will show the strain. Choosing plants that tolerate both periods of drought and the eventual downpour can be a challenge for the gardener.

Fortunately, once their root systems are established, many fine plants will thrive during dry periods as well as wet winters. Star performers include native New Jersey tea *(Ceanothus americanus)*, sweet shrub *(Calycanthus floridus)*, Adam's needle *(Yucca filamentosa)*, coreopsis, prairie grasses such as switch grass *(Panicum virgatum)*, and prairie dropseed *(Sporobolus heterolepis)*. These plants have evolved to survive extremes of climate in much the same way cacti have evolved to live in desert zones.

Other dry-summer plants come from the Mediterranean region, southern Africa, Central and South America, or Australia—parts of the world where dry summers are normal. Yarrow, artemisia, most herbs, and some junipers are all drought-tolerant species from other countries.

To create a flower border that will need little extra irrigation after the first year, combine introduced and native perennials. In fact, it is a good idea to group together the drought-tolerant plants in your garden and give them excellent drainage. Most will perform better with little or no summer irrigation. You also save time and money by not watering these sections. When designing islands of plants with low water needs, site them where irrigation equipment would be difficult to install or maintain.

A. Hardy, rugged shrubs are the "bones" of any garden. Some good choices for drought tolerance are eastern red cedar *(Juniperus virginiana)* and deciduous barberries. Barberry's brilliantly colored foliage is also useful in flower arranging.

B. Among the medicinal and culinary herbs are many that are drought tolerant. Often fragrant, their scent concentrates when their essential oils are not diluted by additional water. This herb garden includes artemisia and lavender.

C. Many native perennials are tough and drought tolerant. Here, variously colored butterfly weed *(Asclepias* species) and purple coneflowers *(Echinacea)* brighten up a traditional border. Both are excellent wildlife plants.

A WATERWISE BORDER

The Plants

A. Achillea filipendulina 'Coronation Gold'
FERNLEAF YARROW (**2**)

B. A. 'Moonshine'
YARROW (**7**)

C. Asclepias tuberosa
BUTTERFLY WEED (**7**)

D. Catananche caerulea
CUPID'S DART (**2**)

E. Coreopsis lanceolata 'Goldfink' (2)

F. Echinacea purpurea 'Bright Star'
PURPLE CONEFLOWER (**1**)

G. Erigeron × hybridus
FLEABANE (**4**)

H. Euphorbia epithymoides
CUSHION SPURGE (**12**)

I. Geranium endressii 'Wargrave Pink'
CRANESBILL (**1**)

J. Lavatera thuringiaca 'Barnsley'
TREE MALLOW (**2**)

K. Liatris spicata 'Kobold'
GAYFEATHER (**6**)

L. Pennisetum alopecuroides
FOUNTAIN GRASS (**9**)

M. Penstemon gloxinioides 'Apple Blossom'
BORDER PENSTEMON (**3**)

N. Perovskia 'Blue Spire'
RUSSIAN SAGE (**6**)

O. Stachys byzantina 'Silver Carpet'
LAMB'S EARS (**5**)

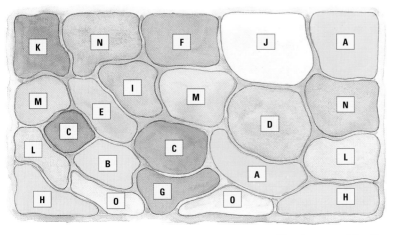

Planting area: 11' × 6'

JEWELS OF THE WOODLAND

Three hundred years ago, the vast northeastern forest wilderness caused deep consternation to the early settlers. One reported home to Europe of a land daunting, terrible, clothed in infinite thick woods filled with bears and bobcats, and strange beasts: squirrels that flew, frogs that whistled, and snakes that rattled.

White birches in the Adirondacks, New York

But soon the parks of the Old World were home to the jewels of the New World woodlands: sugar maples, white birches, and hemlocks, fragrant wild azaleas and smelly skunk cabbage, delicate trilliums and lilies. Today the Northeast woodlands draw visitors year-round to their stunning autumn beauty, snowy peace in winter, colorful burgeoning in spring, and shady cool in summer.

Spring is a window of opportunity for woodland plants. As winter releases its grip, the snow cover melts and the ground begins to thaw, and spring ephemerals that have been dormant since the previous summer now stir into growth. Overhead, the tree canopy is open to the sky, allowing the sun to reach the ground. Skunk cabbage and marsh marigolds appear along creek beds, the first places to thaw. Tiny frogs called spring peepers fill the night with sound. Small bulbs and tubers come into bloom, such as bloodroot *(Sanguinaria)* and dogtooth

Fiddlehead ferns

Trillium erectum

Erythronium dens-canis

No woodland garden would be complete without fiddlehead ferns rising in spring above newly melted snow. It should also harbor fragile treasures like trilliums, the official flower of Ontario, and dogtooth violets *(Erythronium)*. Both are spring ephemerals that go dormant and disappear in summer.

Lilium canadense

violets *(Erythronium)*, as well as sweet violets. Later come the taller bulbs and perennials: mayapples, trilliums, white foamflower *(Tiarella)*, Solomon's seal, meadow rue *(Thalictrum)*, and red-and-yellow columbines. And everywhere there are tender green ferns.

As the deciduous trees fill in their foliage, the middle story of the woodland comes into bloom. White-flowered dogwood and redbud join viburnums, native azaleas, spicebush *(Lindera)*, mountain laurel *(Kalmia)*, and *Clethra* to fill the woods with color and fragrance. Spring rains give way to dry summer, and in clearings and on the woodland's edges the stately bloom of native Canada and Turk's cap lilies join with cardinal flower and scarlet bee balm *(Monarda)*. Asters, goldenrod, and sweet autumn clematis, with its cloud of white flowers, follow in fall.

But it is probably autumn's fireworks that most distinguish the northeastern woodland. Every plant is a player in the autumn pageant, but probably none more than the deciduous trees and shrubs, flashing deep orange and gold, scarlet to burgundy, lemon yellow, lush purple to deepest mahogany. Then the white trunks of the birches, the colorful stems of shrubby willows and dogwoods, and vermilion sumac berries sparkle in the winter woodland.

Woodland walk. A winding path of wood chips leads a visitor across a wooden bridge and deep into a shady woodland garden near Charlottesville, Virginia. Ferns and wildflowers carpet the forest floor under a canopy of maple trees.

Shade- and moisture-loving flowers such as Northeast natives white wood aster *(Aster divaricatus)* and mayapple *(Podophyllum peltatum)*, and bleeding heart *(Dicentra spectabilis)* from Asia, round out the seasons, beginning with mayapple in early spring, then bleeding heart in early summer, and asters in fall.

White wood aster

Mayapple

Bleeding heart and primrose

237

A

B

C

BULBS

Some of the best-loved garden flowers, such as tulips and daffodils, arise from bulbs—or from corms, tubers, rhizomes, or tuberous roots. Although traditionally associated with spring, some bloom in late winter, summer, or fall, making bulbs ideal for single displays and for mixed borders.

Bulbs are inexpensive, and to get a good splash of color, you should plant them by the dozens. Bulbs that multiply and spread from year to year, such as grape hyacinths, can be naturalized under trees or in meadows.

In naturalized settings, grassy cover disguises bulb foliage, which must be left until it has yellowed and can easily be pulled away. In formal gardens, overplant newly planted bulbs with annuals such as pansies or forget-me-nots. The flowers will bloom simultaneously, but the long-blooming annuals will camouflage the wilting bulb foliage.

In fall, plant bulbs in containers, in flower boxes, or along a walkway or path for spring color. Spring-planted bulbs such as gladiolus can be set out at four-week intervals to provide an ongoing source of cut flowers. Autumn-blooming bulbs, such as autumn crocus, saffron crocus, and spider lily, offer special bursts of late-season color.

A. When thickly massed, a display of tulips requires hundreds of bulbs. Here, annual blue forget-me-nots, their seeds sown just after the tulip bulbs were planted, furnish a lacy filler and extend the color as the tulips fade. When the show is over, both plants can be dug out and the bed refilled with summer annuals.

B. Among the oldest known form of daffodils, multiflowered tazettas bear clusters of three to six delicate, sometimes scented, blossoms on each stem. Tazettas are relatively small, growing from 6 inches to 14 inches tall. They naturalize well and make good cut flowers.

C. A mixed border of Asiatic lilies in pink, yellow, peach, and red blooms in early summer at the same time as delphiniums, roses, and Peruvian lilies *(Alstroemeria).* They reach from 2 to 4 feet; the taller Oriental hybrids can climb to 8 feet and bloom from mid- to late summer.

A LATE-SPRINGTIME SHOW

The Plants

A. Artemisia schmidtiana 'Silver Mound'
ANGEL'S HAIR (**12**)

B. Hyacinthus 'Gypsy Queen' and 'Blue Giant'
HYACINTH (**16, 12**)

C. Iris 'Apple Blossom Pink' (10)

D. Iris 'Heavenly Rapture' (10)

E. Iris 'Wedgwood' (30)

F. Myosotis
FORGET-ME-NOT (**10**)

G. Narcissus 'Polar Ice'
DAFFODIL (**40**)

H. Primula polyantha
PRIMROSE (WHITE) (**20**)

I. Primula polyantha
PRIMROSE (MULTICOLOR) (**20**)

J. Rosa 'Iceberg'
ROSE (**1**)

K. Tulipa 'Blushing Beauty'
TULIP (**18**)

L. Viola × wittrockiana Imperial Antique Shades
PANSY (**24**)

M. Viola × wittrockiana (white)
PANSY (**10**)

N. Wisteria sinensis 'Alba'
CHINESE WISTERIA (**4**)

Peach, blue, and white dominate this springtime garden corner. The roses and wisterias serve as a sparkling backdrop for hyacinths, irises, and tulips. As the bulbs die back after flowering, primroses, violas, and forget-me-nots will fill in around them, extending the life of the border.

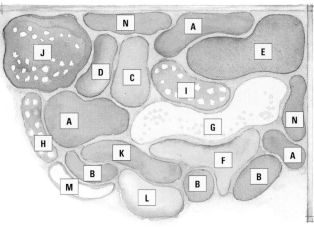

Planting area: 14' × 9'

COLOR IN

Color gives a garden its personality. The success of a garden's overall plan depends to a large extent on how well plant color arrangements harmonize and how well they fit the site. Like beauty, pleasing color combinations are in the eye of the beholder; there are no hard-and-fast rules for using color successfully, so feel free to experiment in your own beds and borders.

You can mass flowers of a single color for elegant simplicity or mix several different shades of one color together for subtle plays of light against dark. Combine hot colors like red, orange, and yellow for sizzle in sunlight, or slow the pace and soothe the eye with

Sizzlers

Bright gold, yellow, orange, and red look spectacular in bright sunlight. Against a quiet background they combine well with one another, and individually each pairs well with blue. The sizzlers are for emphasis, color, and warmth.

Primary colors

All colors derive from red, yellow, and blue. These combine well together, especially when tempered with gray.

Neon brights

Brilliant scarlet, hot pink, and orange are dazzling in sunlight. Together they make a strong statement, if used carefully—in their own bed or pot, for example. The neon brights don't work well with softer colors because they steal the spotlight.

Midnight shades

Dark purple, burgundy, and near black are regal yet somber colors that combine well. However, they disappear in shade. At dusk they glow next to lighter colors, such as lime green or white.

THE GARDEN

cool pastels. Tame aggressive colors with gray, add sparkle with white, or wake up somber burgundies or deep purples with lime green. Pair plants with blue and yellow flowers for a classic combination. Make sure that flowers with contrasting colors, such as red and white, bloom at the same time.

When choosing your palette, take a cue from the colors of surrounding walls, garden furnishings, or the landscape beyond your garden. Pick a flower of one color and hold it next to other plants to see what works. Or plant a container with likely combinations, and, if the colors are pleasing, try them in beds and borders.

Cool pastels
Pale lavender, pink, blue, and apricot are romantic colors. They're excellent in cottage gardens and billowy perennial borders. All harmonize with soft blue, silver, and pale yellow.

Earth tones
Green, straw, gold, and amber, colors found in nature, are most effective in gardens by the seashore, near oak woodlands, or on grassy hillsides—or in naturalistic gardens near wild land.

The Anchors
These are a color gardener's best friends. They play a variety of roles in the garden and are capable of enhancing a wide array of other colors with equal aplomb.

Snow white
White keeps pastels from fading into oblivion, diffuses the potential clash of strong hues, and prevents jewel tones from losing their richness in the sun's glare. In the shade or twilight, it supplies welcome illumination and adds sparkle to greens.

Gray
The temperers, gray- or silver-foliaged plants, mellow the heat of reds, oranges, yellows, and magentas. They're also diplomats: flower colors that would war if planted directly next to each other coexist peacefully if separated by a buffer zone of gray.

Lime green
Yellow-green foliage is handsome as a foil, backdrop, or spotlight. It brightens somber colors like deep purple or blue. And it provides a lively backdrop for marine blue flowers, such as summer forget-me-nots, or clear pink flowers.

Blue
From sky-colored to royal hues, blue blends well with most colors, even strong ones like scarlet. It complements yellow and enhances lavender. Sky blue and soft coral, and blue-violet and yellow combine especially well.

HERBS

Gardeners have known the culinary and medicinal value of herbs for thousands of years. Today, herbs are equally valuable as adornments—planted in a kitchen window box, mixed with other plants in a scented garden, or used as a low hedge along a garden path. Most herbs are easy to grow, and many develop a more intense flavor and fragrance when given little water.

The compact herb garden below, which edges a patio just outside a kitchen, was designed to look good and to deliver snippets for flavoring soups, salads, and grilled meats. It pairs foliage and flowers in a classic yellow and blue combination. A terra-cotta pot adds a Mediterranean touch, and the miniature rose 'Sunsplash' supplies a colorful accent from May through August.

A FRAGRANT NOOK

The Plants

A. Allium schoenoprasum
CHIVES (3)

B. Artemisia dracunculus
FRENCH TARRAGON (4)

C. Nepeta × faassenii
CATMINT (3)

D. Origanum majorana
SWEET MARJORAM (1)

E. Origanum vulgare
OREGANO (2)

F. Rosa 'Sunsplash'
ROSE (1)

G. Rosmarinus officinalis 'Collingwood Ingram'
ROSEMARY (3)

H. Salvia officinalis 'Icterina'
COMMON SAGE (3)

I. Santolina chamaecyparissus 'Nana'
LAVENDER COTTON (3)

J. Thymus citriodorus 'Aureus'
LEMON THYME (1)

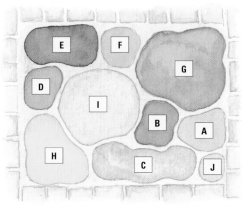

Planting area: 8' × 6'

A FORMAL CIRCLE

The Plants

HERBS

A. Chamaemelum nobile
CHAMOMILE **(22)**

B. Salvia officinalis 'Icterina'
COMMON SAGE **(8)**

C. Salvia officinalis 'Purpurascens'
COMMON SAGE **(16)**

D. Salvia officinalis 'Tricolor'
COMMON SAGE **(16)**

E. Thymus citriodorus
LEMON THYME **(16)**

F. Thymus vulgaris
COMMON THYME **(16)**

G. Thymus vulgaris 'Argenteus'
SILVER THYME **(16)**

SHRUB

H. Buxus sempervirens 'Suffruticosa'
TRUE DWARF BOXWOOD **(40)**

Formal herb plantings vary in design, from intricate "knot" gardens filled with geometrical planting beds and gravel paths to "sundial" gardens composed of flowering herbs that open at different times of the day. Formal gardens require precision in planting: begin hedges with small plants spaced close together, and place herb plants according to a carefully designed pattern. Maintaining such an orderly garden requires more work than for informal borders, but an arrangement of neatly edged plants creates a uniquely peaceful setting.

A formal herb garden need not be large, but it must be in a sunny spot for the herbs to thrive. In the formal circle shown above, the different textures and tones of the foliage— yellows, greens, and grays—offer interesting contrasts and harmonies, creating a "stained-glass window" effect. The warm tones of flagstone and brick, traditional paving materials for this type of garden, blend well with the herbs and lend an air of antiquity to the site.

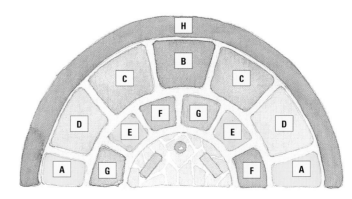

Planting area: 26' × 13'

FRUITS AND VEGETABLES

Creating a garden that is both edible and attractive is well within the reach of even novice gardeners. Fortunately, most nurseries in the East supply a wide range of fruit trees, vegetables, and herbs, and a number of these plants have ornamental appeal. Many gardeners also mix edibles with flowering perennials and annuals. Using vegetables as ornamentals in the landscape allows you to enjoy small amounts of home grown produce without a big commitment of time and garden space.

Herbs, with their distinctive fragrances and interesting colors, can line pathways. Long-lived vegetables such as cabbages can fill decorative containers. The colors and textures of leafy greens such as Swiss chard enliven late-season borders, while the sculptural images of plants such as artichoke or rhubarb lend an exotic touch to a border.

For the best effect when mixing vegetables and flowers, cluster plants in groups of three or more. Vary plant heights and add accents such as fennel or dill. To avoid a busy look, repeat a few of the dominant plants throughout the bed.

Many vegetables and fruits require extra cosseting, generally in spring; others are virtually maintenance free. Do not plant disease-susceptible ornamentals—those that require spraying—with edible plants.

A. The bright flowers and circular leaves of climbing nasturtiums add a peppery flavor to salads. This annual vine looks best when allowed to grow unchecked; it will quickly cover any object it encounters.

B. A river of gold signet marigolds winds among blue-green and red cabbages, curly-leafed Savoy cabbages, and smoky-colored kale, blurring the line between decorative and edible.

C. Brussels sprouts and lettuces create a panoply of leaf shapes and colors, punctuated by bright marigolds and red salvia.

A Kitchen Garden

The Plants

A. **Apple, dwarf** (2)

B. **Asparagus** (4)

C. **Blueberry** (2)

D. **Calendula officinalis**
POT MARIGOLD (**8**)

E. **Chives** (6)

F. **Monarda didyma
'Cambridge Scarlet'**
BEE BALM (**2**)

G. **Pepper** (5)

H. **Rhubarb** (2)

I. **Rosmarinus officinalis
'Prostratus'**
DWARF ROSEMARY (**1**)

J. **Salvia officinalis
'Icterina'**
COMMON SAGE (**1**)

K. **S. o. 'Purpurascens'**
COMMON SAGE (**1**)

L. **S. o. 'Tricolor'**
COMMON SAGE (**1**)

M. **Sweet basil
'Dark Opal'** (6)

N. **Thymus citriodorus
'Aureus'**
LEMON THYME (**4**)

O. **Tropaeolum majus**
GARDEN NASTURTIUM (**4**)

*Accessible and varied, this richly
textured garden contains a cornucopia of
herbs, vegetables, and fruits. The focal point
is the "living fence" created by two
espaliered apple trees, easily reached from
the pathway. The other plants are also edible.
The garden is shown here in late spring.*

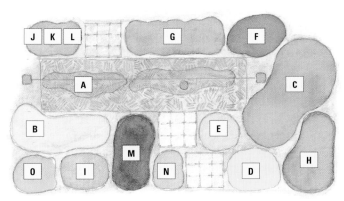

Planting area: 30' × 12'

ORNAMENTAL GRASSES

If you are looking for special effects in your garden, consider planting ornamental grasses. These versatile plants offer beauty and grace but demand only minimal care. Once used almost exclusively in prairie or native gardens, they are now finding their way into elegant and even formal landscapes.

Ornamental grasses can be divided into two types, according to their growth habit. Runners, such as ribbon grass *(Phalaris arundinacea)*, spread by rhizomes and can be invasive. If contained, however, these grasses make wonderful ground covers. The growth of clumpers, such as fountain grass and blue fescue, is not rampant. With their handsome upright or tufted shapes, they blend well in perennial flower borders with irises, daylilies, and plants that have softly spired or daisy-shaped flowers.

Massed groups of clumping grasses, as shown here, can create the same color impact as landscape shrubs. The taller plants, such as zebra grass *(Miscanthus sinensis* 'Zebrinus') or giant reed *(Arundo donax)*, can make effective hedges and privacy screens.

In small gardens, use ornamental grasses as specimens or as accents in borders. In large gardens, fill wide borders with grasses that have airy textures and interesting colors. If you have a pond in your garden, try planting some moisture-loving grasses such as purple moor grass *(Molinia caerulea)* close to the water's edge, where they will help to establish a naturalistic setting.

Most ornamental grasses are perennial and live for many years. Consult the chart at right for help in finding choices that would be suitable for your garden.

The showy, plumelike flower clusters of maiden grass lend an imposing presence to the summer border.

AN ORNAMENTAL GRASS SAMPLER

NAME	LIGHT	BLOOMS	DESCRIPTION/LANDSCAPE USES
Arrhenatherum elatius bulbosum 'Variegatum' Bulbous oat grass	Sun or partial shade	Summer	White-striped foliage. Showy, erect, oatlike flower spike. Short-lived in hot inland areas. Dormant in summer. Effective as accent in perennial borders and large rock gardens.
Briza media Quaking grass	Sun or partial shade	Spring	Heart-shaped florets resemble rattlesnake rattles; good for cutting. Green foliage. Evergreen. Use as accent or in groups in shrub and perennial borders.
Calamagrostis acutifolia 'Stricta' Feather reed grass	Sun	Late spring to fall	Bright green foliage. Tall, erect flower spikes, but bloom varies, depending on climate. Good for cutting. Deciduous in colder areas; semievergreen in mild areas. Makes strong vertical accent plant; in groups, plant at rear of a border.
Carex buchananii Leatherleaf sedge	Sun or partial shade		Coppery red-brown foliage with curled leaf tips. Evergreen. Use as accent, in groups, or combined with blue, gray, or dark green foliage.
C. morrowii 'Goldband' 'Goldband' Japanese sedge	Shade or partial shade		Lustrous bright yellow striped foliage. Evergreen. Use as accent, alone or in groups, in borders.
Festuca amethystina, F. glauca Blue fescue	Sun or partial shade	Spring	Foliage may be green, blue, or gray. *F. a.* 'Superba', with blue-green weeping foliage and pink flowers, is best bloomer. Evergreen. Use as ground cover, in groups, or as a single accent. Makes good edging for borders.
Imperata cylindrica 'Rubra' Japanese blood grass	Sun; partial shade in heat		Leaves are bright green with blood red tips; turn reddish brown in fall. Spreads slowly.
Stipa tenuissima Mexican feather grass	Sun or partial shade	Summer	Fine-textured green foliage clumps. Tall, tan in winter. Flowers fine-textured, filmy, green turning tan. Can become invasive.
Helictotrichon sempervirens Blue oat grass	Sun	Late summer to fall	Blue-gray foliage with sharply pointed tips. Showy flowers; blooms best in cool areas. In hot areas, in wet, heavy soil, root rot may occur. Evergreen. Makes good accent alone or in groups, in borders and rock gardens.
Miscanthus sinensis 'Gracillimus' Maiden grass	Sun or shade	All year	Narrow green foliage. Showy beige flowers; good for cutting. Evergreen. Use as a specimen or plant at back of a border.
Pennisetum setaceum 'Rubrum' Purple fountain grass	Sun	Summer to fall	Purple foliage topped by red-purple plumes; good for cutting. Evergreen to deciduous. Cold hardiness varies greatly. Noninvasive type. Effective as accent or in groups in perennial or shrub borders. Striking with blue and gray plants.
Stipa gigantea Giant feather grass	Sun	Summer	Gray green foliage, golden flower spikes dangle from stems; good for cutting. Evergreen. Use as a specimen or in groups, particularly in perennial borders.
Cortaderia selloana 'Gold Band' or 'Sun Stripe' Yellow pampas grass	Sun	Late summer to fall	Yellow-green leaves with yellow stripes. Erect, creamy white flower spikes; good for cutting. Noninvasive type. Evergreen. Use as dramatic accent with shrubs or in background plantings. Hardy in mild areas only. 'Pumila' is hardiest form.
Miscanthus sinensis Eulalia	Sun or shade	Summer to fall	Green foliage, some with white or yellow. Cultivars differ greatly. Showy plumes; good for cutting. Deciduous. Use as specimen or in groups.

(Left vertical labels: ▼ UNDER 2 FEET | ▼ 2 TO 4 FEET | ▼ OVER 4 FEET)

Calamagrostis acutifolia 'Stricta'

Imperata cylindrica 'Rubra'

Stipa tenuissima

Helictotrichon sempervirens

GRASSY BORDERS

Though a solitary clump of ornamental grass can create a focal point among other garden plants, you can enliven an entire border—or a whole garden—by skillfully combining several or even a dozen kinds of grasses. The photographs at left present some particularly showy types, illustrating the color range of these plants and offering ways to combine them or to mix them with more traditional border plants such as shrubs and perennials.

A. Massed grasses in bold hues bring color and excitement to this garden border. The plumes of dwarf fountain grass nod over clumps of yellow *Pennisetum alopecuroides* 'Hameln' and orange *Panicum virgatum* 'Heavy Metal'.

B. A soft look is achieved by mixing drifts and clumps of ornamental grasses with small-flowered pink shrub roses. Red Japanese blood grass, blue wild rye *(Elymus glaucus),* and large bursts of golden sedge *(Carex elata* 'Bowles' Golden') create a colorful year-round display. The roses, allowed to ramble, offer a brief but glorious midsummer show of profuse blossoms.

C. Like bursts of fireworks, the flower spikes on giant feather grass *(Stipa gigantea)* shoot skyward. The yellowish flowers shimmer on 3- to 4-foot stems in late spring, set off against bluebeard *(Caryopteris)*. They show off especially well when backlit by early morning or evening light, and the slightest breeze makes them wave softly to and fro.

A Medley of Grasses

The Plants

A. Briza media
PERENNIAL QUAKING GRASS (5)

B. Calamagrostis arundinacea 'Karl Foerster'
FOERSTER'S FEATHER REED GRASS (5)

C. Festuca amethystina 'Superba'
AMETHYST-FLOWERING FESCUE (13)

D. Festuca glauca 'Blausilber'
BLUE-SILVER FESCUE (11)

E. Helictotrichon sempervirens (Avena sempervirens)
BLUE OAT GRASS (5)

F. Imperata cylindrica 'Rubra'
JAPANESE BLOOD GRASS (13)

G. Miscanthus sinensis 'Gracillimus'
MAIDEN GRASS (1)

H. Miscanthus sinensis 'Yaku Jima' ('Yakushima')
JAPANESE SILVER GRASS (1)

I. Pennisetum alopecuroides 'Moudry'
BLACK-FLOWERING PENNISETUM (1)

J. Stipa tenuissima
MEXICAN FEATHER GRASS (13)

This all-grass island planting, seen here predominantly from one side, demonstrates the variety that can be found among a single group of plants. Heights vary from under 1 foot to nearly 5 feet; colors range from silvery blue to blue-green to deep green with red tints. The airy floral panicles bring the entire composition alive with movement.

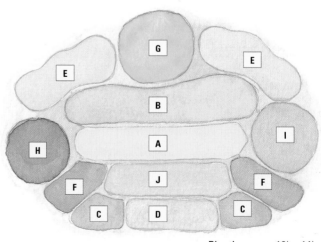

Planting area: 18' × 14'

DWARF CONIFERS

Much of the Northeast is prime country for growing conifers, and winter is the season when we appreciate how much they contribute to the landscape. But many conifers are forest giants; having them in your garden would be akin to keeping a whale in a bathtub. Fortunately, a group of smaller plants—the dwarf conifers—is ideally suited to home gardens.

You can buy dwarf conifers at nurseries in 1- and 5-gallon cans. They are typically classified into four sizes: miniature (plants that seldom grow taller than a foot); dwarf (plants that will be between 3 and 6 feet tall in 10 years); intermediate (6 to 15 feet); and large (more than 15 feet tall). The dwarf types fit best into home gardens or containers. They stay compact, are long-lived, and remain relatively free of diseases and pests.

When choosing a conifer for your landscape, consider the plant's form and color. Do you want a species that grows upright, or one that cascades or sprawls near the ground? Would you prefer a plant with foliage that's green, gold, or blue?

Also take into account the seasonal colors of neighboring plants: a 'Blue Star' juniper or a golden cedar may be a handsome focal point in a winter landscape, but would look insipid and out of place in summer surrounded by pink petunias.

Use a colorful conifer to anchor a perennial planting, to dress up an entryway, or to provide contrast in a mixed border. Or cluster several conifers in a large pot for a low-maintenance, year-round spectacle. Some gardeners in cold-winter areas like Buffalo or Cleveland use dwarf conifers beautifully as backbones of a border, then fill in around them with spring and summer annuals and perennials that have compatible colors. In winter, a light dusting of snow turns conifers into a magical presence in the garden.

A. This poolside mix of colors and textures is provided by a bonsai black pine (right), a weeping deodar cedar (upper left), and various species of pine and *Chamaecyparis*.

B–D. Choice specimens include *Chamaecyparis obtusa* 'Fernspray Gold' backed by *Picea likiangensis* 'Purpurea' with *Chamaecyparis thyoides* 'Andelyensis' in front (**B**); mounding *Pinus mugo* 'White Bud' (**C**); and graceful, spreading *Cedrus deodara* 'Prostrate Beauty' (**D**).

Colorful conifers

GREEN FOLIAGE

Cryptomeria japonica 'Tansu'
JAPANESE CRYPTOMERIA

Pinus mugo mugo 'Sherwood Compact'
MUGO PINE

Pseudotsuga menziesii 'Loggerhead'
DOUGLAS FIR

Thuja occidentalis 'Hetz Midget'
AMERICAN ARBORVITAE

Tsuga canadensis 'Cole's Prostrate'
CANADA HEMLOCK

GOLDEN FOLIAGE

Chamaecyparis obtusa 'Nana Lutea'
HINOKI FALSE CYPRESS

Juniperus horizontalis 'Mother Lode'
JUNIPER

Picea glauca 'Rainbow's End'
WHITE SPRUCE

Thuja occidentalis 'Rheingold'
AMERICAN ARBORVITAE

BLUE FOLIAGE

Abies lasiocarpa 'Glauca Compacta'
ALPINE FIR

Juniperus communis 'Compressa'
JUNIPER

Picea pungens 'R. H. Montgomery'
COLORADO SPRUCE

E. A colorful palette. Clockwise from top, gray green *Picea sitchensis* 'Tenas Papoose'; yellow *Chamaecyparis obtusa* 'Nana Lutea'; slate blue *Picea pungens* 'R. H. Montgomery'; gold and orange *Thuja occidentalis* 'Rheingold'; golden *Juniperus horizontalis* 'Mother Lode'; *Pinus strobus* 'Blue Shag'; and steel blue *Abies balsamea* 'Nana'. In the center are *Juniperus squamata* 'Blue Star' (left) and *Thuja occidentalis* 'Hetz Midget' (right).

E

SUCCULENTS

Because they are often spaced uniformly—and unimaginatively—in a conventional bed of rocks or gravel, succulents have had their reputation unfairly maligned. But with drought and water-conservation measures occurring more often in the East, gardeners are discovering new ways to use them as landscaping plants, either in the ground or, especially for those that won't survive the cold winters, in a variety of containers.

The list of succulents that are hardy in the Northeast is short—just four species—yet full of variety: it is dominated by the indomitable sedum. One of the most versatile plants around, sedum is valued for both its foliage and its flowers, which contribute color and rich texture to a garden over a long period. Leaves can range from the maroon of *Sedum* 'Vera Jameson' to the blue-green of *Sedum cauticolum* to the red-edged leaves of *Sedum spurium* 'Dragon's Blood'. Flowers may be yellow to gold to white or pinkish mauve. *Sedum* 'Autumn Joy' is prized for its blooms—rosy pink in midsummer, deepening to red then bronze-red in fall, and turning golden brown if left in place for the winter. Sedums are tough plants that tolerate almost any well-drained soil.

To help your succulents make a strong impact in a landscape setting, mass plants of the same kind, taking care to vary the leaf color and shape of each adjacent group. For added height and bulk in the garden, try using a few taller drought-tolerant plants, such as yarrow, potentilla, and *Yucca filamentosa*.

Nearly all succulents can survive several weeks without water, but most will have a plumper, lusher look if given regular watering during dry summers. Some, such as *Sedum* 'Autumn Joy', are perfectly at home in an irrigated flower bed. Verify the water needs of succulents before planting them.

A. On a steep slope that faces southwest, two autumn crocuses *(Colchicum)* stand in stark contrast to the carpet of succulent *Sedum spurium* 'Fulda Glow' around them. Drought-tolerant 'Golden Sword' yucca (foreground) and the spiky fronds of blue fescue *(Festuca glauca)* lend a vertical element to the plantings, which also include vinca (right foreground) and the large quilted leaves of 'Helene von Stein' lamb's ears (right).

B. In midsummer the pink-mauve flowers of *Sedum* 'Autumn Joy' cut a cheerful swath in this bed of yucca, blue fescue, and, in the foreground, hen and chickens.

C. Low, dense prickly pear cactus *(Opuntia)* plays off the delicate bright green foliage and white blooms of *Baptisia alba* (white false indigo) in this drought-tolerant planting. *Baptisia* adapts to almost any well-drained soil.

D. Later in the year the bronze-red color of *Sedum* 'Autumn Joy's blooms matches that of the maturing fruit on the *Opuntia*.

Hardy Succulents

Opuntia humifusa
PRICKLY PEAR
Mat-forming plant; thick, fleshy,
padlike leaves

O. polyacantha
PLAINS PRICKLY PEAR
Mat-forming plant; thick, fleshy,
padlike leaves and prominent
downward-pointing spines

Sedum acre
Green leaves, yellow flowers

S. 'Autumn Joy'
Green leaves, pink-mauve flowers

S. cauticolum
Blue-green foliage, pink flowers

S. kamtschaticum
Green leaves, yellow-gold flowers

S. k. 'Variegatum'

S. k. 'Weihenstephaner Gold'
Green leaves, gold flowers

S. sieboldii
Gray green leaves, pink flowers

S. s. 'Frosty Morn'
Gray green leaves, white flowers

S. spurium 'Album Superbum'
Green leaves, white flowers

S. s. 'Dragon's Blood'
Red-edged leaves, red stems,
red flowers

S. s. 'Tricolor'
Green, white, and pink leaves,
red stems, pink flowers

S. telephium 'Vera Jameson'
Maroon leaves, pink flowers

Sempervivum arachnoideum
COBWEB HOUSELEEK
Fleshy leaves in compact rosettes
densely covered with white hairs

S. tectorum
HEN AND CHICKENS
Fleshy leaves in compact rosettes

Yucca filamentosa 'Bright Edge'
Swordlike leaves broadly edged in
rich yellow

Y. gloriosa 'Garland's Gold'
Swordlike leaves with prominent
central gold stripe

Y. glauca
Sharply pointed gray-green
swordlike leaves

You can combine flowering annuals such as rosy pink petunias with erect, blue *Salvia farinacea* 'Victoria' and white African daisies. Or match the rosy pink floribunda rose 'Nearly Wild' with annual red and pink *Dianthus deltoides* (maiden pink). To design large mixed plantings, select the foundation plant first, then choose plants with flowers that complement its growth habit and colors. Annuals are perfect for planting in containers, thanks to their shallow roots and vigorous growth, but most plants will perform well as long as the container is large enough to accommodate the plant's soil needs.

Select your container first, because its shape and size will help determine the plants you'll grow. If the pot is simple, the plants it holds can dominate. But if the container is strong in character, you may want to fill it with a simple plant—a single rose, for example. And remember, all containers are not alike. Plastic pots conserve moisture better than clay ones, but clay pots provide better air circulation and drainage. For this reason, soil may dry out faster in clay pots, so you'll need to check your plants daily if they are sited in full sun.

A. The tropics come to New Jersey as massive *Canna* 'Grande' plants and variegated ficus trees provide the background for containers filled with tender perennials, including *Caladium bicolor* 'Little Miss Muffet', New Guinea impatiens, and *Pelargonium* 'Persian Queen'. The vivid colors of the pots underscore the tropical theme.

B. Delicate maidenhair fern (Adiantum) and lacecap hydrangea arch gracefully over pink polka-dot plant (*Hypoestes phyllostachya*) and snow bush (*Breynia nivosa*) in a 13-inch-wide Italian terra-cotta pot.

C. Marching up the steps to a deck, pots of brilliant red geraniums share a sunny spot with a cheerfully painted blue Adirondack chair. Because the pots can be moved to take advantage of sunny sheltered areas, the plants will last well into fall.

D. Pots of all shapes and sizes, from troughs to strawberry pots to bonsai containers, form an eclectic container garden ringing this island bed.

WILDFLOWERS

Doll's eyes, rattlesnake master, and Quaker ladies—these are just of few of the many wildflowers that grow in the East. With their evocative names and brilliant colors, wildflowers offer the gardener a chance to bring pioneer history, Native American lore, and ecological conservation into the garden.

Wildflowers are the perfect subjects for a miniature meadow. A 4- to 8-foot border of coneflowers, cardinal flowers, butterfly weed, and asters creates a cheery transition between lawn and woods. You can grow patches of these natives in gaps between ground covers. Or simply designate a corner of your property as a "wild" patch where children can explore and play.

Although wildflowers seem right at home in a naturalistic meadow, don't be afraid to include them in a formal border. Good candidates are coneflowers *(Echinacea purpurea)* and threadleaf coreopsis *(Coreopsis verticillata)*. And feel free to intersperse native species and their modern hybrid offspring—such as *Monarda didyma* (bee balm) and its cultivars 'Marshall's Delight', 'Jacob Kline', and 'Cambridge Scarlet'—with exotic garden flowers.

Specialty seed companies offer regional mixes of showy eastern natives to sow into meadows. You can also create your own mix by buying and mixing seeds of the flowers you prefer.

In this West Virginia meadow, an expanse of native blue flax (Linum perenne) *is punctuated by naturalized daisies and coral verbena.*

Starting a Meadow

There is more than one way to start a wildflower meadow. An easy, inexpensive way is to broadcast seed. If you are using a seed mixture specific to your region, you will have to remove existing vegetation and prepare the soil as for any garden. These measures are equally necessary when you start your meadow from small grass and wildflower plants, plugged into a prepared bed at 1-foot intervals.

Perhaps the easiest method, however, is to do nothing. Some eastern

gardeners report surprisingly good results when they simply let an area grow and then selectively remove any woody volunteers and unwanted plants. The upside of this method is that wildflowers—interspersed with grasses—seem to pop up out of nowhere. The downside is that bloom is not as dense as in seeded mixtures.

In any case, small areas must be kept weeded and be cut back at the end of the growing season. Meadows require mowing once or twice each year as well as selective cutting out of unwanted plants. Because much of the land in the East reverts easily to forest, young trees and vines such as bittersweet sprout quickly and, if allowed to grow, will soon shade out wildflower patches and meadows.

A last tip from expert gardeners: Never gather plants or take cuttings or seeds from

plants in the wild. Many native plant species are in danger of extinction and others are threatened.

A WILDFLOWER SAMPLER

	NAME	LIGHT	BLOOMS	DESCRIPTION
YELLOW	*Chrysogonum virginanum* Green-and-gold	Sun to shade	Spring, summer	Bright flowers on low, 6-in. spreading ground-cover plant.
	Coreopsis verticillata Threadleaf coreopsis	Sun	Summer	Hundreds of small, golden daisylike flowers on 2-ft. mounds of fine foliage.
	Helianthus mollis Sunflower	Sun	Late summer	Small yellow-centered sunflowers on tall, 6-ft. fuzzy foliage.
	Oenethera macrocarpa Ozark sundrops	Sun	Summer	Large, floppy lemon yellow blooms on low, 1-ft. sprawling plants. Thrives in hot spots.
RED AND ORANGE	*Asclepias tuberosa* Butterfly weed	Sun	Summer	Flat orange flowers attract butterflies; grows 30 in. tall. Not fussy about soil as long as it is well drained.
	Aster novae-angliae 'Alma Potschke'	Sun to part shade	Late summer, fall	Riveting coral red profuse flowers on 3-ft. plants. Easy to grow.
	Echinacea purpurea Coneflower	Sun to part shade	Summer	Big purple-pink daisy flowers bloom profusely on 3- to 4-ft. stems.
	Monarda didyma Bee balm	Sun to part shade	Summer	Spidery scarlet flowers on 3- to 4-ft. aromatic foliage.
	Ratibida columnifera Mexican hat	Sun	Summer	Drooping, red-ray flowers touched with yellow surrounding a prominent central cone. Grows to 3 ft. tall.
BLUE AND VIOLET	*Baptisia australis* False indigo	Sun	Summer	Clear blue spikes of pea flowers on 4-ft. gray green foliage.
	Linum perenne Blue flax	Sun	Summer	Pale blue flowers on 2-ft. stems of fine, bright green foliage.
	Phlox divaricata Blue phlox	Part shade	Spring	Blue flowers on low, 9-in. plants.
WHITE	*Baptisia alba* White baptisia	Sun	Summer	Drooping white flowers on black stems. Grows 3 ft. tall.
	Iris cristata 'Alba' White crested iris	Part shade, shade	Spring	Small, flat flowers on 6-in. stems.
	Penstemon digitalis Foxglove penstemon	Sun	Summer	Spikes of plump flowers on 15-in. glossy-leaf plants.
FERNS	*Osmunda claytoniana* Interrupted fern	Part shade, shade		Soft green fronds radiate from a central clump. Grows to 2 ft.
	Polystichum acrostichoides Christmas fern	Part shade, shade		Shiny dark green leathery evergreen fronds with cinnamon-colored spore cases under the leaves. Grows to 2 ft.

Aster novae-angliae 'Alma Potschke' | *Ratibida columnifera* | *Osmunda claytoniana* | *Iris cristata* 'Alba'

FINISHING TOUCHES

A garden's personality comes not only from its plants and structures. Much depends on the gardener's knack for adding finishing touches—a copper lantern, a bright glazed pot, a collection of folk-art birdhouses. From a teak bench to a lacy hammock or a well-placed boulder, these decorative elements can create a focal point in your garden, complement a grouping of foliage and flowers, or simply delight the eye.

Luckily, garden accessories have never been as plentiful and as varied as they are today. Furniture is available in a variety of styles, umbrellas come fitted with lights or with canvas walls that block the wind, and birdbaths range from rustic to sculptural in form. Resourceful gardeners are turning humble boulders into striking sculptures and adding flair with painted walls, birdhouses, statuary, and outdoor lighting. Giving your garden a distinctive look is as simple as letting your imagination lead the way.

BIRDBATHS

While birds will happily frolic in a streambed or puddle, a birdbath is their preferred watering hole. If you set one out in your garden, it's a sure bet feathered visitors will come flocking—especially on warm summer days.

Birdbaths run the gamut from simple to elaborate. Some are basic bowls that sit on the ground or atop pedestals, or hang from chains. Others are designed as much for the people who watch the birds as for the birds themselves—you can display these birdbaths as garden art.

Once birds discover your bath as a reliable water source—placed in the right spot, kept filled and clean—your garden will come alive with their color, music, and activity. And you'll discover the quiet pleasure of watching sparrows, wrens, and other songbirds swoop into the bath for a splashing good time.

While a dip cools birds in summer, it can also help them keep warm in winter: frequent bathing insulates birds by keeping their feathers clean and fluffed. So keep your birdbath filled and ready for whatever flies your way.

B

Birdbath Basics

Keep it shallow but roomy. *Ideally, baths should be 2 to 3 inches deep and 24 to 36 inches across. The sides should slope gradually .*

Consider materials. *Plastic and metal are often too slippery for birds. Some plastics can crack with age; metal dishes, if used, should be stainless steel or other rust-resistant material.*

Keep it clean. *Use a strong jet of water from the hose to clean the bowl. If the bottom is dirty, scrub it.*

Keep it safe. *Put the birdbath next to shrubs or trees that provide cover and escape routes. Place ground-level baths*

where they have 10 to 20 feet of open space around them—but no more, or you'll leave damp birds exposed to hawks, owls, and cats.

Keep it moving. *Running water attracts birds. Some baths come with built-in fountains. Or you can create a small fountain by adding a submersible pump with a spray head.*

Keep it from freezing. *In cold climates in winter, add a heating element to keep the bath water thawed.*

E

D

F

G

A. Irregularly shaped and close to the ground, this mossy stone bowl marries perfectly with the low stone wall and plantings of blazing red salvia.

B. This fanciful stone bowl, embellished with salamanders, can rest on a pedestal or a boulder.

C. As much sculpture as birdbath, this copper basin stands out against a fountain of ornamental grasses.

D. This homemade bath is a glazed terra-cotta saucer resting atop a pot.

E. A steel sundial encircles the copper basin in this dual-purpose structure.

F. A yellow toy sailboat adds a whimsical touch to this birdbath—a cast-concrete bowl, perched atop a tree stump.

G. Suspended near a window, this glazed stoneware bath provides a delightful show of songbirds.

BIRDHOUSES

Like weather vanes and sundials, birdhouses can be as much garden art as functional pieces. They come in many styles, from gaily painted wooden antiques to sleek metal models. However delightful they may be to look at, however, you'll want to make sure the birds find them attractive as well.

Only cavity-nesting birds (those that nest in tree hollows) use birdhouses. This group includes bluebirds, chickadees, nuthatches, swallows, and wrens. The kind of house you install determines the kinds of birds you'll attract, but this is a most inexact science: while a birdhouse may be intended for a wren or a bluebird, it will be fair game for any birds of similar size.

Small birds like chickadees, nuthatches, and most wrens prefer a hole that's 1⅛ inches across. Medium-size birds like bluebirds, swallows, and purple martins need a nest box with a hole 1½ inches wide. White-breasted nuthatches need 1¼ inches.

Larger birds, such as flickers and kestrels, take boxes with 2½-inch entry holes. Flickers usually like to dig out their own nests, but sometimes you can attract them with a large nest box. Fill it with wood chips; they'll dig it out.

A. This whimsical flying stork birdhouse doesn't fool many birds.

B. Attached to a wooden post and camouflaged by a clematis vine, this inviting house is ready to host a bird family.

C. Built to Audubon specifications, these sleekly designed birdhouses sit atop tall poles.

D

E

D. Wren house has a 1⅛-inch entry hole and a short chain to minimize swinging.

E. Chickadee house mimics the birds' favored hollow conifer.

F

F. This terra-cotta "bird bottle" accommodates wrens, sparrows, and swallows.

G. Made of metal, this birdhouse condo can house a crowd.

H. Bluebird box with 1½-inch entry hole has a removable side for easy cleaning at season's end.

G

Birdhouse Basics

To keep birdhouses safe *from raccoons and cats, mount the houses atop metal poles. If you want to put a birdhouse in a tree, hang it from a branch.*

Keep houses away *from feeders (the mealtime bustle makes nesting birds nervous).*

Face the entrance *away from the prevailing weather, and remove any perch your birdhouse came with (it's unnecessary, and house sparrows may sit on it to heckle birds inside).*

Birdhouses *should be made from materials that insulate well, such as 1-inch-thick wood (plastic milk bottles and milk cartons are too thin and have poor ventilation; heat can bake chicks inside or make them fledge too early).*

Nest boxes *need an openable side or top for easy cleaning, drain holes on the bottom, and, in hot-summer areas, ventilation holes high in the sides.*

If you put up *more than one, keep houses well separated and out of sight of one another. Houses must go up early, since migrant birds start returning in late February and look for nest sites soon after they arrive.*

H

BOULDERS

With mountains studding nearly every state in the Northeast, it's no surprise that most gardeners are never more than a stone's throw from a rock or a boulder. While some gardeners fight to rid their land of rocks, others embrace them, lacing their properties with stone walls, steps, benches, edgings, pathways, and more. And those gardeners who live in the cities or close-in suburbs where rocks don't occur naturally are no exception: they merely import rocks into their gardens as accent pieces.

Quarries and rock yards can supply a great variety of decorative rock, from small flagstones and cobblestones to huge boulders and columns.

Before you buy, consider your site. (Put a 2-ton rock in the wrong place, and you're stuck.) It's wise to work with a landscape architect, designer, or contractor with plenty of experience in installing rock. And if you live on a sloping lot, you may need to consult a landscape contractor or architect to ascertain the ability of the slope to hold the rocks securely.

A. Blending beautifully with the naturally occurring rock nearby, these flat stepping-stones make a functional and organic pathway.

B. The horizontal and vertical shapes of these large boulders seem to mirror the growth habits of the plants and trees sharing this island bed.

Boulder Basics

Try to work with rock naturally available in your region. It will be relatively in-expensive and more likely to suit your landscape.

At the rock yard, flag the rocks you want with colored ribbon. Figure out exactly where each will go in the garden—and which side will go up (taking snapshots of the rocks can help you place them at delivery time).

Most rock is sold by the ton, though some is also sold by shape (slabs and columns, for example). If you want rocks covered with moss or lichen, expect to pay extra, but beware: moss doesn't always survive the move from mountainside to back-yard patio.

Don't put large rocks on top of small ones. Unless you do it artfully, the large rocks will look unstable. Rocks with flat tops are useful as informal benches or for holding container plants.

Allow for the settling of large rocks (the amount can be significant).

Rocks look better with time. Scars from transport and handling disappear, and lichen will grow on them if you live where the air is relatively unpolluted.

Artificial boulders offer a lighter-weight alternative, but they can be more expensive. Typically made of concrete over metal lath, they're shaped, colored, and textured to look like the real thing.

C. Naturally occurring rocks and boulders vary in shape, size, and color (below), but if you're looking for a particularly large slab, you may be better served by an artificial stone like the one shown above. Lighter in weight than a true boulder, artificial slabs are easier to maneuver and position in the garden.

FURNITURE

There's an enduring graciousness to outdoor furniture. It evokes images of rolling lawns, intimate gardens, and lemonade in the afternoon. But deciding which furniture to buy can be a challenge.

Many styles are available, in materials that include teak, woven willow, and cast iron. Rustic furniture blends well with natural surroundings. Other styles are more finely crafted to complement patios and decks. Still other outdoor "furniture" comes not from a showroom but from a gardener's imagination: well-placed boulders, stones, or wooden planks can also provide outdoor seating.

Manufactured lounges, chairs, and tables are often designed in sets, with pieces priced individually or in a grouping. In general, wooden furniture is more expensive than its cast-resin or metal counterparts.

Whichever type you choose, keep in mind that ourdoor furniture must withstand the elements—sun, rain, insects—and the heavy wear and tear people dole out. Deck and patio furniture can be stored or covered over the winter, but check with the manufacturer if you plan to leave benches, chairs, or other items in the garden year round.

A. With its handsome supports and marble top, a classic bench doubles as garden sculpture in this formal setting.

B. An unobtrusive addition among the plantings of primula and *Rodgersia,* this stone slab bench blends beautifully with the low wall surrounding the pond in this Vermont garden.

C. Painted wooden rockers invite visitors to sit a spell and enjoy conversation and views from the porch.

D. The gently curved seat of this weather-resistant teak garden bench ensures comfort.

E. Tucked in a grassy nook and surrounded by *Coreopsis verticillata,* this antique green filigree bench creates an eye-catching focal point for the garden.

F. A delicate wooden bench painted in an interesting design beckons visitors to relax by the fishpond in this garden.

A CAMP GARDEN

Gardeners often pay homage to a time and place. The sight and smell of familiar plants will conjure up a favorite garden, a beloved gardener, or, in the case of Ellen Penick, the summer camp of her childhood. Faithful to her memory of Camp Okahahwis and her camp mates of 50 years ago, Penick has re-created those days in a corner of her 3-acre garden near Richmond, Virginia. There she used logs to build an open pavilion overlooking a grove of loblolly pines and a lake beyond. She added a mock outhouse, complete with a crescent moon carved in the door. And even though Indian tribes of the mid-Atlantic did not make totem poles, Penick commissioned a local artisan to re-create the pole that once stood at Camp Okahahwis.

Penick designed the garden to blend into its site at the edge of the lake, with water on one side and boggy forest on the other. Native and exotic perennials and shrubs, such as Carolina allspice *(Calycanthus),* with ribbony brown scented flowers, beautyberry *(Callicarpa japoni-ca),* with pink or purple berries, and deciduous azaleas add color and texture to this wild garden. Penick says she is looking forward to her first campout, but admits "I haven't gotten that brave yet."

C. A stone path leads up to an open pavilion made of logs and named Sewalka Cabin after one of Penick's camp cabins. Variegated manna grass (*Glyceria maxima* 'Variegata') and 'Buff Dancer' iris border the pathway.

D. A wooden sign to the "Main Lodge" directs visitors over a bridge and to the house. Yellow *Achillea* 'Moonshine', gray-leafed lamb's ears (*Stachys byzantina* 'Helen von Stein'), and red bee balm crowd together in the sun.

A. **Wearing the Camp Okahahwis uniform**, Ellen Penick (kneeling, second from right) relives her camp days with former camp mates. "Lighting the fire circle was always a great honor," she recalls.

B. **A totem pole** towers over a bed of hostas and *Tiarella* 'Echo Dark Stain', flanked by a young dogwood and a loblolly pine. Local folk artist Larry Butler, of Doswell, Virginia, carved the pole from a photograph supplied by Penick.

A

LIGHTING

For most busy homeowners, evening comes just as they're ready to settle down for some time in the garden—after a busy workday or following a weekend day of chores. But lighting that is thoughtfully chosen and placed can extend your hours of enjoyment outside.

Outdoor lighting allows you to accentuate certain areas of the garden and leave others in shadow to enhance the drama. It can also visually enlarge rooms inside your house: if you peer out at an unlighted garden at night, your windows seem little more than dark mirrors. Landscape lighting

B

makes the windows transparent again, and your home feels more spacious because the eye is drawn outdoors.

Good lighting has a practical use, too. Lights can illuminate a dark driveway, make paths safe for walking, and brighten dark areas to discourage intruders.

Lighting can be subtle, dramatic, and anything in between. Lighting a pond underwater or silhouetting a single shrub or tree can add ethereal magic to a nighttime garden. Carefully placed lights can even mimic the play of moonlight and shadow across pavings.

Lighting Basics

Outdoor lighting fixtures are either decorative or functional. Decorative lights—lanterns, hanging and post- or wall-mounted units, path lights, and strip lights—can add some fill light, but they're primarily meant to be seen and to set an architectural tone.

A functional fixture's job is to light the garden unnoticed. Although some manufacturers make attractive versions, the less visible these fixtures are, the more successful your lighting will be.

Backlighting a lacy shrub makes it glow delicately.

Path lights can flank walks or go high under eaves.

Sidelighting dense trees defines their details.

"Grazing" lights aim upward to highlight architecture.

Uplighting trees reveals form; canopy reflects glow.

Shadowing magnifies plant silhouettes on walls.

"Moonlighting" casts soft pools of light below trees.

A. Ground-level path lights illuminate the entrance to the terrace and light a pathway through this small Branford, Connecticut, garden. Floodlights positioned low to the ground provide uplighting that washes over the bridge that connects the deck to the garden, and to the stone wall and plantings that define it.

B. The glow from this small Japanese-style lantern accentuates the glistening snow-laden branches of nearby shrubs.

C. Cleverly placed strip lighting—recessed in a notch on the underside of the cedar deck railing—provides a soft illumination that invites guests to relax and enjoy the nighttime scene.

A

B

C

Standard Current or Low-voltage?

Outdoor lighting can be powered by standard 120-volt current or by low-voltage systems with transformers that reduce household current to 12 volts.

Standard current

Well suited for large projects or for lighting tall trees with a strong blast of light, standard-voltage fixtures are often better built and longer lasting than low-voltage models. However, they're also larger, harder to hide, more costly to install, more difficult to move, and harder to aim.

Any standard-voltage installation requires a building permit, and codes require that circuits be wired through ground-fault circuit interrupters (GFCIs). Wires must be encased in rigid conduit unless they're at least 18 inches underground, and all junctions must be encased in approved outdoor boxes.

Low voltage

The advantages of low-voltage fixtures are many, including energy conservation, easier installation, portability, and better control of light beams. Also, some fixtures are solar powered.

On the down side, these fixtures are often merely staked in the ground and can be dislodged easily. They're also expensive, and the number of lamps that can be attached to one transformer is limited.

A. Because it's lightweight, this low-voltage copper cylinder is easy to hang from trees.

B. Graceful lines mark this Craftsman-style copper lantern.

C. This low-voltage handcrafted copper lantern hangs from a curved staff.

D. A "mushroom" path lamp lights the way for safe passage.

E. This two-tiered pagoda stands tall among shrubs.

F. Unobtrusive and ideal for "grazing," this low-voltage unit casts light upward.

D

E

F

G

H

I

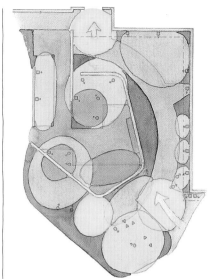

J

L

K

G. This wall-mounted decorative spot
provides a vertical shaft of light.

H. The swivel spot casts a narrow beam
wherever you need it.

I. Mounted on a wall or ceiling, this low-
voltage square spot supplies a pale glow.

J. Designed to illuminate steps and
decks, this 12-volt light measures only
3½ inches across.

K. This flush-mounted light tucks
beneath steps, staying out of harm's way.

L. Placed underwater, this low-voltage
unit may be aimed upward at statues,
plants, or small waterfalls.

Light Placement

*Whether your garden is large or small,
start by determining how much of it
you want to light. Most lighting designers divide the garden into three zones:
a foreground, which is usually given
midlevel brightness; a middle ground,
with low-level light and an interplay of
shadows; and a background—often
the brightest of all—to draw the eye
through the garden.*

*The concept plan above shows these
different zones. Pathways are marked,
and entryways are indicated by arrows.
Individual lights are indicated by tri-
angles (tree mounts), circles (ground
lights), and squares (wall mounts);
arrows show the direction of the light
they will cast. Fine-tuning for placement and brightness should be done
under actual conditions.*

*Lighting should never be spotty. It
should define, not disguise. For example,
uplighting gives the mantle of a tall tree
a dramatic form, but it can also make
the top appear to hover ghostlike above
the earth. To visually anchor the trunk,
have the light (or an additional one)
illuminate the trunk near ground level.*

*Finally, be aware of how your lights
may affect your neighbors. Some communities even have ordinances regu-
lating "light trespass."*

A

PORTABLE LIGHTING

Special occasions such as holidays or outdoor parties often call for temporary lighting that can be put into place almost instantly. A broad range of lanterns is available, from hurricane lamps that burn oil to glass-sided lanterns that house candles. Classic New Mexican luminarias—open paper bags that contain votive candles set in sand—have now been electrified, adding to the growing field of specialty outdoor lighting. Tiny hat lights on strings can bring a carnival atmosphere to a patio or deck. And lanterns on stakes can add drama along the path to a gate or door.

A sampling of lights you might find in stores and catalogs that sell home accessories is pictured here. Keep in mind that selections change from year to year.

No matter which lantern you choose, you'll need to place it with care; this is especially true for lanterns with open flames. Unless snow covers the ground around them, avoid placing lanterns along a path or among foliage where they can pose a fire hazard. Also, make sure that they're sturdy and will not topple in a breeze. And avoid putting metal lanterns that could become hot near dry plant material.

B

A. Strings of white holiday lights laced through wisteria provide a warm ambiance for dining on this cozy deck.

B. Galvanized steel-hat lights dance across a patio.

C–G. Variations on the hurricane theme, these lanterns protect candles from evening breezes. All are glass and metal, except for the terra-cotta "beehives" (**E**).

H. Four lights nestled at the top of the center pole of this umbrella cast a warm glow on those dining or relaxing on the terrace.

I. Festive paper-bag luminarias light the way into this garden.

J. A cast-iron Japanese lantern casts a flickering glow across night gardens.

GARDEN ILLUSIONS

There are times when a gardener's best tool is a paintbrush. When a portion of a walled-in garden is too dark or inhospitable for healthy plants, when the wall itself is drab or in disrepair, when you yearn for a view that could never be or want a little self-expression, it's time to let your imagination rule. Several coats of brightly colored paint can liven up a dark corner and set off the plants in front of it. Attaching a large mirror to a wall can reflect light into a shaded spot and give the impression the garden is deeper and more filled with plants than it is.

If you have true artistic leanings, you can create a tropical paradise filled with butterflies and birds in chilly Massachusetts, a bower of climbing vines in a narrow city alley, or a view of the Tuscan hills complete with atmospheric perspective worthy of Leonardo da Vinci. Even if you are not an artist, there are a variety of stencils with garden themes available at craft supply shops or through the mail (check the home-decorating sections of home improvement magazines for listings).

A. In the heart of Philadelphia, a mural with a superimposed trompe l'oeil trellis appears to lead the viewer out of this small brick-walled garden through a pergola and into a flower-filled, fountained lawn.

B. A faux limestone wall in Washington, D.C., makes a warm-textured backdrop for the dark foliage of an oakleaf hydrangea, pale pink azalea blossoms, and tulips in white and salmon red.

C. The confines of this narrow balcony in Washington, D.C., become elongated by an arched painted view of a pond with cattails and trees. Blue-flowered climbing vines at right soften the hard geometry of the brick wall and help to create a garden where potted plants are all that can grow.

A. Water from this formal, pedestal-style fountain recirculates from the small pool. Surrounded by low plantings that tie it to the rest of the garden, the fountain becomes the focal point of the scene.

B. Its honeycomb shape allows water to flow into the small pool from openings all around this low, circular fountain.

C. Neck outstretched, this garden swan releases a graceful arc of water into a shallow pool.

D. Combining birdbath with fountain, this simple basin pleases on many levels: it offers a feast of flowers—the annual strawflower 'Silverbrush'—splashing birds, and flowing water.

A Pond in a Pot

You can create your own simple water feature. All you need is a glazed ceramic pot at least 30 inches in diameter, without a drainage hole, or a half barrel fitted with a heavy plastic liner. Fill the container about two-thirds full with water, then add plants such as miniature water lilies and water irises, each in its own pot (set plants on inverted pots to raise them). Then fill the rest of the tub with water.

If you already have fish in a larger pond, add them to your pot. Mosquito fish (gambusia) or goldfish will control mosquito larvae and will also feed on the algae in the pot. You'll need about six fish for a 30-inch container. If you are not using fish, put in a submersible pump to create a burbling fountain.

Unless you have an area indoors, such as a greenhouse, where you can overwinter the container, you will have to empty the pond and retire it until spring. Return the fish to the deep pond, discard the plants and the plastic liner, and clean the pot and the pump.

REGIONAL PROBLEMS AND SOLUTIONS

Mountains and seacoast, cities and rural areas: each contributes greatly to the character of the Northeast. And each brings with it challenges for a gardener, from searching out plants that thrive in higher altitudes or along coastlines to protecting seedlings from hungry deer and other pests. Closer to the city, privacy is a pressing issue, and air quality can also cause problems. The pollen of certain plants aggravates allergies, for example; others do not grow well in smog. And across the Northeast, the seasonal extremes of winter, with frost and snow, and summer, with searing heat and periods of drought, can drive even the most experienced gardener to despair.

But every problem brings an opportunity for a new approach. Thoughtful landscape design and maintenance can help a gardener sidestep regional problems and transport the garden to a new level.

MANAGING WETLANDS

Water in a fountain or a pond can add an extra dimension to a garden. Water that stands in puddles and saturates the soil can be a problem. Poor drainage and saturated soil can cause root rot and may suffocate plants not adapted to such conditions. Because excess water displaces the oxygen in the soil, it deprives plant roots of that essential element. And without oxygen, most plants cannot fuel photosynthesis; eventually they die.

Many gardens have a patch where the runoff water from storms collects and the soil stays wet longer than elsewhere on the property. However a wet, boggy area that rarely—if ever—dries out is another matter. In that case, you have several options.

AMEND CLAY SOIL. Clay soil is dense and drains slowly. If rainfall is heavy or if there is a lot of water seeping into the area, clay will remain soggy for a long time. Lighten the soil with organic amendments such as well-rotted manure and compost to promote aeration and drainage.

RISE ABOVE THE PROBLEM. If the ground is always moist but not boggy, you can surmount the problem by building a raised bed. The height to which you need to go depends on what you intend to plant. Shallow-rooted annuals and perennials can make do with an 8- to 10-inch soil depth; deep-rooted plants, including trees and shrubs, may need as much as 2 or 3 feet. A low raised bed can support itself, especially if you plant around the edge to hold the soil in place. For deeper raised beds, provide retaining walls, and be sure to include drainage holes at the bottom if the structured sides have no gaps for water to seep through.

CHANNEL EXCESS WATER. There are several methods for channeling excess water to a convenient place for disposal. Flexible drainpipes attached to downspouts are easy to install. Bury the pipe, allowing it to resurface at a spot where the water can run off safely. Another option is a channel of drain tiles, which are also positioned underground. You'll need to dig a trench sloped at a rate of 1 inch for every 8 feet of length. Then lay down a 2-inch-deep layer of gravel, and top with tiles set end to end. Cover the tile joints with tar paper to keep out soil and debris, and finish with a 4- to 6-inch layer of gravel. You can either leave the channel as is or cover it with soil.

Wrap t
nurser

SHIELI
snow f
with a
with bi
on the
may da

USE SA
walkwa
growin
may he
plants l
plants a
shield.
rather t
spring,
salted o

Specia

In the c
tions. P
light mu
even in
nique th
driving s
Once th
mounde

Other

Water ga
containe
ground i
winter m

WATER (
shapes.
drained f
the wate
area such
cover it v
at least 1
pool itsel
water fre
Still, the p

CONTAIN
ceramic p
them in a
fluctuatio
just as yo

A. **A boardwalk** built over
marshy ground provides access
to a larger part of the garden—and an intimacy with
the plantings that flank it.
Here feathery astilbe plumes
and floral sprays of coral bells
(Heuchera) beckon the eye.

B. **Extending out** over the
bank and stream, this deck
increases the usable garden
and recreation space on the
sloped property, and provides
a pleasing view of the untamed
soggy land below.

C. **A simple arched bridge**
spanning a pond is an attractive
garden focal point; the marshy
area proves fertile ground for
a variety of plants.

PLANT A BOG GARDEN. Transform a liability into an asset by turning a muddy spot of standing water into a beautiful bog garden.
Some garden plants, such as hosta, astilbe, and daylilies, get along
in normal soil but really prosper when they are given continual
moisture. There are a host of other beautiful plants that need wet
conditions. See the list on page 305 for some ideas.

BUILD A BOARDWALK. Create easy, comfortable access through
your bog or water garden with a boardwalk built just above the
level of the wet ground. The wood surface is pleasing underfoot,
and the dry path offers an opportunity to view up close particularly
choice plants and wildlife that would normally remain remote.

CREATE BOGGY CONDITIONS. If you yearn for a bog garden but
don't have a suitable environment, you can create one. Dig out the
soil to a depth of 12 to 18 inches (the depth depends on the plants
you want to use), line the hole with heavy plastic that is punctured
in a few places for slow drainage, backfill the hole, water well, and
plant. Because it isn't a natural bog, you'll need to watch for signs
of drying out and water as necessary.

th
re

P
Su
of
gr
on
fr
fr
re
re
tr
da

Preparing for the thaw

Late winter and early spring bring some of the greatest dangers to the garden. Temperatures can be quite warm during the day, and the timing of the last freeze is unpredictable. In fact, at this time of year the garden is vulnerable to a particular type of freeze that occurs in isolated spots on clear, still, dry nights. Known as a radiation freeze, this happens when the warmth that was stored in the ground during the day rises quickly and is replaced by cold air.

Young plants set out in the spring are most susceptible to radiation freezes. To protect plants, cover them with plastic, burlap, or newspaper, which slows the loss of heat and insulates against the cold. Prop up the material in such a way that it doesn't touch plant leaves.

A. A burlap snow fence (above) shields these azaleas from the drying effects of winter winds, which can strip them of moisture and cause moderate to severe injury.

B. Resting under a layer of mulch 4 to 6 inches deep, these raised beds have been prepared for winter (right). The beds will also warm quickly in the spring and may be planted earlier than flat beds.

WINTERIZING A WATER GARDEN

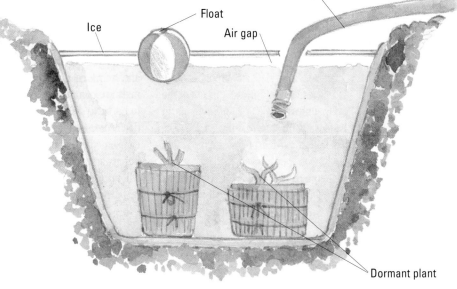

Ice · Float · Air gap · Garden hose

Dormant plant

For a pool more than 12 inches deep, lower aquatic plants to the bottom of the pool to protect them. Place a compressible float of some type, such as a rubber ball, on the surface of the water to decrease the pressure exerted by ice as it forms. The plants will need air throughout the winter months, so once ice has covered the surface, create a hole big enough to insert a section of hose; use the hose to siphon out some water, which creates an air gap beneath the ice.

PROPER MULCHING TECHNIQUE

When mulching, avoid piling it directly against the plant stems, as this encourages rot and other diseases. Instead, apply the mulch in a volcano-like mound around the plant. Don't mulch any deeper than necessary; that would only encourage winter pests and inhibit air, water, and nutrients from reaching your plants.

Pest-control chart

Various methods are used to keep animal pests out of the garden, including barriers, repellents, habitat alteration, and traps. Any of these methods can be effective. However, if you are unwilling to use a lethal trap or kill a trapped animal humanely, trapping is not recommended. Many pests carry viral diseases that may be transmitted to humans. Releasing a pest in another location will reduce the food supply available to that species in that area and possibly burden another garden with the problem you are trying to solve.

METHOD OF CONTROL

ANIMAL	TYPE OF FENCING	TREE GUARDS	REPELLENTS USED	TYPE OF TRAP	ENVIRONMENTAL CHANGES
Raccoons	Electric fence for ponds			Live	Eliminate food sources. Prune tree limbs.
Woodchucks	Fence at least 3' high and 2' deep			Live	Clear garden of tall grass.
Moles	Line planting beds with wire mesh.			Lethal	Plant lavender, rosemary, or salvia. Eliminate grubs by treating lawn with milky spore disease.
Voles	Line planting beds with wire mesh.	Plastic or mesh extending 6" below ground		Lethal	Eliminate food sources. Keep lawn mowed. Work sharp gravel into soil. Get a cat.
Deer	At least 7' high or electrified		Commercial repellents must be applied weekly or after a rainfall.		Try using plants deer avoid.
Rabbits	Use a small mesh fence 2' high and 6" below ground.	Plastic or mesh extending 6" below ground	Commercial repellents must be applied weekly or after a rainfall.	Live	Clean up thickets and brush piles. Get a cat.
Squirrels		Netting over bushes and fruit trees. Use wire mesh on planters.	Use mothballs at the base of trees. May be harmful to pets, however.	Live or lethal	

Miscanthus sinensis (eulalia)

Deer-resistant Plants

Very few ornamentals are absolutely invulnerable to deer, but there are some that appear to be the food of last resort. This list includes plants that are known to be poisonous, and therefore less appealing, and plants that have been reported either in studies or anecdotally as being deer resistant in the northeastern states. This list is only a guideline, however. Remember, what deer find distasteful one year or in one area they may find irresistible at another time or in another location. The best method for finding deer-resistant plants for your area is trial and error. Plants with thorns (but not roses) or spiny projections, such as holly and barberry, are the most deer resistant, so you may want to start with these.

GROUND COVERS

Convallaria majalis
LILY-OF-THE-VALLEY ◊

Liriope
LILYTURF*

Pachysandra
PACHYSANDRA

Vinca minor
PERIWINKLE ◊

GRASSES

Calamagrostis*

Chasmanthium latifolium
NORTHERN SEA OATS

Festuca ovina glauca
BLUE FESCUE ◊

Miscanthus purpurascens
FLAME GRASS

M. sinensis*
EULALIA

PERENNIALS

Aconitum species
MONKSHOOD ◊

Artemisia*

Astilbe
FALSE SPIREA *

Calamintha nepeta
LESSER CATMINT ◊ *

Cimicifuga americana
AMERICAN BUGBANE ◊ *

Delphinium species ◊

Perched atop a stone wall, this aromatic Calamintha nepeta *is a plant deer avoid.*

Dicentra peregrina◊

Digitalis purpurea
FOXGLOVE ◊

Helleborus species
CHRISTMAS ROSE,
LENTEN ROSE ◊

Hyacinthus orientalis
HYACINTH ◊

Iris species ◊

Kniphofia
RED-HOT POKER*

Lavandula
LAVENDER*

Liatris spicata
SPIKE GAY-FEATHER*

Narcissus species ◊

Ranunculus species ◊

Santolina chamaecyparissus
LAVENDER COTTON*

Sedum ◊ *

Tanacetum vulgare
TANSY ◊

VINES

Hedera helix
ENGLISH IVY

Trachelospermum jasminoides
STAR JASMINE

SHRUBS

Berberis
BARBERRY*

B. thunbergii 'Atropurpurea'
RED-LEAF JAPANESE
BARBERRY*

Buxus sempervirens
COMMON BOXWOOD ◊

Ceanothus americanus
NEW JERSEY TEA

Cephalotaxus fortunei
CHINESE PLUM YEW*

Cornus racemosa*

Cotoneaster
COTONEASTER*

Cydonia oblonga
QUINCE*

Forsythia
FORSYTHIA*

Ilex aquifolium
ENGLISH HOLLY ◊ *

I. glabra
INKBERRY*

I. opaca
AMERICAN HOLLY ◊ *

I. verticillata
BLACK ALDER,
WINTERBERRY ◊

Kalmia species ◊
MOUNTAIN LAUREL

Leucothöe fontanesiana
DROOPING LEUCOTHOE

Ligustrum
PRIVET ◊ *

Pieris floribunda
MOUNTAIN PIERIS*

Prunus serotina
BLACK CHERRY ◊

Sambucus canadensis
BLACK ELDERBERRY ◊

S. pubens
SCARLET ELDERBERRY ◊

Spiraea species
BRIDAL WREATH*

Spiraea × Vanhouttei
VANHOUTTE SPIREA*

Stewartia species*

Vaccinium corymbosum
HIGHBUSH BLUEBERRY*

Viburnum carlesii
KOREAN SPICE VIBURNUM*

V. dilatatum*

V. opulus
SNOWBALL BUSH*

V. rhytidophyllum*

V. sieboldii*

V. tomentosum
SNOWBALL VIBURNUM*

V. wrightii*

Weigela florida*

TREES

Abies fraseri
FRASER FIR*

Acer rubrum
RED MAPLE*

Betula papyrifera
WHITE BIRCH*

B. pendula
WEEPING BIRCH*

Cornus amomum
SILKY DOGWOOD*

C. florida
FLOWERING DOGWOOD*

C. kousa
KOUSA DOGWOOD*

C. mas
CORNEL,
CORNELIAN CHERRY*

C. sericea
RED OSIER DOGWOOD*

Laburnum anagyroides
GOLDEN CHAIN ◊

Picea abies
NORWAY SPRUCE*

P. glauca
WHITE SPRUCE*

P. pungens
COLORADO BLUE SPRUCE*

Pinus cembra
SWISS STONE PINE*

P. mugo
MOUNTAIN PINE*

P. nigra
AUSTRIAN PINE*

P. resinosa
RED PINE*

P. strobus
WHITE PINE*

P. sylvestris
SCOTCH PINE*

Populus nigra 'Italica'
LOMBARDY POPLAR*

Pyrus communis
PEAR*

Robinia pseudoacacia
BLACK LOCUST ◊

◊ POISONOUS PLANTS DEER
MAY AVOID
* PLANTS DEER HAVE BEEN
KNOWN TO AVOID IN THE
NORTHEAST

In a garden filled with deer-resistant plants, pink astilbe colors the foreground, blooming against a backdrop of white Cimicifuga.

POLLEN

Itchy eyes, a runny nose, near-constant sneezing—to many allergy sufferers, this is how spring, summer, and fall are defined. Wind-borne pollen causes about 60 percent of all allergy problems, and most of it comes from trees and summer-blooming grasses. You may opt to stay indoors during the worst of the allergy season, or you could try another approach: plant low-allergen plants in your garden.

Seasonal allergies affect 22 million Americans annually. Trees—especially oaks, maples, and birches—are the major culprits in spring; grasses trigger midsummer problems; and weeds, such as ragweed, bring on symptoms from late summer until the first frost. In addition, some plants cause an itchy skin condition called contact dermatitis when they come into contact with skin.

Reducing pollen

The very nature of wind-borne pollen makes it difficult to escape. You can't replace all the trees and shrubs growing in your neighborhood or eliminate the pollen-rich grasses growing along the roadsides. But you can choose plants for your own garden that are known not to produce wind-borne pollen. By replacing wind-pollinated plants with those pollinated by insects, you can greatly reduce the allergens in your garden.

What to plant?

Happily, the most colorful flowering plants don't produce airborne pollen. Petunias and pansies, for example, are low-allergen plants, as are peonies and daylilies. This is because nature uses color to entice insects. Foraging bees respond to blue and yellow above all other colors, for example. Fragrance also attracts pollinators, so another advantage to planting insect-pollinated plants is the rich perfume they exude.

Planting nonallergenic trees and shrubs will also reduce pollen in the garden. If possible, you should also eliminate or minimize hedges and lawns: many are allergenic, and they can also trap pollen and mold spores.

Among the plants listed at right are those that produce little pollen, as well as some of the most notorious troublemakers. In addition, there is a list of plants known to cause contact dermatitis in some people. An allergist can tell you about your particular sensitivity to plants, and recommend other nonallergenic plants suitable for planting in your area.

Tips for a Sneeze-free Garden

DISPATCH WEEDS REGULARLY
  Many weeds are highly allergenic. Keep them mowed, spray with an herbicide, or hoe them or pull them out by hand before they bloom.

TRIM GRASSES
  Lawn grasses, particularly Bermuda grass, are among the most common causes of allergies. Mow your lawn frequently at the proper height so that seed heads don't form. Keep grass growing vigorously with regular water and fertilizer to prevent it from going to seed. Try to avoid mowing the lawn yourself. If grass causes your allergies to flare up too much, replace the lawn with a substitute ground cover (see pages 224–225).

USE A RAKE
  Nothing makes dust, pollen, and fungal spores spread faster than leaf blowers. Try a rake instead.

CONSIDER OTHER CAUSES
  Fungal spores, dust mites, and animal dander cause many allergies, particularly in fall. Consult an allergist to identify the cause of your symptoms before you undertake any relandscaping.

Pinus contorta

Nonallergenic plants

Very few annuals and perennials produce wind-borne pollen; those that do are listed under "Other allergenic plants."

TREES

Aesculus
HORSE CHESTNUT AND BUCKEYE

Catalpa

Celtis
HACKBERRY

Cercis
REDBUD

Cladrastis lutea
YELLOWWOOD

Cornus
DOGWOOD

Crataegus
HAWTHORN

Ginkgo
MAIDENHAIR TREE

Halesia
SILVER BELL

Ilex
HOLLY

Liriodendron
TULIP TREE

Magnolia

Malus
CRABAPPLE

Oxydendrum
SOURWOOD

Prunus
FLOWERING CHERRY

Pyrus
FLOWERING PEAR

Sorbus
MOUNTAIN ASH

Stewartia

Styrax
SNOWBELL

SHRUBS

Berberis
BARBERRY

Buddleia
BUTTERFLY BUSH

Calycanthus
ALLSPICE

Camellia

Chaenomeles
FLOWERING QUINCE

Cotoneaster

Daphne

Deutzia

Euonymus

Forsythia

Hamamelis
WITCH HAZEL

Hydrangea

Kalmia
MOUNTAIN LAUREL

Kolkwitzia
BEAUTY BUSH

Leucothöe

Lonicera
HONEYSUCKLE

Nandina
HEAVENLY BAMBOO

Philadelphus
MOCK ORANGE

Pieris
ANDROMEDA

Pyracantha

Rhododendron

Rosa
ROSE

Spiraea

Viburnum

Allergenic plants

TREES AND SHRUBS

Acer
MAPLE

Alnus
ALDER

Betula
BIRCH

Carya
HICKORY AND PECAN

Castanea
CHESTNUT

Fagus
BEECH

Fraxinus
ASH

Juglans
WALNUT

Juniperus
JUNIPER

Liquidambar
SWEET GUM

Morus
MULBERRY

Pinus
PINE

Platanus
PLANE TREE

Populus
POPLAR

Quercus
OAK

Salix
WILLOW

Ulmus
ELM

Other allergenic plants

Amaranthus
LOVE-LIES-BLEEDING

Ambrosia artemisifolia
RAGWEED

Aster

Carex
SEDGES

Chrysanthemum

Grasses (many)

Marigold

Sunflower

Zinnia

Plants that can irritate the skin

Angelica

Dictamnus albus
GAS PLANT

Heracleum
GIANT HOGWEED

Rhus radicans
POISON IVY

R. vernix
SWAMP SUMAC

Ruta graveolens
RUE

Liquidambar

PRIVACY

For most people today, privacy is an increasingly valuable commodity. Noisy streets and bright lights shining through your bedroom window at night—these are just some of the intrusions brought about by houses that are built close together on small lots or located near roadways.

Fortunately, most privacy problems can be solved with creative landscaping. Well-positioned hedges, fences, or walls can shield your house from the street or from neighbors. A tree or an arbor can block the view of your property from the hillside above. A combination of walls or berms, plants, and maybe a fountain or other water feature can even soften the noise of the busy street nearby.

In addition to shielding you from the outside world, creating privacy has some extra benefits. Walls and berms, carefully placed, can create outdoor "rooms" and add interest to the garden.

Identify the intrusions

Before you can create privacy, you must determine exactly what you want to block out or be shielded from. Walk around your property, identifying areas that require covers or screens. Also try to evaluate how plantings and additional structures will affect your neighbors, the patterns of sun and shade in your garden, and any views you want to preserve.

A particularly annoying privacy problem might seem to call for a stand of fast-growing, closely spaced trees or shrubs. But don't overdo it. You may end up replacing or removing such plants because fast growers are often not long-lived. You can, however, plan for selective removal, such as every other shrub in a closely spaced hedge. Or combine both fast- and slow-growing plants, knowing that you'll remove the less desirable ones as the better species mature.

A. Looking out across rocks and mounds of *Picea abies* 'Globosa' in this New Hampshire garden, the eye comes to rest on a row of espaliered McIntosh apple trees; these screen the view to a parking lot beyond.

B. Rapid and dense in its growth, *Ligustrum* (privet) is the ideal hedge plant. Sheared into a formal hedge, as shown here, privet screens views, mitigates noise, and withstands difficult conditions such as dry soil and city pollution.

C. Hidden from the street by a privacy gate, this New York home retains its attractive front while shielding its entranceway from the glances of passersby. The open-work of the gate not only creates a welcoming front, it allows air circulation as well.

D. Enclosing this rooftop creates a private spot for gardening and entertaining. The wooden planter box, overflowing with brightly colored chrysanthemums, is crafted from the same material as the walls that screen the rooftop from its neighbors.

E. A beautifully symmetrical hedge of arborvitae alternating with 'New Dawn' and 'William Baffin' roses clothes the fence separating two properties. The dense arborvitae lends added screening from sights, sound, and wind.

HIGH-ALTITUDE GARDENING

High winds, freezing temperatures, and thin soil give Northeast gardeners in high-altitude regions some tough challenges. The mountains along the Appalachian chain rise no higher than 6,000 feet, but the growing conditions are nonetheless extreme, with arctic winds bringing subzero temperatures as far south as the Ozarks in winter and blowing away the insulating snow cover. Wind and rain also remove topsoil; what soil is left in rock crevices and gulches tends to be acidic. Alpine shrubs and trees such as firs and spruces compete aggressively for growing space, creating shade and clogging the soil with roots.

And yet a gardener can be richly rewarded by an alpine garden in the Northeast. The mountains receive steady precipitation, in the form of 30 to 50 inches of snow, rain, and fog yearly. Trees help protect alpines from scalding sun and desiccating wind in summer and winter, and the rocky soil ensures good drainage. Best of all, there is a wide array of dwarf trees, shrubs, perennials, bulbs, and ground covers like mosses that thrive best in rigorous alpine conditions. Even gardeners in lower elevations, such as the rocky coast of Maine, can draw from the palette of alpine plants.

The term *alpine plants* properly refers only to plants that grow above the timberline on a mountain; included here are also plants from meadows, bogs, woodlands, prairies, and the shore. What these plants have in common is a need for excellent drainage and an intolerance for water-retentive clay soil—especially in winter. Given the right conditions, these tough plants resist drought and the effects of bitter winter by developing a low-to-the-ground profile, and by going dormant during the harshest weather. Lovely flowers—if diminutive—and fine foliage also characterize these plants, as well as true alpines.

Blue Serbian bellflower (Campanula poscharskyana) *with Johnny-jump-ups* (Viola tricolor) *and a* Lewisia *(top), and cushion spurge* (Euphorbia epithymoides) *with spurred bell-flower* (C. alliariifolia) *(bottom).*

You can locate a rock garden for high-altitude plants anywhere there is a slope with good drainage. The best vantage is in full sun, but in the Northeast partial shade under trees may be the best you can do. However, there are many shade- and moisture-tolerant alpines from which to choose.

Extra topsoil will give your plants a good start. The preferred alpine soil is a mix of equal parts loam, clean sharp sand, leaf mulch, and limestone chips; add a larger proportion of leaf mulch for a shady garden. You may also have to shift around some rocks and boulders to achieve a good effect, but they will become a dramatic foil for your plants and make them look right at home.

This sun-dappled rock garden in Maine was made by scraping away the thin topsoil from the rocks and inserting plants among them. These include cabbagelike *Bergenia cordifolia*, a native of Siberia with pink flower spikes in early spring; magenta-flowered hardy geranium in the foreground; and other perennials. Low-growing evergreens maintain a year-round presence.

High-altitude plants

SUN LOVERS

Allium cyaneum

Anemone pulsatilla
PASQUEFLOWER

Aster alpinus
ALPINE ASTER

Aurinia saxatilis
BASKET-OF-GOLD

Berberis candidula
PALELEAF BARBERRY

Calluna vulgaris
HEATHER

Campanula carpatica
CARPATHIAN HAREBELL

Cotoneaster

Crocus

Daphne cneorum
ROSE DAPHNE

Dianthus alpinus
DWARF ROCK PINK

Erica
HEATH

Genista tinctoria
COMMON WOADWAXEN

Geranium macrorrhizum
HARDY GERANIUM

Iberis sempervirens
CANDYTUFT

Iris cristata
CRESTED IRIS

Juniperus and Pinus
JUNIPER AND PINE CULTIVARS

Narcissus species
SPECIES DAFFODIL

Oenethera species
EVENING PRIMROSE

Papaver alpinum
ALPINE POPPY

Sedum
STONECROP

Sempervivum tectorum
HEN AND CHICKENS

Thymus
THYME

Tulipa species
SPECIES TULIPS

Vaccinium angustifolium
LOWBUSH BLUEBERRY

SHADE TOLERANT

Abies, Taxus, Thuya, and Tsuga
DWARF FIR, YEW, ARBORVITAE, AND HEMLOCK CULTIVARS

Allium moly
LILY LEEK

Anemone canadensis
MEADOW ANEMONE

Aquilegia canadensis
CANADIAN COLUMBINE

Asarum europaeum
EUROPEAN WILD GINGER

Corydalis lutea
YELLOW FUMATORY

Cyclamen hederifolium
NEAPOLITAN CYCLAMEN

Dicentra eximia
FRINGED BLEEDING HEART

Dodecatheon meadia
SHOOTING STAR

Erythronium species
TROUT LILY

Ferns

Gaultheria procumbens
WINTERGREEN

Geranium ibericum
CAUCASUS GERANIUM

Heuchera species
ALUMROOT

Hosta

Leucojum
SNOWFLAKE

Phlox divaricata
WILD BLUE PHLOX

Polygonatum
SOLOMON'S SEAL

Primula
PRIMROSE

Pulmonaria angustifolia
LUNGWORT

Rhododendron
DWARF SPECIES AND CULTIVARS

Sanguinaria canadensis
BLOODROOT

Scilla bifolia
TWINLEAF SQUILL

Tiarella cordifolia
FOAMFLOWER

Trillium grandiflorum
SNOW TRILLIUM

Viola
VIOLET

WATERWISE GARDENING

I n the minds of most northeasterners, recurring drought and water-conservation methods are challenges faced only by those living in desert areas and on the West Coast. But with the increasing frequency of dry summers and the threat—if not the reality—of water restrictions becoming a familiar scenario for the Northeast, gardeners are coming face-to-face with the need to plan landscapes that are as water thrifty as possible.

By following the eight fundamental principles for a waterwise garden that appear below, you'll not only have the pleasure of knowing you're a responsible gardener, you'll be rewarded with a garden that requires far less maintenance: by choosing drought-tolerant plants adapted to your region, improving your soil, and mulching regularly, for example, you will save countless hours weeding, mowing, trimming—and watering—your plants.

USE WATER-CONSERVING PLANTS. Some plants need a lot of water to survive; others perform better with less. You can find water-thrifty trees, shrubs, flowering plants, ground covers, and even some grasses for your garden. Some provide seasonal color, others year-round green. The key is to choose plants that are well adapted to the natural conditions of your region. Lists of plants with low water needs appear in the *Sunset National Garden Book.*

GROUP PLANTS WISELY. Place thirsty plants together and drought-resistant plants elsewhere. Then put plants that need regular watering on a separate irrigation system and schedule.

LIMIT TURF AREAS. A lawn requires more irrigation than almost any other landscape feature. Limit its size to just what you need for your purposes and choose a grass or grass mix adapted to your climate (see pages 220–223). Consider replacing at least part of your lawn with hardscape materials or alternative plants.

IRRIGATE EFFICIENTLY. Make sure that your watering practices and devices use water as efficiently as possible. Information on choosing an irrigation system can be found on the following pages; installation guidelines appear on pages 396–397.

IMPROVE YOUR SOIL. Routinely cultivate your soil and incorporate organic matter. You'll improve the soil's ability to resist evaporation and retain moisture.

MULCH. Place a layer of organic or mineral material over soil and around plants. Mulch greatly reduces moisture loss through evaporation, reduces weeds, and slows erosion.

MAINTAIN YOUR GARDEN. Tighten faucets so they don't drip. Water plants only when needed, not by the clock or the calendar. Avoid runoff, which wastes water.

CONTROL WEEDS. These garden intruders consume water needed by more desirable plants.

A. This pleasing combination of the daisylike flowers of *Echinacea purpurea* (purple coneflower) in white and purple, the feathery bottle-brush blooms of *Liatris,* and a scattering of spiky ornamental grasses has the added bonus of tolerating heat, drought, and wind.

B. Perfect for drier parts of a planting area or in a wild garden, *Monarda fistulosa* (wild bergamot) is a versatile plant: it is quite drought resistant but also performs well in moist soil.

C. Cultivars of *Miscanthus sinensis*, including 'Strictus', which has yellow-striped leaves, and 'Gracillimus', with feathery plumes above clumps of fine-textured foliage, grow enthusiastically in this Connecticut garden. The grasses are very low maintenance, preferring well-drained soil and full sun.

SEACOAST PLANTINGS

Coastal gardens can be both a blessing and a curse, as one Connecticut garden designer puts it. The growing season is long, but the plants must be able to withstand such special conditions as salt-laden winds, fog and humid air, and low sun intensity. Coastal soil is sandy and salty, and it retains very little moisture. But for gardens directly or largely influenced by the ocean, the tough plants listed here can take these inhospitable conditions and thrive in all but the most exposed situations. Some, including rosemary, gaillardia, bayberry, rugosa rose, and sea lavender, can survive even if they suffer direct hits of spray-laden wind.

Rosa rugosa

Buffeted by constant winds, plants on a coastal slope need to be tough to survive. This illuminated pathside garden is filled with a mix of colors and textures that includes the purple flower heads of statice and the striking form of aloe.

Seacoast plantings

TREES

Albizia julibrissin 'Rosea'
SILK TREE

Acer pseudoplatanus
SYCAMORE MAPLE

Aesculus hippocastanum
HORSE CHESTNUT

Amelanchier canadensis
SHADBUSH

Crataegus crus-galli
COCKSPUR THORN

Cryptomeria japonica
JAPANESE CRYPTOMERIA

Ilex opaca
AMERICAN HOLLY

Juniperus virginiana
RED CEDAR

Nyssa sylvatica
TUPELO

Picea pungens 'Glauca'
COLORADO BLUE SPRUCE

Pinus rigida
NORTHERN PITCH PINE

P. sylvestris
SCOTCH PINE

P. thunbergii
JAPANESE BLACK PINE

Quercus alba
WHITE OAK

Asclepias tuberosa 'Gay Butterflies'

Gaillardia × grandiflora

Quercus marilandica
BLACKJACK OAK

Robinia pseudoacacia
BLACK LOCUST

Thuja occidentalis
AMERICAN ARBORVITAE

Tilia cordata
LITTLELEAF LINDEN

Ulmus parvifolia
CHINESE ELM

SHRUBS

Aronia arbutifolia
RED CHOKEBERRY

Baccharis halimifolia
GROUNDSEL BUSH

Chamaecyparis pisifera cultivars
SAWARA FALSE CYPRESS

Clethra alnifolia
SUMMERSWEET

Comptonia peregrina
SWEET FERN

Cornus sericea
RED OSIER DOGWOOD

Cotoneaster species
COTONEASTER

Cytisus scoparius
SCOTCH BROOM

Elaeagnus angustifolius
RUSSIAN OLIVE

Halimodendron halodendron
SALT TREE

Hibiscus syriacus
SHRUB ALTHEA

Hydrangea macrophylla cultivars
HOUSE HYDRANGEA

Ligustrum species and cultivars
PRIVET

L. morrowii
MORROW HONEYSUCKLE

Lonicera tatarica
TATARIAN HONEYSUCKLE

Myrica pensylvanica
BAYBERRY

Pinus mugo and cultivars
MUGO PINE

Prunus maritima
BEACH PLUM

Rhus species
SUMAC

Rosa rugosa
RUGOSA ROSE

R. virginiana
VIRGINIA ROSE

R. wichuraiana
MEMORIAL ROSE

Rosmarinus officinalis
ROSEMARY

Sambucus canadensis
ELDERBERRY

Spiraea species
SPIRAEA

Syringa vulgaris cultivars
LILAC

Tamarix species
TAMARISK

Taxus species and cultivars
YEW

Viburnum dentatum
ARROWWOOD

VINES AND GROUND COVERS

Arctostaphylos uva-ursi
BEARBERRY

Calluna vulgaris cultivars
HEATHER

Celastrus scandens
AMERICAN BITTERSWEET

Clematis paniculata
SWEET AUTUMN CLEMATIS

Delosperma species
ICE PLANT

Hydrangea anomala petiolaris
CLIMBING HYDRANGEA

Juniperus conferta
SHORE JUNIPER

J. horizontalis
CREEPING JUNIPER

Parthenocissus quinquefolia
VIRGINIA CREEPER

Polygonum aubertii
SILVER FLEECEVINE

Thymus species and cultivars
THYME

PERENNIALS AND ANNUALS

Artemisia stelleriana
BEECH WORMWOOD

Asclepias tuberosa
BUTTERFLY WEED

Aurinia saxatilis
BASKET-OF-GOLD

Centaurea cyanus
CORNFLOWER

Cerastium tomentosum
SNOW-IN-SUMMER

Chrysanthemum species and cultivars

Dianthus species and cultivars
PINKS, CARNATIONS

Dictamnus albus
GAS PLANT

Eschscholzia californica
CALIFORNIA POPPY

Gaillardia × grandiflora

Gypsophila paniculata
BABY'S BREATH

Hemerocallis
DAYLILY

Iberis sempervirens
CANDYTUFT

Lychnis coronaria
ROSE CAMPION

Papaver orientale
ORIENTAL POPPY

Pelargonium species and cultivars
GERANIUM

Santolina chamaecyparissus
LAVENDER COTTON

Sedum species and cultivars
STONECROP

Sempervivum species and cultivars
HEN AND CHICKENS

Tropaeolum majus
NASTURTIUM

Veronica species and cultivars
SPEEDWELL

Pinus sylvestris 'Glauca Nana'

Hydrangea macrophylla

LANDSCAPE PLANS

A garden reflects your interests as well as your needs. Perhaps you love to cook, and want a steady supply of fresh greens, fruits, and vegetables. Perhaps you have an active family, with children who like to romp on lawns, jump on play structures, eat barbecue fare, and swim. Perhaps you prefer a wild garden of rambling shrubs, trees, and flowers that attract butterflies and birds. Or maybe you're not a gardener at all, and want just a patio, a water feature, and a few containers.

In every case, you need a plan. The following plans show gardens developed to suit the differing homesites and needs of eastern gardeners, using plant varieties that flourish in most northeastern climate zones. Follow a plan exactly, or adapt a few features that appeal to you.

Once you know precisely what you want, you're ready to start, whether that means peeling up sod to make room for flower beds and a path, or building a new garden from the ground or the concrete up.

The Plants

A. Acer palmatum
JAPANESE MAPLE

B. Syringa vulgaris 'Monge'
LILAC

C. Pachysandra terminalis
PACHYSANDRA

D. Quercus rubra
RED OAK

E. Ginkgo biloba (grafted male)
MAIDENHAIR TREE

F. Rosa rugosa
RUGOSA ROSE

G. Cytisus scoparius 'Hollandia'
SCOTCH BROOM

H. Malus 'Donald Wyman'
CRABAPPLE

I. Kolkwitzia amabilis
BEAUTY BUSH

J. Viburnum × carlcephalum
FRAGRANT SNOWBALL

K. Yucca 'Golden Sword'
YUCCA

L. Stewartia pseudocamellia
JAPANESE STEWARTIA

M. Prunus sargentii
SARGENT CHERRY

N. Scabiosa 'Butterfly Blue'
PINCUSHION FLOWER

TWO ENTRY GARDENS

The area in front of a house is often too public for sitting, entertaining, or other more typically backyard pursuits. But these two plans show what is possible when homeowners decide to take back the front for themselves.

In the design above, the landscape architect created a private enclave by surrounding the garden with a 5-foot-high fence, softened by an open grid and climbing vines. Inside this space, the garden makes a series of transitions from the public to the private world. The first transition occurs at the gate, to the left of the driveway. The second is at the front steps, where visitors can either enter the patio or continue to the front door.

Lush growth surrounds the pavement. A red oak and a cherry tree provide shade for most of the day. Their bright autumn leaves add seasonal interest; in winter their bare silhouettes allow sun to warm the area. Perennials planted along the edges provide further

A Second Entry Garden

An alternative plan for the same garden is shown below. Here the landscape architect has created a low-maintenance design filled with shrubs, ground covers, and natural boulders. Most of the shrubs are broadleaf evergreens; deciduous shrubs provide colorful accents in spring and summer. A fescue is a good wear-tolerant choice for the small lawn.

Tall variety thujas planted in a row along the southwest side of the garden create a sense of enclosure. A 6-foot-wide walk, accented with brick steps and clusters of large terra-cotta pots, creates a welcoming transition in a short space.

The Plants

A. Hemerocallis 'Catherine Woodbury'
DAYLILY

B. Arctostaphylos uva-ursi
BEARBERRY

C. Cercis canadensis
EASTERN REDBUD

D. Thuja plicata
GIANT ARBORVITAE

E. Iris tectorum
JAPANESE ROOF IRIS

F. Euonymus alatus 'Compactus'
WINGED EUONYMUS

G. E. fortunei 'Emerald Gaiety'

H. Indigofera kirilowii
KIRILOW INDIGO

I. Vinca minor
COMMON PERIWINKLE

J. Ilex cornuta 'Compacta'
COMPACT INKBERRY

K. Juniperus chinensis procumbens 'Nana'
JUNIPER

L. J. sabina 'Tamariscifolia'
TAMARIX JUNIPER

M. Hibiscus syriacus 'Woodbridge'
SHRUB ALTHEA

N. Forsythia viridissima 'Bronxensis'
BRONX FORSYTHIA

O. Lavandula officinalis
TRUE LAVENDER

P. Koelreuteria paniculata
GOLDEN RAIN TREE

Q. Pieris japonica
JAPANESE ANDROMEDA

R. Quercus robur 'Fastigiata'
PYRAMIDAL ENGLISH OAK

S. Rhododendron 'PJM'
PJM RHODODENDRON

T. Salvia nemorosa 'East Friesland'

U. Verbena 'Homestead Purple'

NORTH ◢

seasonal color. Beside the driveway, a line of fragrant white viburnums softens the property line, and a crabapple displays creamy bloom in spring and scarlet fruits in fall and winter.

A key element in this design is the use of brick set in woven patterns in the colored concrete, to further define spaces. The front steps and raised planters are brick as well.

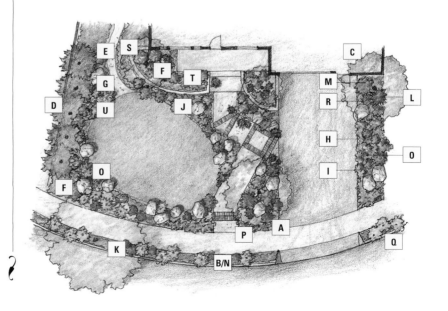

Two Side-yard Gardens

S ide yards are design challenges—
long, narrow spaces that are difficult
to make attractive, let alone useful. In
these two plans—one for a sunny area, the
other for shade—the garden designer rose
to the challenge.

On the sunny east side of this house, the
side yard is only 6 feet wide, except for an
alcove off the kitchen. In the plan shown at
left, the designer took advantage of the
wonderful morning light there by creating a
breakfast nook large enough to accommodate a table and a passageway. Connecticut
bluestone surfaces the area, while the rest
of the side yard is paved with brick to match
a brick wall, and inset with bluestone.
Raised brick planters bring colorful plants
such as impatiens to eye level and further
define the nook. Two rough-bark Japanese
maples (*Acer palmatum* 'Sangokaku')
provide seasonal interest.

Trees cast dense shade on the west side
of the house, and here the designer developed a serene garden filled with shade-
loving plants (illustrated at right). French
doors from the living room face symmetrical wrought-iron arches that echo the
arched entrances to both side yards. The
grid running the length of the garden wall is
also wrought iron. To infuse the garden—
and the living room—with a quiet burbling
sound, fountainheads spout water into
limestone bowls. Lush greenery, including
Japanese andromeda, mountain laurel,
and Japanese spurge, spills from a raised
bed along the fence and fills ground-level
planting areas. Dark green winter creeper
softens the wall. The side yard is paved with
waterwashed flagstone; rupturewort grows
between the stones.

NORTH

a limited number o
L shape separates the
relaxing or entertainin

    Shade is cast by an
concrete slab; tile cov
fence is painted a lig
planters contain lirio
flowering shrubs. Col
and petunias. Colorfu
collection contribute a

The Plants

A. Acer japonicum 'Aconitifolium'
    A. palmatum 'Sangokaku'
    Fernleaf fullmoon maple
    Japanese maple

B. Anemone hybrida
    Japanese anemone

C. Buxus sempervirens 'Green Velvet'
    Boxwood

D. Dryopteris erythrosora
    Autumn fern

E. Euonymus fortunei 'Vegetus'
    Winter creeper

F. Herniaria glabra
    Rupturewort

G. Hydrangea macrophylla
    Bigleaf hydrangea

H. Impatiens wallerana

I. Kalmia latifolia
    Mountain laurel

J. Menispermum canadense
    Moonseed

K. Pachysandra terminalis
    Japanese spurge

L. Pieris japonica
    Japanese andromeda

A DECKSIDE RETREAT

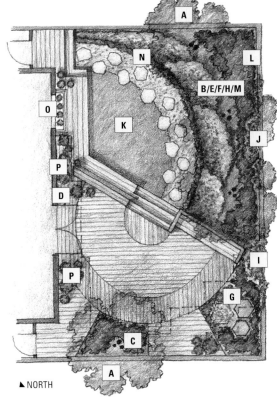

▲ NORTH

The Plants

A. Betula nigra 'Heritage'
HERITAGE RIVER BIRCH

B. Anemone blanda 'White Splendor'

C. Bulbs: 'Thalia' and 'Golden Cheerfulness' daffodils, Tulipa tarda

D. Annuals

E. Heuchera 'Palace Purple'
PURPLE ALUMROOT

F. Crocus speciosus 'Alba', C. vernus 'Snow Storm'

G. Asarum europaeum
WILD GINGER

Cyclamen hederifolium
HARDY CYCLAMEN

H. Gaultheria procumbens
WINTERGREEN

I. Clematis montana 'Tetrarose'

J. Hydrangea petiolaris
CLIMBING HYDRANGEA

K. Lawn grass

L. Sarcococca hookerana var. humilis
SWEET BOX

M. Trillium grandiflorum
WAKE ROBIN

N. Viola cucullata 'Freckles'
SWEET VIOLET

O. Mixed herbs

P. Mixed perennials

Limited space
shown here
ferent sites.
water features, an

Lavish use of
design shown on
a pattern inspire
half the 25-by-4
chores. Container
close to the hous
deck overlooks a
mortared into a p
lis mask intrusive
areas. A fountain
columns, with the

A GRASSY GLADE

The Plants

TREES

A. Prunus subhi
AUTUMN HIGA

B. Oxydendrum
SORREL TREE

C. Pinus wallic
HIMALAYAN PI

D. Halesia mon
PINK MOUNTA

E. Cornus kous
KOUSA DOGW

SHRUBS AND

F. 'Concord' gr

G. Cornus flori
FLOWERING D

The Plants

A. Pinus mugo
MUGO PINE

B. Lonicera sempervirens 'John Clayton'
YELLOW HONEYSUCKLE

C. Pachysandra terminalis

D. Cupressocyparis leylandii
LEYLAND CYPRESS

E. Campsis × tagliabuana 'Mme. Galen'
TRUMPET VINE

F. Kalmia latifolia
MOUNTAIN LAUREL

G. Mahonia aquifolium
OREGON GRAPE

H. Molinia caerulea 'Karl Foerster'
MOOR GRASS

I. Pennisetum alopecuroides 'Hameln'
FOUNTAIN GRASS

J. Acer griseum
PAPERBARK MAPLE

K. Succulents

L. Lawn grass

▲NORTH

A
FOR

Bouquet
almost
dedicat
array of bloo
Not only trac
shrubs and
material for f

Most of tl
beds facing t
grape arbor.
help screen
view. Beyond
bulbs, and n
feverfew defin

Spring fav
sythia, azale
lilac, and Fr
dogwood usl
hollyhock, r
In autumn, tl
of viburnum
esting branch
supply mater

A KITCHEN GARDEN

Blending practicality and beauty, this garden puts food crops at center stage. In just 40 by 60 feet there is space for more than two dozen kinds of vegetables and herbs, as well as for fruit trees and vines.

The grassy walkways give physical and visual access to the whole garden. Overall, however, the garden's layout draws visitors to its center, whether for a moment of planning and reflection or to set up a barbecue and create a garden meal on the spot. The garden is productive for much of the year: some root vegetables and hardy greens are harvested in late autumn, and early spinach and peas may be planted as soon as the ground can be worked in spring.

To save space, the semidwarf apple trees, which reach only 5 to 6 feet tall, are espaliered. Likewise, grapes and berries are trained on trellises of 4-by-4 posts with horizontal heavy-gauge wire; 2-by-2 crosspieces would also work. Concentric semicircles contain beds of perennial and annual herbs in the center, with tomatoes, eggplant, melons, and sunflowers toward the outside. Tall crops such as corn and pole beans grow in the long beds at each corner where they won't shade other plants.

A compost bin behind the apple trees takes most garden waste and provides some of the mulch lavishly spread around the crop plants. The double-dug, mounded beds are drip-watered: in-line emitters are used for the circles, perforated tubing for the straight beds.

The varieties in the plant list at right are suggestions only: feel free to plant your own favorites instead.

The Plants

A. Apples: 'Red Stayman Winesap'

B. Beans, bush: 'French Fillet', 'Roma II', 'Blue Lake 274', 'Sequoia' (purple)

C. Beans, pole: 'Kentucky Wonder', scarlet runner

D. Beets: 'Detroit Dark Red', 'Golden Beet', 'Sangria'

E. Berries: Blueberries (early, mid-season, late), jostaberry, raspberry, thornless blackberry, day-neutral strawberry

F. Carrots: 'Imperial Chantenay', 'Nantes Scarlet'

G. Corn: 'Silver Queen', 'Ambrosia'

H. Eggplant: 'Vittoria', 'Ichiban', 'Rosa Bianca', 'Bambino'

I. Grapes: 'Delaware' (red, mid-season) 'Catawba' (red, late), 'Interlaken' (seedless, green)

J. Greens: lettuce 'Simpson Elite', 'Mighty Red Oak', 'Gourmet Blend'; arugula 'Wild Italian Rocket'; swiss chard 'Bright Lights'

K. Herbs: basil, chives, cilantro, dill, fennel, oregano, parsley, sage, savory, sweet marjoram, tarragon, thyme (English, lemon silver)

L. Melons: 'Sweet 'n' Early', 'Ambrosia'

M. Onions: 'Spanish Yellow', 'Walla Walla Sweet', 'Snow White'

N. Peppers, hot: 'Habanero', 'Jalapa'

O. Peppers, sweet: green, red, orange, yellow, purple

P. Potatoes: 'Kennebec', 'White Cobbler'

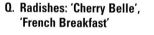

Q. Radishes: 'Cherry Belle', 'French Breakfast'

R. Squash, summer: 'Peter Pan' (scallop), 'Seneca Butterbar' (yellow), 'Spineless Beauty' (green zucchini), 'Butterstick' (yellow zucchini)

S. Squash, winter: 'Butter Boy', 'Nicklow's Delight', 'Buttercup'

T. Sunflowers: both tall and short varieties

U. Tomatoes: 'Celebrity', 'Better Boy', 'Sweet Tangerine', heirloom varieties, 'Juliet', 'Sweet Million', 'Sungold' (cherry), 'Roma', 'Viva Italia' (paste)

V. Turnips: 'Tokyo Cross'

W. Broccoli, cabbage, cauliflower, garlic, leeks, mint, New Zealand spinach, rhubarb

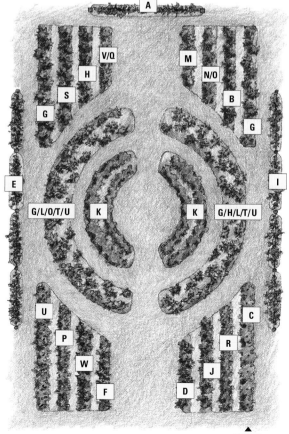

NORTH

A FAMILY GARDEN

New family, new house, new garden: planning a landscape that's good for all three is a real challenge. In this garden, a rectangle of 55 by 65 feet, plantings and hardscape have been designed to suit a range of family interests, minimize maintenance, and allow for changes as the children grow.

Washed concrete and an area of brick form the entry to the lawn and pool—with the pool fenced for safety, of course. The central area of lawn is large enough for romping or a summer barbecue. Rimming the lawn are evergreen rhododendrons that flower in late spring; leafy hostas underplant the shrubs. On the right, a long flower bed cloaking the pool's fence is planted with annuals and perennials. With spring-flowering bulbs tucked under the other plants, this flower bed will blaze with color 9 months of the year.

The trees here have been chosen for durability, beauty, and play potential. Both the white pine and the red oak are splendid climbing trees, and the oak could make a good base for a tree house when the children reach that stage. The weeping mulberry is a perfect place for hide and seek or secret picnics. Its graceful form focuses the view from the house, and birds can nibble on the berries.

The swing set with slide and climbing bars is close enough to the playhouse to make a "children's complex." When the kids outgrow this area, the playhouse can become a storage shed for garden tools or sports equipment, while the plot where the swing set stood can be tilled into a vegetable garden or planted with flowering shrubs. Long-blooming, practically indestructible rugosa roses nestle against the right side of the playhouse. Bright red rose hips develop

The Plants

A. **Quercus rubra**
   RED OAK

B. **Prunus sargentii**
   SARGENT CHERRY

C. **Pinus strobus**
   WHITE PINE

D. **Vaccinium corymbosum 'Jersey',
   'Patriot, 'Bluecrop'**
   BLUEBERRY

E. **Morus alba 'Pendula'**
   WEEPING MULBERRY

F. **Mixed annuals: Pelargonium,
   Zinnia, Tagetes**

G. **Mixed perennials: Echinacea, Phlox,
   Iris, Sedum telephium, Pennisetum**

H. **Container plants:
   Petunia, Portulaca,
   Impatiens,
   'Tumbler' tomato**

I. **Fragaria 'Tri-Star'
   or 'Ever Red'**
   STRAWBERRY

J. **Rhododendron
   'Blue Peter'**

K. **Rosa rugosa**

L. **Lonicera sempervirens**
   HONEYSUCKLE

M. **Hosta cultivars**

N. **Rhododendron 'Boule
   de Neige'**

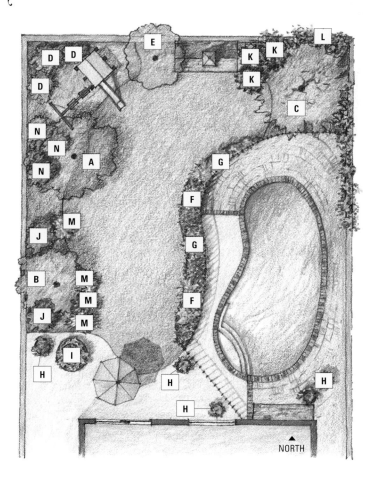

after the blooms fade, making these plants attractive from early spring into the winter.

Container plants—placed near the pool and outdoor seating—offer both colorful ornamentals and minivegetables like patio-type tomatoes. A trilevel planter at the edge of the concrete is a good way to grow strawberries close to the kitchen. Three blueberry varieties (at least two must be planted for good fruit production) form attractive edible landscaping choices behind the swing set. These mid-size bushes flower delicately in spring, set delicious fruit in summer, and blaze into orange and yellow glory in the autumn.

A GARDEN FOR SHADE

The Northeast is a wonderful place for trees, with both native and imported species flourishing here. But as gardens mature, growing trees increase the amount of shade, often at the expense of flower beds and traditional, sun-based plantings. This garden proves that color and contrast need not be lost beneath the trees: flowering shade is achievable over a long season if plants are carefully chosen.

The garden is rimmed by large deciduous trees—oaks, maple, tulip, and the Kentucky coffee tree that is hardy well north of Kentucky. Connected beds of massed spring-blooming shrubs underplant the trees. Many of these, including rhododendrons, laurels, daphne, and mahonias, are evergreen, so they color the garden's rim all through the year. The viburnum's leaves brighten to orange in the autumn, while the leucothöe's pink-green-white foliage remains winter and summer. The viburnum also offers the attraction of scarlet berries. Low-growing ground covers and perennials are planted around the shrubs; the epimediums flowering in pink and white, and the gaultheria in white followed by red berries. The flowering herbaceous species were chosen to allow a changing focus of color throughout the warm seasons, with the bleeding heart and iris blooming early and the heuchera, eupatorium, and hostas later in the summer.

Variety of shape and texture is another attractive feature of these plantings. Delicate fern foliage is set against the large, sculptural leaves of the oakleaf hydrangea. Shiny, stiff hellebores hold their leaves erect beside the arching, green-gray fronds of bleeding heart at the left of the paving, and slender iris leaves adjoin broad, pleated hostas. Overall bold, flowing swaths of plants accent the placement of the trees and encourage viewing the garden from many different vantage points.

The Plants

A. **Heuchera 'Persian Carpet'**
ALUMROOT

B. **Iris tectorum**
JAPANESE ROOF IRIS

C. **Kalmia latifolia**
MOUNTAIN LAUREL

D. **Rhododendron**
EXBURY AZALEA

E. **R. yakusimanum 'Yaku Princess'**

F. **Dicentra spectabilis**
BLEEDING HEART

G. **Mertensia virginiana**
VIRGINIA BLUEBELL

H. **Daphne × burkwoodii**
'Carol Mackie'

I. **Epimedium × youngianum**
'Niveum'
BARRENWORT

J. **Mahonia aquifolium 'Compacta'**
HOLLY GRAPE

K. **Hosta 'Frances Williams'**

L. **Leucothöe fontanesiana**
'Girard's Rainbow'
FETTERBUSH

M. **Dicentra spectabilis**
'Adrian Bloom'
BLEEDING HEART

N. **Hypericum calycinum**
AARON'S BEARD,
ST.-JOHN'S-WORT

O. **Iris pallida**
DALMATIAN IRIS

P. **Gautheria procumbens**
WINTERGREEN

Q. **Viburnum setigerum**
TEA VIBURNUM

R. **Hydrangea quercifolia**
OAKLEAF HYDRANGEA

S. **Gymnocladus dioica**
KENTUCKY COFFEE TREE

T. **Quercus rubra**
RED OAK

U. **Liriodendron tulipifera**
TULIP TREE

V. **Acer griseum**
PAPERBARK MAPLE

W. **Quercus alba**
WHITE OAK

X. **Athyrium niponicum 'Pictum'**
JAPANESE PAINTED FERN

Y. **Helleborus foetidus**
BEAR'S FOOT HELLEBORE

Z. **Rhododendron 'Scintillation'**

AA. **Helleborus orientalis**
LENTEN ROSE

BB. **Epimedium grandiflorum**
'Rose Queen'
BARRENWORT

CC. **Adiantum pedatum**
MAIDENHAIR FERN

DD. **Dryopteris erythrosora**
AUTUMN FERN

EE. **Eupatorium rugosum**
'Chocolate'
WHITE SNAKEROOT

FF. **Iris cristata**
CRESTED IRIS

◄ NORTH

A LOW-MAINTENANCE FORMAL GARDEN

Many gardeners today like the classical appeal of a formal garden, but lack the time to maintain it. The garden shown here, once installed, needs little care beyond the basics of sweeping up leaves, trimming shrubs, and feeding, pruning, and spraying the roses.

All the shrubs are underplanted with ground covers: evergreen pachysandra and felt-leaved lamb's ear. Many of the shrubs and trees are evergreens to keep the garden's look consistent through the changing seasons—rhododendrons, laurels, thujas, junipers, and magnolias.

Color variation is provided year-round through the use of red-berried hollies, red-fruited kousa dogwoods, and "Crimson Pygmy"

barberries that sport deep burgundy leaves. Summer color begins with the lavish blooms of repeat-flowering, disease-resistant rose varieties, backed up by arching shapes of tall buddleias that produce cascades of blossom for several months.

Paving connects the formal vistas of the garden. The long arbor, covered in season with trailing wisteria flowers, leads out from the house to a favorite statue. Within close reach of the house for easy entertaining, guests at the table can enjoy the fountain, completely shielded from neighbors by a dense hedge. The handsome zelkova shades this seating area in summer. Movable planters can be used to display ornamental topiary or the gardener's favorite container varieties, placed in sun or shade as required.

The Plants

A. Thuja occidentalis 'Nigra'
ARBORVITAE

B. Berberis thunbergii 'Crimson Pygmy'
BARBERRY

C. Juniperus virginiana 'Skyrocket'

D. Ilex pedunculosa
LONG-STALK HOLLY

E. Rosa 'Graham Thomas'

F. Rosa 'Heritage'

G. Cornus kousa
KOUSA DOGWOOD

H. Magnolia virginiana
SWEET BAY

I. Zelkova serrata 'Village Green'
JAPANESE ZELKOVA

J. Buddleia davidii
BUTTERFLY BUSH

K. Kalmia latifolia
MOUNTAIN LAUREL

L. Rosmarinus officinalis
ROSEMARY

M. Hibiscus syriacus 'Diana'
SHRUB ALTHEA

N. Rhamnus frangula 'Tallhedge'
BUCKTHORN

O. Iris sibirica
SIBERIAN IRIS

P. Pennisetum alopecuroides 'Hameln'
FOUNTAIN GRASS

Q. Wisteria floribunda 'Macrobotrys'
WISTERIA

R. Stachys byzantina 'Big Ears'
LAMB'S EAR

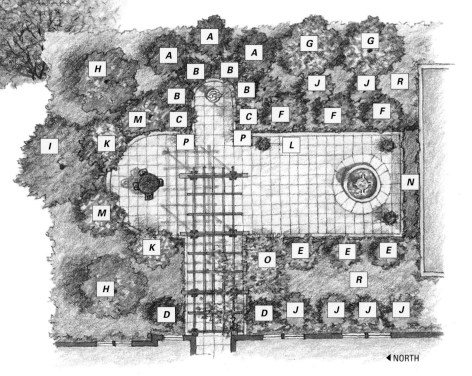

◀ NORTH

MATERIALS AND TECHNIQUES

You've dreamed, schemed, and planned your new landscape. Now it's time to lay some brick and pound a few nails. When it comes to garden structures, just what's involved? What kind of lumber is best for raised beds? How do you make a gravel pathway? Which fasteners are best for overheads? Should you use homemade concrete or ready-mixed concrete?

Whether you use tried-and-true materials like wood or brick, or try out new products like molded concrete "flag-stones," remember that a little local knowledge goes a long way. After you have read the step-by-step instructions given here, seek advice at your local building department, lumber-yard, or garden center.

Should you do the work your-self? Although it's satisfying and can be more economical, some projects take hard work and require construction or woodworking experience. If you decide to do it yourself, read over the safety guidelines given at the end of the chapter.

LUMBER

Many landscaping projects begin with lumber, including decks, fences, steps, and raised beds. Given here is an overview of lumber products you'll need for garden construction projects, along with the fasteners and finishes that are available for them. Step-by-step directions illustrate the most common wooden garden projects: an attached deck (see pages 366–367), a basic board fence (see pages 368–369), and a freestanding overhead (see page 370).

Lumberyard tools and materials

Because wood comes in so many sizes, species, and grades, a visit to a lumberyard can be a daunting experience for the beginning do-it-yourselfer. Busy salespeople may not be very helpful if you are unfamiliar with basic building terminology, so it's a good idea to familiarize yourself with the terms you'll need to know for your projects *before* asking an employee for help.

As a rule, softwoods are much less expensive, easier to tool, and more readily available than hardwoods. In fact, nearly all outdoor construction is done with softwoods. Hardwoods such as oak, hickory, and poplar are generally used for indoor projects.

SPECIES. Woods from different trees have specific properties. Redwood and cedar heartwoods (the darker part of the wood, cut from the tree's core), for example, have a natural resistance to decay. This characteristic, combined with their beauty, makes them attractive candidates for decks and natural-finish lath roofing. But these woods are expensive, and can easily run double the cost of a structure built from pressure-treated pine, the most common decking lumber (opposite). In addition, redwood and cedar contain tannins that break down steel nails; if you choose to build with these woods, you must use stainless steel nails and fasteners.

For structural members or for elements that will be painted or stained, many landscape professionals substitute less expensive woods such as spruce or ponderosa pine. You can also apply a protective finish to make wood more durable (see page 365).

LUMBER GRADES. Wood is sorted and graded at a lumber mill according to several factors: natural growth characteristics (such as knots), defects resulting from milling errors, and commercial drying and preserving techniques that affect each piece's strength, durability, and appearance. A stamp on the lumber identifies its moisture content and its grade and species mark, as well as the mill that produced it and the grading agency.

In general, the higher the grade, the more you will have to pay. One of the best ways to save money on a structure is to identify the best grade (not necessarily the highest grade) for each element.

Structural lumber and timbers are rated for strength. The most common grading system includes the grades Select Structural, No. 1, No. 2, and No. 3. For premium strength, choose Select Structural. Often, lumberyards sell a mix of grades called No. 2 and Better. Other grading systems used for some lumber (typically 2 by 4s) classify wood as Construction, Standard, and Utility, or as a mixture of grades called Standard and Better.

Redwood is usually graded for its appearance and the percentage of heartwood versus sapwood it contains: Clear All Heart is the best and the most expensive. B Heart, Construction Heart, and Merchantable Heart, in descending order of quality, are typical grades of pure heartwood; lesser grades are likely to contain more knots, splits, and other flaws.

Cedar grades, starting with the highest quality, are Architect Clear, Custom Clear, Architect Knotty, and Custom Knotty. These grades don't indicate if wood is heartwood or sapwood.

Pressure-treated timbers serve well as edging for raised beds or steps and for building gates and decks; use construction-grade lumber—typically spruce, pine, or fir—for framing a garden shed or greenhouse. From left to right above: pressure-treated 6 × 6 and 4 × 4; landscaping timber; construction-grade 2 × 6; cedar and construction-grade 1 × 4s; pressure-treated and construction-grade 2 × 2s.

BUYING LUMBER. Lumber is divided into categories according to size: *dimension lumber,* which is from 2 to 4 inches thick and at least 2 inches wide; *timbers,* heavy structural lumber at least 5 inches thick; and *boards,* which are normally not more than 1 inch thick and 4 to 12 inches wide.

Lumber is sold either by the *lineal foot* or by the *board foot.* The lineal foot, commonly used for small orders, considers only the length of a piece. For example, twenty 2 by 4s, 8 feet long, would be the same as 160 lineal feet of 2 by 4s.

The board foot is the most common unit for volume orders. A piece of wood 1 inch thick, 12 inches wide, and 12 inches long equals one board foot. To compute board feet, use this formula:

Thickness (in inches) × width (in feet) × length (in feet).

So a 1 by 6, 10 feet long, would be computed as follows:

1 inch × ½ foot (6 inches) × 10 feet = 5 board feet.

When you place an order at a lumberyard, you must give the exact dimensions of the lumber you need.

NOMINAL SIZES. Remember that a "2 by 4" does not actually measure 2 by 4 inches. Its *nominal size* is designated before it is dried and surface-planed; the finished size is actually 1½ by 3½ inches. Likewise, a nominal 4 by 4 is actually 3½ by 3½ inches.

Rough lumber is usually closer to the nominal size because it is wetter and has not been surface-planed. If your measurements are critical, be sure to check the actual dimensions of any lumber you are considering before you buy it.

DEFECTS. Lumber is subject to a number of defects due to weathering and milling errors. When choosing lumber, lift each piece and look down the face and edges for any defects. The most common problems are cupping and bowing—warps and hollows on the board. In addition, be on the lookout for problems such as rotting, staining, splits, and missing wood or untrimmed bark along the edges or corners of the piece, called wane. Also look for insect holes and reservoirs of sap or pitch.

Pressure-treated Lumber

Most woods that come into contact with soil or water—with the exception of redwood and cedar, which have a natural resistance to decay and termites—will rot and lose strength. To avoid this problem, less durable types of lumber, such as southern pine, are often factory-treated with chemical preservatives that guard against rot, insects, and other sources of decay. Once treated, they can be used for surface decking, gates, and steps, as well as for structural members such as posts, beams, and joists.

Working with treated lumber has drawbacks. It can be hard and brittle, and as it dries—which can take up to a full year— it can warp or twist. Moreover, some people object to its greenish brown color, although applying paint or a semitransparent stain on the wood after it dries can conceal it.

The primary preservative used in pressure-treated lumber contains chromium, a toxic metal. As a precaution, therefore, you should wear safety glasses and a dust mask when cutting this type of lumber, and you should never burn the scraps. In addition, wear gloves when handling pressure-treated wood for prolonged periods.

Although studies suggest that it is safe to use pressure-treated lumber for outdoor structures such as vegetable beds and play yards, you can opt for heartwood in potential contact areas, or line planters with impermeable plastic or sheet metal. For additional information, check with your local lumberyard or building supply center.

Some salvaged wood, such as railway ties, has been treated with creosote, a toxic chemical. In some parts of the country the sale and use of creosote-treated lumber has been banned, and this wood is not recommended for garden construction.

Practical needn't be plain. Color surrounds these steps, which are fronted with heavy pressure-treated timbers. The attractiveness of these risers belies their durability; they will last long after foot traffic and rain would have rotted untreated wood.

Fasteners and Hardware

Nails, screws, and metal framing connectors are essential for constructing sturdy outdoor structures. The hardware you would typically need for a garden project includes:

NAILS. Hot-dipped galvanized, aluminum, or stainless steel nails are essential for outdoor construction because they resist rust. Common and box nails are similar but the former have a thicker shank, making them more difficult to drive but increasing their holding power. Both types are sold in boxes (weighing 1, 5, or 50 pounds) or loose in bins. Standard nail sizes are given in "pennies" (penny is abbreviated as "d," from the Latin *denarius*). The higher the penny number, the longer the nail. Equivalents in inches for the most common nails are as follows:

4d=$1\frac{1}{2}$ in. 6d=2 in. 8d=$2\frac{1}{2}$ in.
10d=3 in. 16d=$3\frac{1}{2}$ in. 20d=4 in.

Choose nails that have a length two or three times the thickness of the material you will be nailing through. Most decking, fence, and overhead framing is secured with 8d and 16d nails.

DECK SCREWS. Although they're more expensive than nails, coated or galvanized deck screws have several advantages over nails: they don't pop as readily, their coating is less likely to be damaged during installation, and their use eliminates the possibility of hammer dents in the decking. Moreover, they are surprisingly easy to drive into soft woods, such as redwood and cedar, if you use an electric drill or screw gun with an adjustable clutch and a Phillips screwdriver tip. Screws are not given ratings for shear (or hanging) strength, so use nails, lag screws, or bolts to fasten joists to beams or ledgers, and posts to beams.

For decks, choose screws that are long enough to penetrate joists at least as deep as the decking is thick (for 2-by-4 or 2-by-6 decking, buy 3-inch screws). Screws are sold in small boxes, by the pound, or, at a substantial savings, in 25-pound boxes.

The heavy-duty lag screw, or lag bolt, has a square or hexagonal head and requires a wrench or a ratchet and socket to tighten it.

FRAMING CONNECTORS. The photo at right shows several framing connectors. Galvanized metal connectors can help prevent lumber splits caused by toenailing two boards together. Be sure to attach connectors with the nails specified by the manufacturer.

To eliminate visible fasteners, deck clips can be nailed to the sides of decking lumber and secured to joists. In addition to remaining hidden between the deck boards, these clips also elevate the boards slightly off the joist, discouraging the rot that wood-to-wood contact may breed. However, the clips are more expensive to buy and more time-consuming to install than nails or screws.

BOLTS. For heavy-duty fastening, choose bolts. Most are zinc-plated steel, but aluminum and brass ones are also available. Bolts go into predrilled holes and are secured by nuts. The machine bolt has a square or hexagonal head that must be tightened with a wrench. The carriage bolt has a self-anchoring head that digs into the wood as the nut is tightened. Expanding anchor bolts allow you to secure wooden members to a masonry wall.

Bolts are classified by diameter ($\frac{1}{8}$ to 1 inch) and length ($\frac{3}{8}$ inch and up). To give the nut a firm bite, select a bolt $\frac{1}{2}$ to 1 inch longer than the combined thicknesses of the pieces to be joined.

Framing connectors and hardware, clockwise from top right: post anchors, deck post tie, earthquake straps, rigid tie corner, joist hangers, rigid flat tie, and decorative post tops.

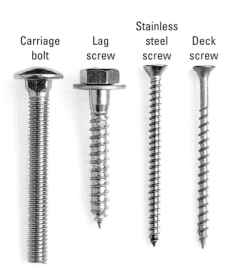

Carriage bolt	Lag screw	Stainless steel screw	Deck screw

Wood Finishes

Structural elements that contact soil or are embedded in concrete do not require a finish. But to protect other parts of a structure and to preserve its beauty, apply a water repellent, a semitransparent stain, or a solid-color stain.

Finishes change a wood's color or tone and may mask its grain and texture. Whatever product you choose, it's best to try it on a sample board first to be sure you like the look. Always read labels: Some products should not be applied over new wood; others may require a sealer first.

Water repellents, also known as water sealers, help prevent decking from warping and cracking. Clear sealers don't color wood but they allow it to gradually fade to gray; some types come in slightly tinted versions. You can buy either oil- or water-base versions, many of which include UV-blockers and mildewcides.

Don't use clear-surface finishes such as spar varnish or polyurethane on outdoor lumber. In addition to their high price, they wear quickly and are very hard to renew.

Semitransparent stains contain enough pigment to tint the wood's surface with just one coat, while permitting the natural grain to show through. They are available in both water- and oil-base versions. In addition to traditional grays and wood tones, you'll find products for "reviving" a deck's color or for dressing up pressure-treated wood.

Solid-color coverings include both deck stains and deck paint. The stains are essentially paints; their heavy pigments cover wood grain completely. Usually, any paint color can be mixed into this base. Even though these products are formulated for foot traffic, you'll probably have to renew them frequently. A word of caution: don't choose stains or paints intended for house siding; they won't last.

Shown here, from top to bottom, are: unfinished pressure-treated pine, clear sealer with UV protection, tinted sealer, semitransparent redwood stain, and gray solid-color stain.

BUILDING A LOW-LEVEL DECK

A low-level, house-attached deck helps to extend the indoor living space. It is also a manageable and economical do-it-yourself project. Before you begin, review the advice given on pages
154–157 and check your local building codes. This type of deck
can be completed over the course of a few weekends, but it will
require the labor of at least two people.

Think ahead about benches or other items that may need to be
integrated with the deck's framing. Be sure the completed deck will
be at least 1 inch below adjacent access doors. If you're planning a
freestanding deck, substitute an extra beam and posts for the ledger
shown; extra bracing at the corners may also be necessary. For
other deck plans, see Sunset's *Complete Deck Book*.

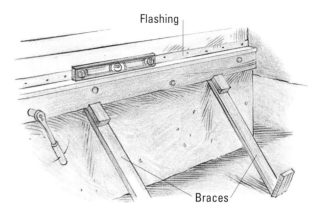

1. Determine the position of the ledger and prop it into place
with 2-by-4 blocks or braces. Drill staggered holes for lag
screws every 16 inches, then fasten ledger in place, making
sure it is level. To prevent rot, either space the ledger off the
wall with blocks or washers, or add metal flashing, as shown.

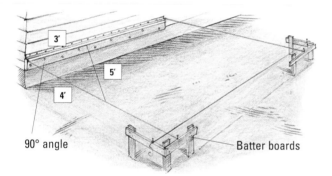

2. Batter boards mark height of deck; build them at outside
corners, level with the ledger top. To mark deck edges, string
mason's line from batter boards to ledger. Corners must be
square; determine using the "3-4-5" triangle method shown.

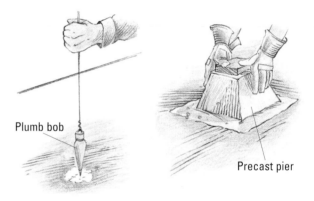

3. Dangle a plumb bob from mason's lines to mark footings.
Dig holes to depths required by code; add gravel, then fill with
concrete (see pages 368–369). Push piers into the concrete,
level their tops, and let concrete set overnight.

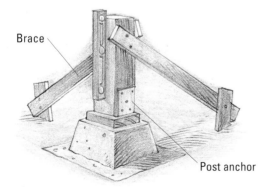

4. Unless piers have integral post anchors, add them now.
Measure and cut posts—for this design, a joist's depth below
the top of ledger. Check plumb on two sides of each post,
temporarily brace each in place, and fasten to piers.

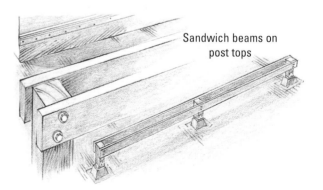

5. Position 2-by beams on each side of post tops, as shown.
After leveling them with post tops, clamp them in place. Drill
staggered holes, then fasten each beam to posts with bolts
or lag screws.

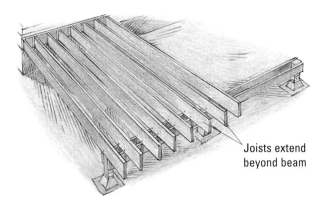

Joists extend
beyond beam

6. Position joists at predetermined span intervals and secure
to ledger with framing connectors, as shown. Set them atop
beams and toenail in place. Brace joists with spacers at open
ends and, if required, at midspan. Add posts for any railings
or benches, or an overhead anchored to deck framing.

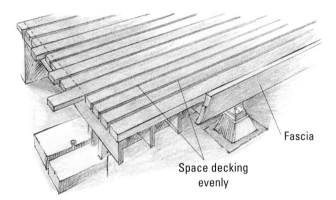

Fascia

Space decking
evenly

7. Align decking boards atop joists, staggering joints (if any).
Space boards, leaving about 3/16 inch—or the thickness of
a 16d nail—for drainage. (Note: This spacing is not necessary
for pressure-treated wood.) Fasten decking to joists with 16d
common nails or deck screws. Trim edges with circular saw.

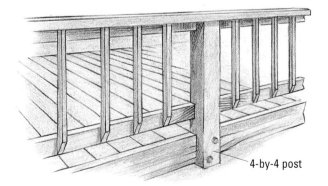

4-by-4 post

8. Finish decking ends and edges as desired with fascia
boards or other trim. If you're planning benches, planters,
steps, or railings that aren't tied directly to the substructure,
add them now.

Decking Patterns

*Decks are designed from the top down, so one of your
first decisions will involve selecting a decking pattern.
The design you choose may affect how the deck's substructure is built. For a house-attached deck similar to
the one shown, it's often simplest to run decking boards
parallel to the house wall. Generally, the more complex
the decking pattern, the smaller the joist spans required
and the more complicated the substructure to support it.*

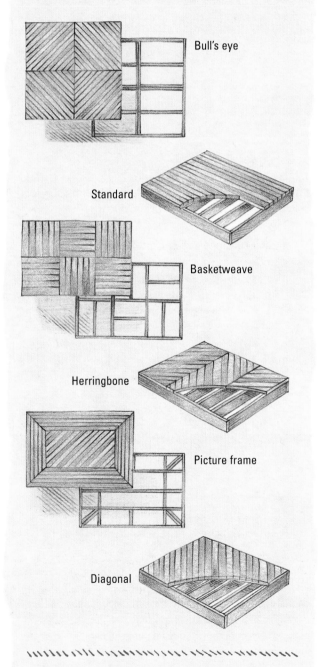

Bull's eye

Standard

Basketweave

Herringbone

Picture frame

Diagonal

BUILDING A BOARD FENCE

In general, fence building is a straightforward task. The hardest part is digging the postholes; the tools shown at right will make this easier. There are many design variations, but the procedure outlined below is a good one for putting up a basic board fence.

Before you set a post or pound a nail, check your local building and zoning codes, as they may influence style, material, setback, and other requirements. Then tackle the building stages: plotting the fence, installing posts, and adding rails and siding.

For fences from 3 to 6 feet tall, plan to set posts at least 2 feet deep—12 inches deeper for end and gate posts. For taller fences, the rule of thumb for post depth is one-third the post length. You can either dig postholes to a uniform depth or cut the posts once they are in the ground. Once the posts are installed, the rest of the job is easy, especially when you have one or two helpers.

If you're planning to hang a gate, too, see pages 160–161 for construction and design pointers.

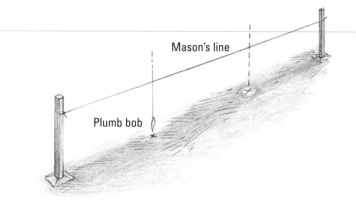

1. First, mark each end or corner post location with a stake. Run mason's line between the stakes, as shown. With chalk, mark remaining post locations on the line. Using a level or plumb bob, transfer each mark to the ground and drive in additional stakes. Then dig holes 6 inches deeper than post depth, making them 2½ to 3 times the post's diameter.

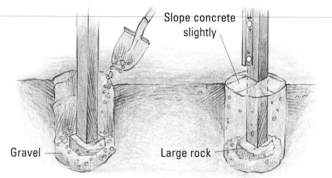

2. Place a rock at the base of each hole and add 4 to 6 inches of gravel. Place a post in a hole and shovel in concrete, tamping it down with a broomstick or capped steel pipe. Adjust the post for plumb with a level. Continue filling until the concrete extends 1 or 2 inches above ground level, and slope it away from the post to divert water.

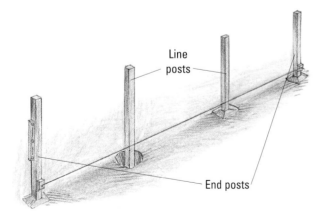

3. To align posts, first position two end or corner posts so their faces are parallel, then plumb them and set them permanently. Use spacer blocks and a mason's line to locate line posts, spacing each a block's thickness from the line. After setting posts in fresh concrete, you have about 20 minutes to align them before concrete hardens. Let cure for 2 days.

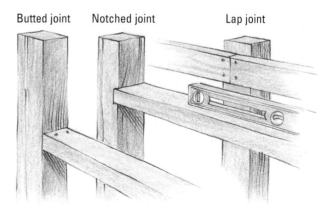

4. Brush on wood preservative where rails and posts will meet. Then fasten one end of each rail; check level with a helper and secure the other end. You can butt them against the post and toenail them, notch them in (cut notches before installing posts), or lap them over the sides or top of each post. If making lap joints, plan to span at least three posts for strength.

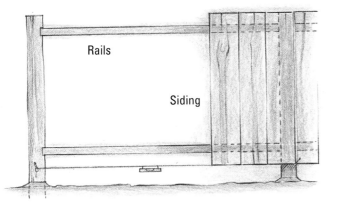

5. Cut siding boards to the same length. Stretch and level a line from post to post to mark the bottom of the siding. Check the first board for plumb, then secure it to rails with galvanized nails three times as long as the board's thickness. Add additional boards, checking alignment as you go.

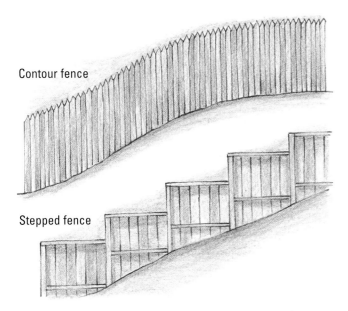

6. On a hillside, post-and-rail and solid fences with pickets or grape stakes make good contour fences. Board, louver, basket-weave, and panel styles work better for stepped fences, which are more difficult to build. For both kinds, make sure that the bottoms of boards 6 inches or wider are cut to follow the contour of the hillside; otherwise, gaps will remain.

Digging Postholes

Although you could use a pick and shovel to dig postholes for fences (or decks and overheads), some heavier equipment will save you time and effort. Two handy tools are shown below.

Posthole, or clamshell, diggers (below left) work in hard or rocky soil. Spread the handles to open and close the blades, which trap soil. This tool is difficult to use for holes more than 3 feet deep, as the sides of the hole interfere with the spreading of the handles.

A power auger, also known as a power digger or earth drill, is recommended whenever you have more than a dozen holes to dig. You can rent models for operation by one or two people (a two-person model is shown below right), and they may be freestanding or vehicle-mounted. Every so often, pull the auger out of the hole to remove the dirt; a posthole digger or a small spade may also be required.

When you turn the handle of a hand-operated auger, the pointed blades bore into the soil, scraping it up and collecting it in a chamber. Once the chamber is full, remove the auger from the hole and empty out the soil. This tool works best in loose soil.

BUILDING AN OVERHEAD

An overhead is essentially a garden structure with a roof, such as an arbor or a pergola, that provides shade or a place for plants to climb. Building an overhead is similar to building a deck, although you'll probably spend a lot more time on a ladder. These illustrations outline the sequence for erecting a freestanding overhead. For a house-attached overhead, see the facing page.

If your overhead will span an existing patio, you can set the posts on footings and piers located outside the edge of the patio, or break through the existing paving, dig holes, and pour new concrete footings (and, if necessary, add piers). If you're planning to install a new concrete patio, then you can pour footings and paving at the same time, embedding the post anchors in the wet concrete.

1. Precut posts to length (or run a level line and cut them later). Set posts in anchors embedded in concrete footing or atop precast piers. Hold each post vertical and nail anchor to it.

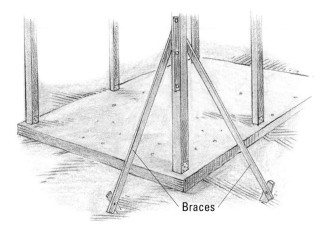

Braces

2. Continue to put up posts, plumbing each post with level on two adjacent sides. Secure each in position with temporary braces nailed to wooden stakes that are driven into ground.

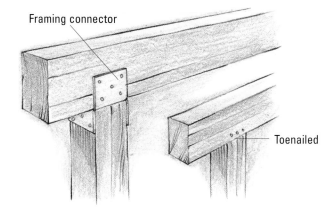

Framing connector

Toenailed

3. With a helper, position a beam on top of posts. Check that posts are vertical and beam is level (adjust, if necessary, with shims); then secure beam to posts.

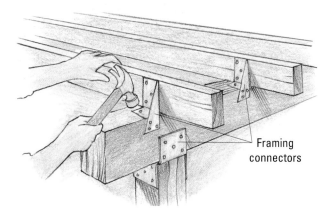

Framing connectors

4. Set and space rafters on top of beams and secure them with framing connectors (shown) or by toenailing to beams. For extra strength, install bracing between posts and beams.

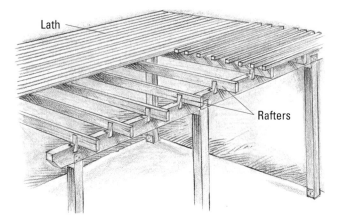

Lath

Rafters

5. Cover rafters with lath, either 1 by 2s or 2 by 2s. Space the lath for plant support or to achieve a specific amount of shade (see facing page).

Overhead alternatives

Although most overheads employ the same basic components (posts, beams, rafters or joists, and some type of roofing), there are many different ways to assemble them. Each, however, must conform to spans determined by local building codes, so be sure to check them before you start to build.

To attach an overhead to your house, you will need to install a ledger, much like a deck ledger (see page 366). Usually made from a 2 by 4 or a 2 by 6, the ledger is typically lag-screwed—either to wall studs, to second-story floor framing, or to the roof. If the house wall is brick or stone, however, you'll need to drill holes and install expanding anchors to bolt the ledger in place.

Rafters can be set on top of the ledger or hung from it with anchors, joist hangers, or rafter hangers. If your overhead's roof will be flat, simply square up rafter ends. Sloped rafters, however, require angled cuts at each end, plus a notch (as shown at right) where rafters cross the beam.

You can also opt for a solid roofing material such as shingles, siding, or even asphalt. If you leave the structure uncovered, treating it with a preservative or other finish can add years to its life.

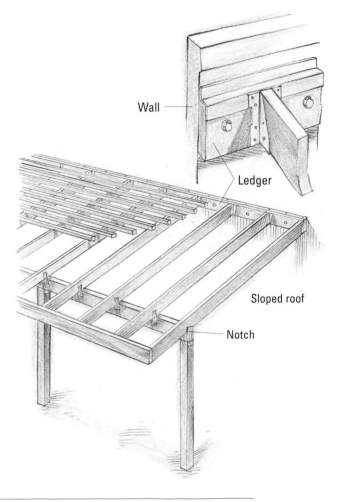

Designing for Shade

If you desire an open effect or plan to cover the overhead with vines, the rafters can act as a roof. For more protection, attach wood laths or louvers, arranged in a lattice pattern or placed at right angles to the rafters. Vary the wood thickness and spacing to cast the shade you desire—thin lath laid flat won't cast as much shade as thicker stock. The direction in which you run the lath depends on the time of day you need the most shade. If you want midday shade, run the lath east-west; for more shade in the morning and early evening, run the lath north-south.

Experiment with the width, spacing, and direction of overhead members by temporarily nailing different sizes to the rafters and observing the effect for a few days.

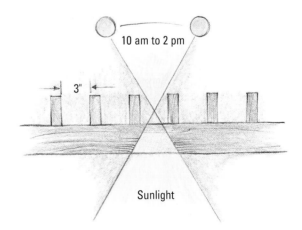

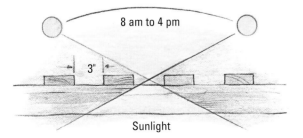

The same boards set 3 inches apart, but at different angles, will affect the extent of shade cast below an overhead. Lath or boards laid on edge diffuse early-morning and late-afternoon sun, but let in plenty of light at midday (above). The same members laid flat (left) allow in more sun in the early morning and late afternoon, but block more midday sun.

MASONRY

This section will guide you through the world of masonry materials and explain the basic techniques for building paths, patios, and walls. Although some stonework requires years of training, these basic masonry projects can be successfully completed by a do-it-yourselfer. The key is to proceed with patience.

However, you should seek advice from your local building department or garden supplier about the best concrete mix, brick types, or base treatment for use in your climate and soil. Speak with your neighbors about the masonry materials they have successfully used in their gardens, and browse through local offerings of masonry products before buying—new products constantly appear.

Loose stones and gravel can be used alone or with other stones of various sizes to create paths or can be seeded into concrete to create an exposed aggregate finish.

the cubic yard, which simplifies ordering; others sell it by the ton. Most suppliers can help you calculate how much you need based on a square-foot estimate.

STONES FOR PAVING. Many stones are precut in square or rectangular shapes; these are fairly uniform in thickness and easy to lay in a grid pattern. Others, however, have random widths and thicknesses.

Granite and marble are both valued for their hardness and durability, though marble is too expensive for most garden construction. Sandstone, limestone, and other sedimentary stones are popular choices; they are more porous than other types and usually have a chalky or gritty texture. Slate, a fine-grained metamorphic rock

Shopping for stone

Stone is particularly appealing because it is a natural material, and most types are very durable. But the availability of stone types, shapes, sizes, and colors varies by locale, and stone's primary drawback is that it can cost up to five times as much as concrete or brick. Geography dictates price: the farther you live from the quarry, the more you'll have to pay. Some dealers sell stone by

that is dense and smooth, is also an excellent choice for paving.

Flat flagstones and cut stone tiles are ideal for formal settings. Technically, flagstone is any flat stone that is either naturally thin or split from rock that cleaves easily. It blends well with plants and ponds or other water features. Furthermore, flagstone is one of the few paving materials that can be set directly on stable soil. However,

outdoor furniture and objects with wheels sometimes get caught on its irregular surface. Also, some types of flagstone become dirty easily and are difficult to clean.

Fieldstone, river rock, and pebbles are less expensive than flagstone or cut tiles. These water-worn or glacier-ground stones produce rustic, uneven pavings that make up in charm what they may lack in smoothness underfoot. Smaller stones and pebbles, for example, can be set or seeded into concrete (see page 378); cobblestones can be laid in concrete or on tamped earth to cover an entire surface; or narrow mosaic panels of very small stones can be used to break up an expanse of concrete or brick.

For economy, good drainage, and a more casual look, don't forget gravel or crushed rock, both of which can provide material for garden paving. Gravel is collected or mined from natural deposits; crushed rock is mechanically fractured and graded to a uniform size. Frequently, gravels are named after the regions where they were quarried.

When choosing a gravel, consider color, sheen, texture, and size. Take home samples as you would paint chips. Keep in mind that gravel color, like paint color, looks more intense when it is spread over a large area.

STONES FOR WALLS. There are two broad classes of stonework that work well for walls: rubble (untrimmed) and ashlar (trimmed). In addition, partially trimmed pieces such as cobblestones can create attractive effects.

The stones used in rubble walls are often rounded from glacial or water action; examples (often igneous in origin) include granite and basalt river rock and fieldstone. Since they are difficult to cut, it's usually easier to search for rocks that are the size you need. Rubblestone is frequently the cheapest kind available.

Fully trimmed ashlar stone is almost as easy to lay as brick. The flat surfaces and limited range of sizes make formal coursing possible and require less mortar than for rubblework.

Ashlar stone is usually sedimentary in origin; the most commonly available type is sandstone. When a tougher igneous stone, such as granite, is cut and trimmed for ashlar masonry, costs are likely to be quite high.

Larger, flat stones are extremely versatile in the garden: use flagstone to create a walkway or terrace, or stack them to create a low decorative wall.

Artificial Rock

Rocks and boulders can lend a rugged texture to a residential landscape. However, big boulders can be hard to find and difficult to transport and install. In some gardens, the site conditions or the landscape design make it impossible to install them. So, some owners are turning to artificial rocks that are shaped, textured, and colored to resemble their natural counterparts.

One rock-forming method starts with a boulder-shaped frame of reinforcing bar. Wire mesh or metal lath is secured to the frame, then several layers of concrete are applied to the shell. To re-create the cracks and fissures of natural rock, the still-wet concrete may be carved with tools or embossed with crinkled aluminum foil, clear plastic wrap, or custom latex molds cast from actual rock formations.

Another popular rock-forming technique calls for latex models to be cast on real rocks. The models are sprayed with a mixture of concrete and strands of fiberglass or polypropylene. When the mixture dries, the forms are removed. The end product is a thin but sturdy panel with a rock-textured veneer. The models yield identical panels, which can be joined together horizontally or vertically so the viewer is not aware of the repeated shape.

True rock is often a pastiche of colors and may also be flecked with lichen or specks of soil. To imitate this look, installers color the concrete by brushing, spraying, or splattering on layers of diluted acrylic stains.

Artificial rocks offer other landscaping opportunities: they can form steps, waterfalls, and pockets for plants, lights, or ponds. Moreover, they can be used to hide pumps and electric or water lines, as well as mask retaining walls.

Because of labor and materials, the cost of artificial rock is usually slightly higher than that of real stone or boulders.

These wide, slightly curved steps and low retaining walls are made of artificial cast stone formed directly on the hillside.

BRICK

rick is one of the most weather-resistant and enduring materials for outdoor projects. Because they are small and uniform in size, bricks are also easy to install and maintain.

Two kinds are used for most garden construction: common brick and face brick. Most paving is done with common brick. People like its warm color and texture, and it is less expensive than face brick. Common brick is more porous than face brick and less uniform in size and color (bricks may vary up to ¼ inch in length). Choose common bricks with fairly smooth surfaces; rough surfaces collect water that can freeze and crack bricks.

Face brick, with its sand-finished, glazed surface, is not as widely available as common brick. More often used for facing buildings than for garden projects, this brick makes elegant formal walls, attractive accents, edgings, header courses, stair nosings, and raised beds—all outdoor projects where its smoothness won't present a safety hazard when it is wet.

Used brick has uneven surfaces and streaks of old mortar that are attractive in an informal pavement. Imitation used or "rustic" brick costs about the same as genuine used brick but is easier to find; it is also more consistent in quality than most older brick.

Low-density firebrick, blond-colored and porous, is tailor-made for built-in barbecues and outdoor fireplaces. It provides interesting accents but doesn't wear as well as common brick.

The standard brick is about 8 by 4 by 2 ³/₈ inches thick. "Paver" bricks, which are solid and made to use underfoot, are roughly half the thickness of standard bricks. All outdoor bricks are graded according to their ability to withstand weathering. If you live in a region where it regularly freezes and thaws, choose common bricks rated SX (SW for face bricks), which means they can stand up to severe weather conditions. To calculate the quantities of brick you'll need for a project, visit a building supplier first, and be sure to have your measuring tape in hand.

The warm tones of the brick walkway above, set in a graceful arcing design, emphasize the abundant green foliage of the garden.

A. Antique brick set in a simple pattern called running bond conveys fluidity and a sense of movement on this garden terrace.

B. A display of brick includes rough common bricks in a range of colors, smoother face bricks for accents and edgings, bullnose types (with rounded edges) for stairs and to cap walls, used or imitation used bricks, and precut bricks (such as the triangle, above right) for patterns.

B

PAVERS

Pavers are an ideal material for do-it-yourself masonry projects. They are easy to install and available in many sizes, colors, and textures. And you'll have a choice ranging from simple 12-inch squares to interlocking pavers in a variety of shapes.

Use square pavers to form part of a grid or even a gentle arc. Squares or rectangles can butt together to create broad, unbroken surfaces, or they can be spaced apart and surrounded with grass, a ground cover, or gravel for textural interest.

Interlocking pavers fit together like puzzle pieces. They are made of extremely dense concrete that is mechanically pressure-formed. Laid in sand with closed (butted) joints, they create a surface that is more rigid than brick. No paver can tip out of alignment without taking several of its neighbors with it, and the surface remains intact even under substantial loads. Some interlocking shapes are proprietary, available at only a few outlets or direct from distributors. To locate these, check the Yellow Pages under Concrete Products.

Modern cobblestone blocks are very popular for casual gardens; butt them tightly together and then sweep sand or soil between the irregular edges.

Turf blocks, which leave spaces for plants to grow through, are designed to carry light traffic while retaining and protecting ground-cover plants. This special type of paver allows you to create grassy patios and driveways or side-yard access routes that stand up to wear.

Cast concrete "bricks," available in classic terra-cotta red as well as imitation used or antique styles, have become increasingly popular as substitutes for the real thing because, in many areas, they're significantly less expensive.

Some landscape professionals cast their own pavers in custom shapes, textures, and colors: adobe, stone, and imitation tile, for example. You can also make forms and pour your own pavers, but they won't be as strong as standard pressure-formed units.

B

C

A. Precast pavers allow you to experiment with designs and shapes, and many imitate tile, brick, or adobe. The assortment shown here includes interlocking puzzlelike shapes, stepping-stones, and turf blocks.

B. Interlocking pavers in two sizes create a level surface for entertaining in this artist's garden in Toronto. The neutral color of the pavers allowed the homeowner to concentrate color and interest in the plantings and furnishings. As a bonus, the pavers were less expensive than flagstone or other natural stones.

C. Granite setts placed in a circular design create a unique island bed in this Purchase, New York, garden. Surrounded by crushed rock, the pavers form a richly textured backdrop for massed pots of geraniums.

INSTALLING A GRAVEL PATH

Gravel—either smooth river rock or the more stable crushed rock—makes a low-cost, fast-draining path that can complement a wide variety of informal and formal planting schemes. The first step in laying a gravel path is to install wooden or masonry edgings to hold the loose material in place. Then put down landscape fabric to discourage weeds. Gravel surfaces tend to shift when walked on, but the movement will be minimized if you use a compacted base of crushed rock or sand.

Edging

Landscape fabric

1. Install edgings first, then put down landscape fabric or plastic sheeting to protect against weeds. Pour decomposed granite or sand over the site, taking care not to dislodge the liner.

Spray nozzle

2. Rake the base material evenly over the path until it is of a uniform 1-inch thickness. As you rake, wet the material with a fine spray.

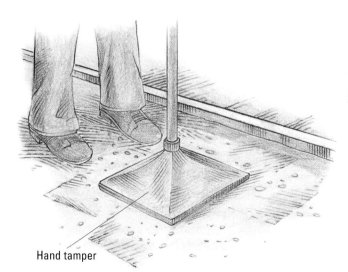

Hand tamper

3. Using a drum roller or a hand tamper, pass over the wet base several times, packing it down firmly. This firm base aids drainage and helps keep the topcoat from shifting underfoot.

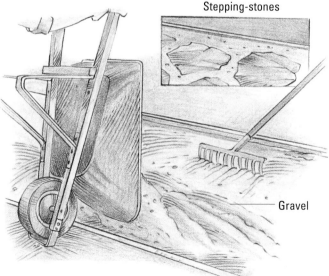

Stepping-stones

Gravel

4. Spread the gravel at least 2 inches thick and rake it evenly over the base. If desired, place stepping-stones on the base so that their tops protrude slightly above the surrounding gravel.

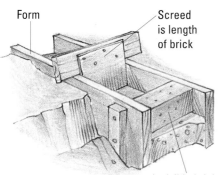

Form

Screed
is length
of brick

Invisible brick

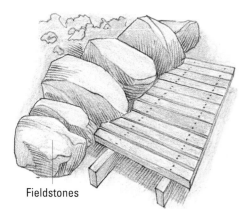

Fieldstones

Concrete mowing strip

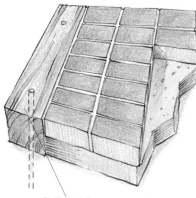

Railroad tie

A look at edgings

Whether you lay it, hammer it, set it, or pour it in place, a patio or walk almost always requires an edging. In addition to visually outlining the surface, an edging confines the pavement within the desired area—which is especially important when you are pouring concrete, working with loose materials such as gravel, or setting bricks or pavers in sand.

Several tried-and-true edging options are illustrated here. The most popular are made of 2-by-4 or 2-by-6 lumber, but for emphasis, you can use 4-by-4 or 6-by-6 material. Heavy timbers and railroad ties make strong edgings and interior dividers, especially when drilled and threaded with steel pipe. If your design calls for gentle curves, try pressure-treated 1 by 4s.

Another effective edging material is poured concrete. It is excellent for constructing invisible edgings underground, serving as a footing for mortared masonry units, or installing flush with a new walk. Bricks also establish a neat, precise edge. Set them directly in firm soil—horizontally, vertically, or even at an angle (but don't expect them to be very durable). And if you have random pieces of uncut stone, bear in mind that they make a perfect edging for a path in a rustic or naturalistic landscape.

Manufactured plastic or aluminum edgings are quite functional. These strips secure bricks or concrete pavers below finished paving height; they can be concealed with soil or sod. Flexible sections are convenient for tight curves.

For curbing paved areas, an edging is often installed after the base has been prepared and before the setting bed and paving are laid. String mason's lines around the perimeter, not only to mark the exact borders of the paving, but also to designate the outside top border of the edging. To achieve the correct edging height, you'll probably need to dig narrow trenches under the lines.

Wooden posts   Finish board

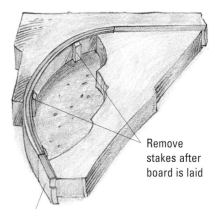

Plastic edging

Remove
stakes after
board is laid

Pressure-treated 1 by 4

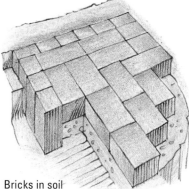

Bricks in soil

POURING A CONCRETE SLAB

Most of the work for a concrete path or patio lies in the preparation, which entails grading and formwork. Lay out stakes and mason's lines to mark the outline of the slab, allowing for at least a 1-inch drop for each 10 feet away from the house for drainage. If the exposed soil is soft, wet it and then tamp it firmly.

Wooden, steel, or copper dividers can be permanent partitions; they also serve as control joints to help prevent cracking and help break up the job into smaller, more manageable pours.

Be sure to add any required reinforcement to formwork before pouring. Check local building codes; usually, 6-inch-square welded wire mesh is the best choice for pavings.

See page 379 for instructions on mixing concrete. Pour large areas in sections and be sure to have helpers on hand to assist with hauling and spreading the wet concrete. You'll need gloves to protect your hands from the concrete's caustic ingredients; wear rubber boots if you have to walk on the wet mix.

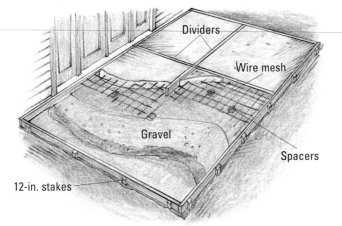

1. For rough grading, dig deep enough to allow for 4 inches of concrete plus 2 to 8 inches of gravel. Construct forms from 2 by 4s secured to 12-inch stakes, placing the form tops at finished slab height. Add welded wire mesh for reinforcement.

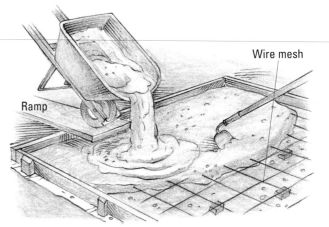

2. Begin pouring concrete at one end of form while a helper spreads it with a hoe. Work concrete up against form and tamp it into corners, but don't press it down too hard. A splashboard or ramp lets you pour the concrete where you want.

3. With a helper, move a 2-by-4 screed across the form to level concrete, using a rapid zigzag, sawing motion. A third person can shovel concrete into any hollows.

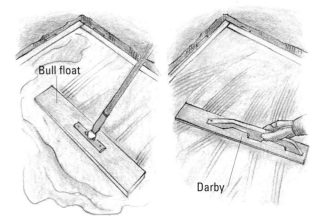

4. Initial floating smooths down high spots and fills small hollows left after screeding. As shown, use a darby for small jobs and a bull float with an extension handle for larger slabs.

Pouring a Footing

You must provide a garden wall with a solid base, or footing. Very low walls (no more than 12 inches) and dry-stone walls (see page 390) may only require a leveled trench or a rubble base; but other walls require a footing fashioned from concrete that is twice as wide and at least as deep as the wall's thickness. In cold-weather areas, extend the footing below the frost line. Add 6 inches to the trench depth for a bottom layer of gravel.

If you need to pour a post footing for a deck, fence, or overhead, see page 368. Use bags of ready-mixed concrete for these small jobs.

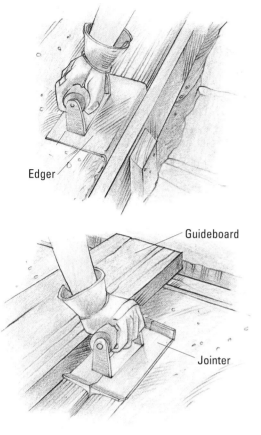

Edger

Guideboard

Jointer

5. Run the edge of a trowel between concrete and form. Then run an edger back and forth to create a smooth, curved edge (top). Make control joints every 10 feet with a jointer (bottom).

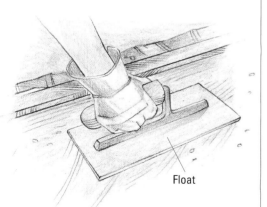

Float

6. Before the surface stiffens, give it a final floating with a wooden float. For a smoother surface, follow with a steel trowel. For a nonskid surface, drag a broom lightly across the concrete, without overlapping.

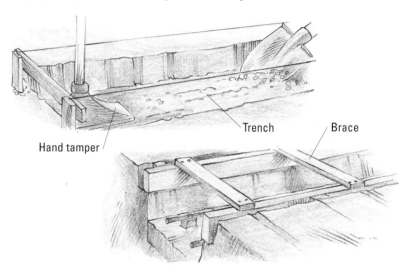

Hand tamper — Trench — Brace

1. Prepare a base for the footing by leveling and tamping the bottom of the trench and adding a 6-inch layer of gravel (top). Trenches in very firm soil may serve as forms; otherwise, build forms with 2-by lumber, stakes, and braces (bottom). Set any required reinforcing bars on a layer of broken bricks or other rubble.

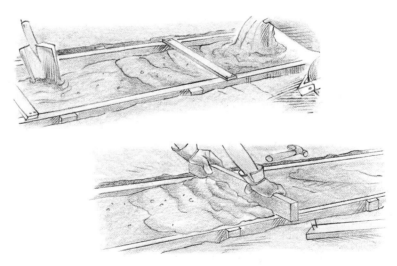

2. Pour concrete (top) and insert any vertical reinforcing bars required by building codes. Screed concrete level with tops of forms (bottom). Cover with a plastic sheet, leave to cure for 2 days, then remove the forms and begin to build the wall.

BUILDING A BLOCK WALL

For fast, inexpensive masonry wall construction, concrete blocks are the ideal material. They are easy to work with, and these rugged units make strong, durable walls.

First, lay out a dry course, or row, of blocks, spacing them 3/8 inch apart, and try to plan the wall so that no block cutting is necessary (you can also draw a plan on graph paper). If cutting is unavoidable, you can use the method described for bricks on page 381. Then you'll need to dig a trench for a strong, level concrete footing (for details, see page 387). Build the wall with a standard wall-building mortar (see page 382), but keep the mix slightly stiff. Otherwise, the heavy blocks may squeeze it out of the joints. A running bond pattern is the simplest to construct (see page 381).

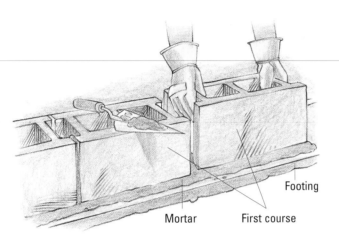

1. Spread a bed of mortar, 2 inches thick and wide enough for three blocks, over the footing. Then place the first-course corner block carefully and press it down to form an accurate 3/8-inch joint with the footing. Butter the ends of the next blocks with mortar, then set each one 3/8 inch from the previous block.

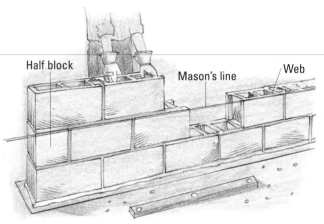

2. Check level often as you build up leads (at least three courses high) at both ends. String a mason's line between corner blocks as a guide to keep blocks straight. Start each even-numbered course with a half block. Butter both webs and edges, making full bed joints.

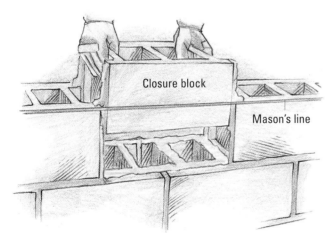

3. Fill in blocks between the leads, keeping 3/8-inch joint spacing. Be sure to check alignment, level, and plumb frequently. To fit the closure block, butter all edges of the opening and the ends of the block, then press it firmly into place.

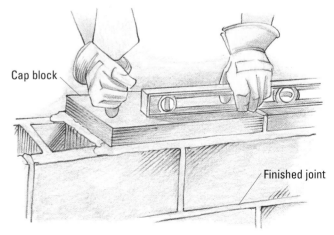

4. As you work, finish joints with a jointer or a wooden dowel. Solid cap blocks, available in various thicknesses, provide the simplest way to top off the last course. Simply mortar them in place on full bed joints, as shown. Tap into place and level.

Applying veneer to a block wall

Many people find concrete block boring or feel that it doesn't blend well with their landscaping. If this is the case, consider dressing up a new block wall by applying a veneer to its surface.

Professional landscapers often take advantage of concrete blocks' low cost and speed of assembly to build a wall, then they cover it with plastering stucco for attractive texture and shape. Though plastering is an acquired technique, an accomplished do-it-yourselfer might reasonably tackle a small garden wall.

Plastering a block wall is a two-part operation. The first layer—or "scratch coat"—should be about ³/₈ inch thick and must be applied after you have painted the wall with concrete bonding agent or covered it with wire lath. Then rough up the scratch coat with a commercial tool or a batch of wires held together (hence the name scratch) to help the finish coat's "bite." Apply the finish coat to a thickness of ¼ inch; it may be precolored or painted later. When the sheen has dulled, give texture to the plaster's surface by floating on the finish coat with a steel trowel (with or without notches), a sponge, or a stiff brush.

For best results, buy plaster premixed. If the color is integral, consult with your supplier about coloring oxides, and plan to use a mix with white concrete and sand in it.

Another way to enhance a block wall is to apply a brick or stone veneer to it (see page 195). Although the resulting wall looks like solid masonry, it requires less labor and expense. You will need to place noncorrosive metal wall ties in the mortar joints in every other row of blocks, spacing them 2 to 3 feet apart. The ties must protrude beyond the blocks to help secure veneer units.

Lastly, mortar the veneer to the core. Bend the wall ties into the joints between the stones or bricks. As you build, completely fill the spaces between the wall and veneer with soupy mortar.

Plastering stucco creates a clean contemporary veneer atop a concrete block wall. Apply the plaster in two coats; the final coat may be precolored or painted when dry. Here, the white plaster finish provides a backdrop for decorative plates and pots.

Building a dry-stone wall

The key to building a stone wall is careful fitting; the finished structure should appear to be a unit rather than a pile of rocks. A dry-stone wall is constructed without mortar and depends upon the weight and friction of one stone on another for its stability. Not only is it simple to build, but it also has the attraction of allowing you to place soil and plants in the unmortared spaces as you lay the stones.

Use the largest stones for the foundation course and reserve the longer ones for "bond" stones—long stones that run the width of the wall. Set aside broad, flat stones to cap the top of the wall.

Most dry-stone walls slope inward on both surfaces; this tilting of the faces is called batter and helps secure the wall. To check your work, make a batter gauge by taping together a 2-by-4 board, a scrap block, and a carpenter's level, as shown below.

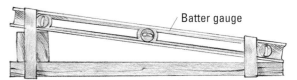

Batter gauge

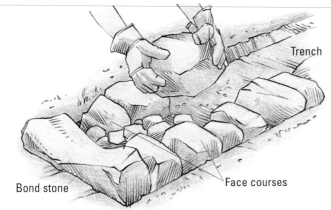

Trench

Bond stone

Face courses

1. Lay foundation stones in a trench about 6 inches deep. First, place a bond stone (one as deep as the wall) at one end; then position the two face courses at both edges of the trench. Choose whole, well-shaped stones for the face courses. Fill in the space between face courses with tightly packed rubble.

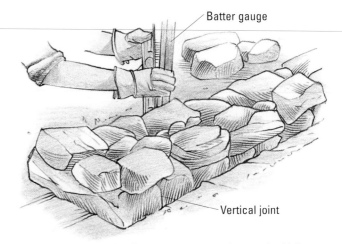

Batter gauge

Vertical joint

2. Lay stones atop the first course, staggering vertical joints. Select stones that fit together solidly and tilt the stones of each face inward toward one another. Use a batter gauge on faces and ends of the wall to check the tilt. Place bond stones every 5 to 10 square feet to tie the wall together.

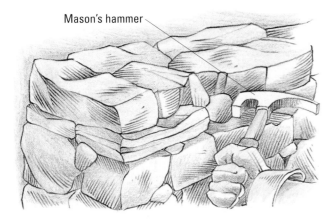

Mason's hammer

3. Continue to add courses, staggering vertical joints and maintaining the inward slope, so that gravity and the friction of the stones set one upon another will help hold the wall together. Gently tap small stones into any gaps with a mason's hammer.

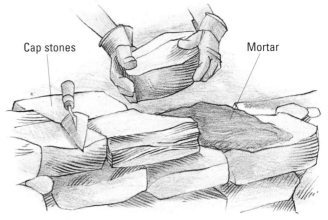

Cap stones

Mortar

4. Finish the top with as many flat, broad stones as possible. If you live in an area that experiences frost, mortar the cap as shown. Don't rake (indent) these joints; level them flush with a piece of scrap wood to prevent water from collecting.

Retaining walls

If your home sits on a sloping lot or a hillside, a retaining wall may be needed to hold back the earth and prevent erosion. Homeowners have a choice of three basic wall-building materials—wood, stone, or concrete—and now a number of new modular masonry systems have been developed with the owner-builder in mind (see below). These proprietary systems come with complete step-by-step instructions for installation.

Simple wood or masonry retaining walls, less than 3 feet high and on a gentle slope with stable soil, can be built by a do-it-yourselfer, but it's a good idea to consult your local building department for even a low retaining wall. Most communities require a building permit for any retaining wall and may require a soil analysis in any area suspected of being unstable.

In general, it's best to site your retaining wall so it results in the least possible disruption of the natural slope, but even so, extensive cutting and filling may be needed. The hill can be held back with a single wall or a series of low retaining walls that form terraces. Though terracing is less risky, both methods disturb the hill and should be designed by an engineer. If space permits, the safest approach is not to disturb the slope at all, but to build the wall on the level ground near the foot of the slope and fill in behind it.

In any case, the retaining wall should rest on cut or undisturbed ground, never on fill. Planning for drainage is also essential. Usually, you'll need a gravel backfill to collect water that dams up behind the wall. Water in the gravel bed can be drained off through weep holes in the base of the wall or through a drainpipe that channels the water into a storm sewer or other disposal area.

Slope is cut away and excess earth is moved downhill. Retaining wall now holds back long, level terrace.

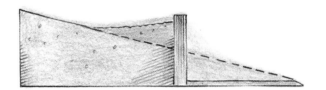

Earth is cut away and moved behind tall retaining wall. Result is level ground below, high, level slope behind.

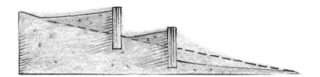

Total wall height is divided between two terraces, resulting in a series of level beds.

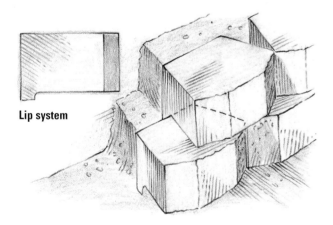

Lip system

For low retaining walls or small raised planters, modular masonry systems are available in various styles and weights. Most use cast "lips" (left) or interlocking pins to establish the

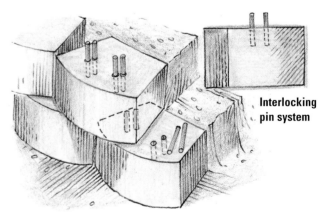

Interlocking pin system

setback and resist outward-pushing forces. Fiberglass or steel pins drop through holes in upper blocks and stop in grooves on units below, joining each to two beneath (right).

Step-building Basics

Laying out low, single, back-garden steps does not involve as much time and effort as planning runs of well-designed formal steps; the latter require an understanding of proper proportions.

The flat part of a step is called the tread; the vertical element is the riser. Ideally, the depth of the tread plus twice the riser height should equal 25 to 27 inches. Based on an average length of stride, the ideal outdoor step should have a 6-inch-high riser and a 15-inch-deep tread, but riser and tread dimensions can vary. Risers should be no lower than 5 inches and no higher than 8 inches; tread depth should never be less than 11 inches. The overall riser-tread relationship should remain the same. All the risers and treads in any one flight of steps should be uniform in size.

To fit steps evenly, you must calculate the degree of slope. Using the drawing at top right as a guide, first calculate the distance from A to B; this is the rise, or change

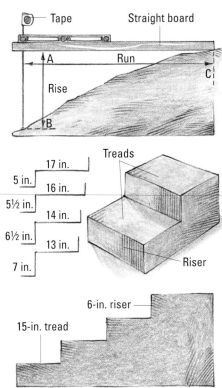

Ideal tread-riser relationship

in level, of the slope. The horizontal distance from A to C is called the run.

To determine the number of steps you will need, divide the desired riser height into the total rise of the slope (in inches). If the answer ends in a fraction (and it probably will), drop the fraction and divide that number into the rise; this time, the resulting figure will give you the exact measurement for each of the risers. Then check the chart (left) to see if the corresponding minimum tread will fit the slope's total run.

Plan on a minimum width of 2 feet for utility steps and 4 feet for most others. If you want two people to be able to walk abreast, allow 5 feet.

Rarely do steps fit exactly into a slope. More than likely, you will have to cut and fill the slope to accommodate the steps. If your slope is too steep for even 8-inch risers, remember that steps need not run straight up and down. Curves and switchbacks make the distance longer but the climb gentler.

Timbers or ties

Both railroad ties and 6-by-6 pressure-treated timbers make simple but rugged steps. To begin, excavate the site and tamp the soil in the tread area firmly. Lay the ties or timbers on the soil, then drill a hole near both ends of each tie or timber. With a sledge, drive either ½-inch galvanized steel pipes or ¾-inch reinforcing bars through the holes into the ground.

Or, for extra support, pour small concrete footings and set anchor bolts in the slightly stiffened concrete. When the concrete has set (after about two days), secure the ties to the footings with the bolts.

Once the tie or timber risers are in place, fill the tread spaces behind them with concrete, brick-in-sand paving, gravel, grass, or another material.

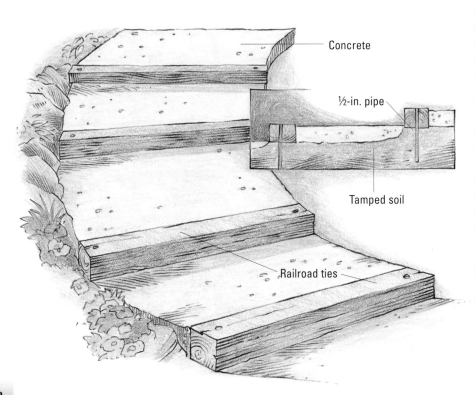

Wooden stairs

Formal wooden steps are best for a low-level deck or for easy access to a doorway. Make stringers from 2 by 10s or 2 by 12s. If the steps are more than 4 feet wide, a third stringer will be needed in the middle.

Use galvanized bolts or metal joist hangers to secure stringers to a deck beam or joist; if you're running stringers off stucco siding or another masonry surface, hang them on a ledger, as shown. Note that when bolts are used, the first tread is below the surface of the interior floor or deck; when joist hangers are the fasteners, however, the first tread must be level with the floor.

Attach the stringers at the bottom to wooden nailing blocks anchored in a concrete footing. Build risers and treads from 2-by material cut to width; treads should overlap the risers below and may hang over slightly.

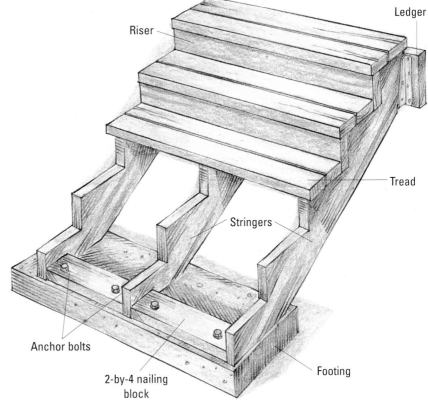

Riser

Ledger

Tread

Stringers

Anchor bolts

2-by-4 nailing block

Footing

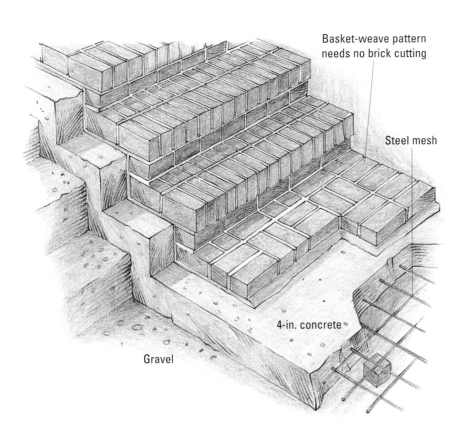

Basket-weave pattern needs no brick cutting

Steel mesh

4-in. concrete

Gravel

Masonry steps

Steps can be built entirely of concrete or, for a finished look, the concrete can be used as a base for mortared masonry units.

First, form rough steps in the earth. Allow space for at least a 6-inch gravel setting bed and a 4-inch thickness of concrete on both treads and risers. (In cold climates you will need 6 to 8 inches of concrete, plus a footing that is sunk below the frost line.) Add the thickness of any masonry units to tread-and-riser dimensions. Tamp filled areas thoroughly.

With 2-inch-thick lumber, build forms like those shown on pages 386–387. Lay the gravel bed, keeping it 4 inches back from the front of the steps; you will pour the concrete thicker at that potentially weak point. Reinforce with 6-inch-square welded wire mesh.

Pour and screed the concrete as for a poured concrete footing. To make treads more weather-safe, broom the wet concrete to roughen its surface, then cure as for a concrete footing (see page 387).

INSTALLING A GARDEN POND

With either a flexible plastic or rubber pond liner and a bit of elbow grease, even a beginner can fashion an average-size garden pond in a single weekend. Of course, plantings and borders will take somewhat longer to establish.

Even a pond with an unusual shape should not present a problem. A liner can take almost any shape, accommodating curves and undulations. It's also possible to weld two pieces of liner together with solvent cement, or have the supplier do it for you.

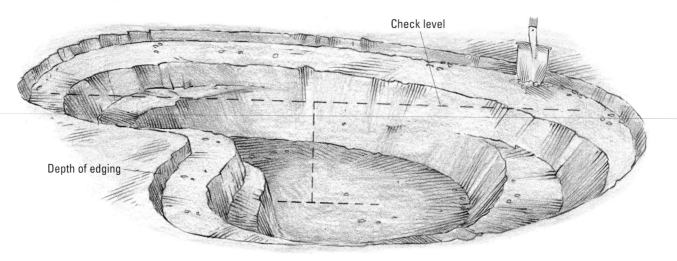

Check level

Depth of edging

1. Mark the pond's outline with a hose or a length of rope. Dig all around the outline with a sharp spade; remove any sod and keep it in a shady spot for later patching. Excavate the hole to the desired depth and width, plus 2 inches all around for a layer of sand. Dig down to the thickness of any edging material. Check level carefully, using a straight board to bridge the rim.

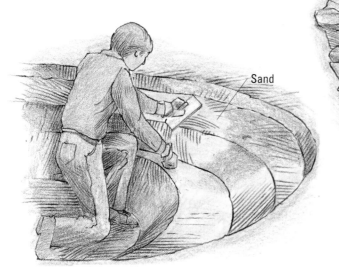

Sand

Liner

3. Open up the liner and let it soften in the sun. Then spread it over the hole, evening up the overlap all around. Place heavy stones or bricks around the perimeter to weigh it down, then slowly begin to fill the pond with water.

2. Next, remove all protruding roots and rocks and fill any holes with soil. Pack a 2-inch layer of clean, damp sand into the excavation. Smooth the sand with a board or a concrete float.

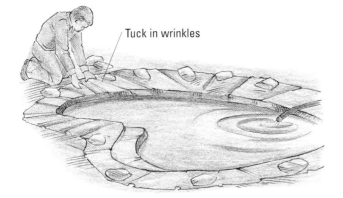

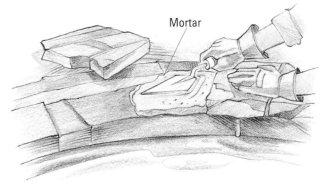

4. Continue filling, tucking in wrinkles all around; as required, make pleats at hard corners (they won't be visible when the pool is filled). You can wade into the pool to tuck in the lining, but the water's weight will make it fit the contours of the hole.

5. When the pond is full, add overhanging edging: lay flagstones or brick in a thin bed of mortar. Next, bring the liner up behind the edging, then trim the liner. Drain the pool and refill it with fresh water.

Fountains and Falls

Water in motion, whether gently spilling, gurgling, or energetically tumbling, is always enchanting. Both fountains and waterfalls help bring the sparkle and the musical sounds of falling water into the garden.

Surprisingly, fountains can be simple to create. A wooden planter box, a metal basin, or a large pot, for example, can easily be converted into a small fountain. Just coat the inside of a wooden container or an unglazed pot with asphalt emulsion or epoxy paint, or use a flexible liner. Then drop in a submersible pump with a riser pipe and add water (in shallow water, a few rocks can conceal the pump).

For larger holding pools, many designers prefer precast rigid fiberglass or reinforced concrete. A wall fountain's raised holding pool is often concrete or concrete block, covered with plaster or faced with brick, tile, or stone above the waterline. A submersible pump and water pipes can be combined to add a fountain to an existing wall. An electric switch, perhaps

located indoors, controls the pump-driven flow; a ball or 3-way valve allows you to alter the flow to suit your taste. To automatically replace water lost through evaporation, hook up a float valve to the water supply line. A drain is also handy.

Waterfalls pose some unique design considerations. The major technical concern is waterproofing. Before plunging into construction, determine which pump, pipes, and other plumbing hardware you'll need to provide the desired flow. For a waterproof channel, use either a flexible liner, free-form concrete, a fiberglass shell or series of splash pans, or a combination of the above.

If you opt for a liner, position waterfall rocks carefully, making sure not to damage or displace the liner. Once the basic structure is complete, secure secondary stones and add loose rocks or pebbles to provide visual accents or to form a ripple pattern. Only creative experimentation will reveal the most pleasing sights and sounds.

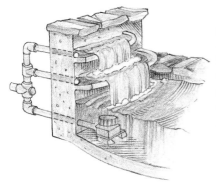

A formal wall fountain combines a raised holding pool, a masonry wall, and decorative spill shelves. Water tumbles from pipe outlets to spill shelves to a holding pool; a submersible pump sends it back around again.

Waterfall design calls for a watertight channel, natural-looking stones, and adequate camouflage for plumbing parts. A flexible liner is the simplest channel option; stone placement conceals the liner.

INSTALLING IRRIGATION SYSTEMS

The benefits of a permanent irrigation system are well known—water and time savings, healthier plants, and reduced maintenance. The information given on pages 330–331 can help you choose the best system for your garden. Shown here are installation procedures for the two main types of irrigation systems—sprinkler and drip.

Most systems can be attached to an existing water supply pipe (1-inch diameter or larger is best). Because drip systems require only low water volume and pressure, you may be able to connect a drip system to a convenient outdoor faucet; the manufacturer's literature will help you determine whether this is best for your situation. You will want to pick out some possible locations to place your valves. Consider how they might be concealed (they can be unsightly) and, if your system will be automated, where you'll put the timer and how far it is from an electrical connection.

No matter how you connect your system to the water supply, you will need proper filter, pressure regulator, and backflow devices. Filters ensure that emitters don't clog. Pressure regulators prevent too much water pressure from building up in the system and possibly forcing the emitter heads off the supply lines. Backflow devices, which are usually required by law, prevent irrigation water from backing into the home water supply.

Whether or not your irrigation system is automated, check it frequently for broken or clogged sprinklers or drip emitters.

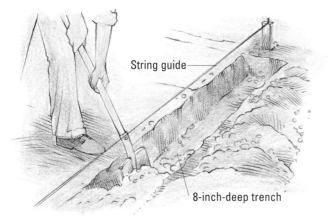

1. A sprinkler system must be laid underground. First, dig 8-inch-deep trenches for pipes. To keep trench lines straight, run string between two stakes.

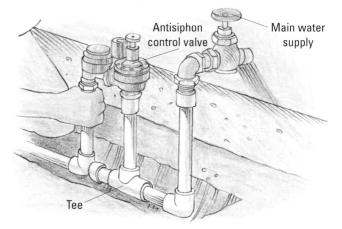

2. Connect pipes to the water supply pipe, then attach control valve (with built-in antisiphon control valve) at least 6 inches above ground. Use thick-walled, ¾-inch PVC pipe.

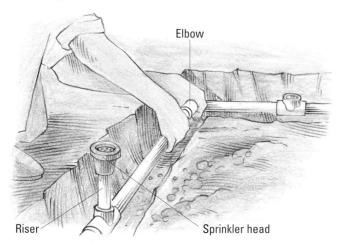

3. Assemble pipes from the control valve outward, fitting risers and sprinkler heads to elbows, tees, and side outlets. Joints may screw together or require PVC solvent cement.

4. Flush out pipes with heads removed. Then fill in trenches, mounding loose soil along center of trench. Tamp the soil firmly with a hand tamper. Avoid striking the sprinkler heads.

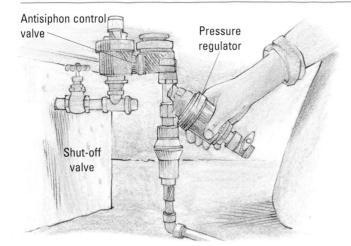

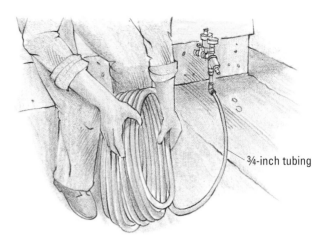

1. Drip irrigation system assembly starts with connecting the antisiphon control valve, filter, and pressure regulator to the water supply line (for hose-end system, use a hose bib).

2. Connect ¾-inch flexible polyvinyl tubing and lay out main lines on the surface of the soil or in shallow trenches. For a sturdier system, use buried PVC pipe for main lines.

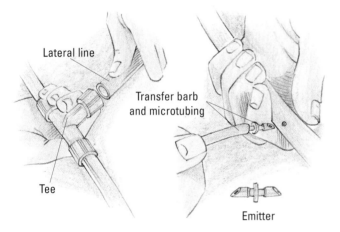

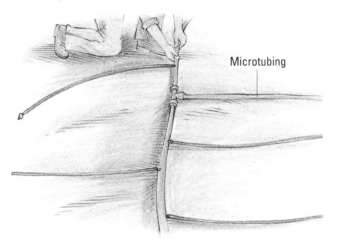

3. Lay out and attach lateral lines using tee connectors (left). Many kinds hold tubing without cement. Attach end caps, then insert emitters or transfer barbs for microtubing (right).

4. Flush system to ensure that all emitters work properly. Cover the lines with a thin layer of mulch, if desired, but leave the emitters and microtubing above ground.

Switching to Drip

If you have an existing sprinkler system with an underground distribution line of PVC pipe, you can simplify the installation of a drip system by retrofitting it. But if you have a galvanized pipe system retrofitting it is less practical than replacing it because over time pieces of flaking metal can clog the drip emitters.

Commercial products make switching to drip easy. At right are two retrofit kits for sprinkler systems. The system you choose depends on the layout of your garden and the number of sprinklers you plan to change.

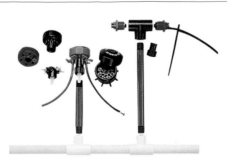

Multioutlet bubbler heads

Capped riser

Generally, it's better to change the entire line on one valve to drip than to mix sprinklers and drip along it (if you have lawns and borders on the same line, for example). Because of different output from sprinklers and drip fittings, trying to adjust watering times on a mixed system is difficult. But in some cases you will have no choice.

The system shown at top delivers water through ¼-inch tubing and multioutlet bubbler heads. The simple retrofit shown at bottom uses only one riser; other risers are capped, as at right.

BUILDING A RAISED BED

Raising your garden above the ground can solve some of the most frustrating problems gardeners face. An easy-to-build bed makes it possible for plants to thrive where soil is poor, wildlife is hungry, or the growing season is short. And if you need easy access to your plants—due to a disability or simply to eliminate back-bending labor—you can sit on the edge of the bed and garden in comfort.

Fill the bed with the best soil you can. Good soil means that plants can be placed closer together, making a small area more productive. Line the bottom of the bed with wire screening to keep out pests, or fit it with a PVC framework for bird netting.

A raised bed can be any size, but if it is more than 4 feet wide it will be difficult to reach the middle from either side. If the sides will double as benches, build the frame 18 to 24 inches high.

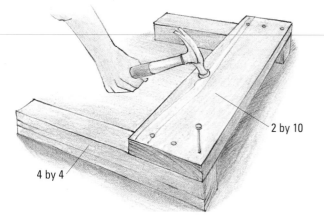

1. Orient a rectangular bed from north to south. For a 4-by-10-foot bed, first nail short sides of 2 by 10s to 3-foot-high 4-by-4 corner posts. Use rot-resistant lumber and galvanized nails.

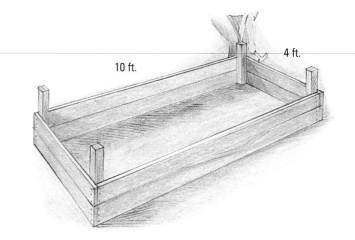

2. Flip over structure and nail 10-foot lengths to corner posts. For added strength, install wooden bracing or metal L-straps. Work on level ground so that bed is as square as possible.

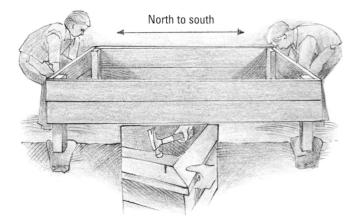

3. Set bed right side up and insert corner posts into predug foot-deep holes. Level if necessary. Cap the top with surfaced redwood 2 by 6s, with ends cut at a 45-degree angle (inset).

4. Place 3 to 4 inches of new soil in the bottom of the bed and mix it into the ground to aid drainage. This 20-inch-deep bed holds about 2½ cubic yards of soil.

RAISED-BED STYLES

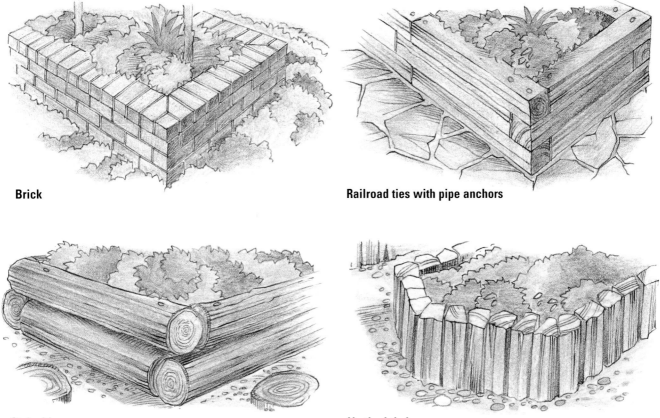

Brick

Railroad ties with pipe anchors

Staked logs

Vertical timbers

Easy-access Gardening

It isn't easy to garden from a wheelchair, but it's not impossible. It takes thoughtful planning to give maximum access to planting areas. Here are some features that make a garden accessible.

Raised beds *can accommodate both flowers and edible plants. To put gardening chores within easy reach of a wheelchair, the beds should be about 16 inches tall and no more than 4 feet wide; they can be long or ∪-shaped, with the opening in the ∪ just wide enough for a chair.*

Paved paths, *about 4 feet wide, can allow a chair to turn, maneuver, and glide easily. Ideally, the paths should be extensions of a paved patio at the rear of the house and a porch or terrace at the front. If the house is at a higher level than the garden, a wide, gently sloping ramp can angle off a back deck.*

Hinged trellises *can be lowered to tend or gather crops such as peas and tomatoes.*

An automatic irrigation system *eliminates the need for routine watering. See pages 330–331 for options.*

Railings *for walks and ramps should be sunk in concrete footings for extra support.*

Special tools *are available with extra-long handles to reach into beds from a chair.*

Mulch *— with fabric or loose materials — reduces the need for frequent weeding, which can be a chore.*

Plant for low maintenance*. Choose trees that don't shed a lot of litter, opt for a reduced lawn — or no lawn at all — and choose plants that don't require frequent maintenance or pest and disease control.*

WORKING SAFELY

Although the garden is not generally a hazardous place, any time you pick up a tool, climb a ladder, or start moving heavy materials, you can injure yourself—or someone else. If you are planning to carry out any of the landscape construction shown in the previous pages, follow the guidelines given here.

Safety accessories and clothing

Many masonry projects call for safety precautions. To protect yourself from flying particles of dust or rock when cutting stone or brick, wear safety goggles or a full face mask. Look for comfortably fitting, fog-free types made of scratch-resistant, shatterproof plastic. Dry portland cement is irritating to the eyes, nose, and mouth, so wear a dust mask when mixing con-

crete. Wet concrete and mortar are caustic to the skin, so wear heavy rubber gloves and tuck your sleeves into them. Also wear rubber boots if you must walk in the concrete to finish it off. Wash your skin thoroughly with water if wet mortar or concrete contacts it.

When using lumber products, protect your hands from wood splinters with all-leather or leather-reinforced cotton work gloves. If you are sanding wood, wear a disposable painter's mask. For work with solvents, finishes, or adhesives, wear disposable rubber or plastic gloves.

Working safely with power tools

Portable power tools can cause injuries in an instant. Handle these tools with respect, and follow some basic safety precautions.

Read the owner's manual before using any tool.

When you operate a power tool, try to do so without interruption or distraction. If possible, block off the work area to keep all visitors away—especially children and pets.

Never wear loose-fitting clothing or jewelry that could catch in a tool's mechanism. If you have long hair, tie it back.

Never use a power tool if you are tired or under the influence of alcohol or drugs.

Before you plug in a tool, check that safety devices such as guards are in good working order. Also tighten any clamping mechanisms on the tool, ensure that the blade or bit is securely installed, and set up any necessary supports or clamps for securing the work.

Ensure that your hands and body—and power cord—are well away from a tool's blade or bit.

Never stand on a wet surface when using a power tool that is plugged into an electrical outlet unless the outlet is GFCI protected (see opposite page).

Never cut wet wood, and if you can't avoid cutting warped boards or must cut through a knot, be on your guard for kickback—when the tool lurches back out of the wood.

Make sure there are no fasteners in any lumber that you are sawing or drilling.

If a blade or bit jams in a piece of wood, turn off and unplug the tool before trying to extricate it. To keep your balance, don't reach too far with the tool; move closer to it and keep a stable footing.

Always allow the bit or blade to stop on its own before setting down the tool.

Unplug a tool before servicing or adjusting it, and after you have finished using it.

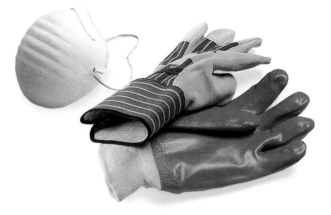

Follow the manufacturer's specifications to lubricate and clean power tools, and make sure all blades and bits are sharp and undamaged.

If you are using a rented concrete mixer, read the instructions carefully. Never reach into the rotating drum with your hands or tools. Keep well away from the moving parts, and do not look into the mixer while it is running.

Working safely with electricity

Tools powered by electricity are essential for most outdoor construction projects. But unless a drill, circular saw, or other power tool is double-insulated, it must be properly grounded or it can give a serious shock. Double-insulated tools should be clearly marked (the plug will have only two prongs). When you are working in a damp area or outdoors, a ground fault circuit interrupter (GFCI) is essential.

When working outside, you will probably need to use an extension cord for your tools. Use the shortest extension cord possible (long cords can overheat, causing a fire hazard), and make sure it's rated for outdoor use. The longer the cord, the less amperage it will deliver, which means less power for the tool's motor. Look for the nameplate on the tool that contains its amperage requirement. Avoid crimping the cord; don't run it through a door that will be continually opened and closed.

A main disconnect allows you to shut down your entire electrical system whenever you need to change a fuse or in case of an emergency. If you need to work on an outdoor switch, circuit, or outlet, you'll need to shut off power to a branch circuit. *Never* work on a live electrical circuit. Two typical disconnects are shown at right. Familiarize yourself with them before you start to work.

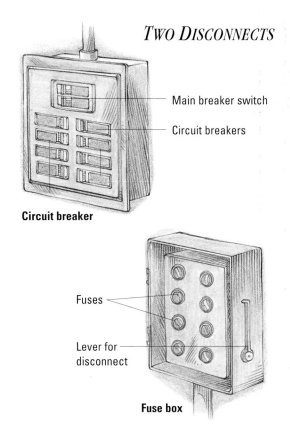

TWO DISCONNECTS

Main breaker switch

Circuit breakers

Circuit breaker

Fuses

Lever for disconnect

Fuse box

To lift heavy objects, spread your feet a comfortable width apart. Then bend your knees and, keeping your back straight, pick up the object—never bend at the waist or you could injure your back. If an object is very heavy, get help.

When working on a ladder, wear sturdy shoes with good traction. Overlap the sections of an extension ladder by three or four rungs and tie the top of the ladder to a stable object. Haul up your equipment using a rope and bucket, as shown.

COMMON NAMES OF PLANTS

A

Aaron's beard—*Hypericum calycinum*
Adam's needle—*Yucca filamentosa*
Alder—*Alnus*
Allspice—*Calycanthus*
Alumroot—*Heuchera*
American bugbane—*Cimcifuga americana*
Andromeda—*Pieris*
Arborvitae—*Thuja*
Arrowhead—*Sagittaria*
Arrowwood—*Viburnum dentatum*
Asarabacca—*Asarum europaeum*
Ash—*Fraxinus*
Autumn fern—*Dryopteris erythrosora*
Azalea—*Rhododendron*

B

Baby's breath—*Gypsophila*
Balloon flower—*Platycodon*
Barberry—*Berberis*
Barrenwort—*Epimedium*
Basket-of-gold—*Aurinia saxatilis*
Bayberry—*Myrica*
Bearberry—*Arctostaphylos uva-ursi*
Beauty bush—*Kolkwitzia*
Bee balm—*Monarda*
Beech—*Fagus*
Bellflower—*Campanula*
Birch—*Betula*
Bittersweet—*Celastrus*
Black alder—*Ilex verticillata*
Black-eyed Susan—*Rudbeckia hirta*
Blanket flower—*Gaillardia*
Bleeding heart—*Dicentra* species
Blueberry—*Vaccinium* species
Blue-eyed grass—*Sisyrinchium*
Blue mist—*Caryopteris*
Bog arum—*Calla palustris*
Bog laurel—*Kalmia polifolia*
Bog rosemary—*Andromeda polifolia*
Boxwood (Box)—*Buxus*
Bridal wreath—*Spiraea*
Broom—*Cytisus; Genista*
Buckeye—*Aesculus*
Buckthorn—*Rhamnus*
Bugleweed—*Ajuga*
Butterfly bush—*Buddleia*
Butterfly weed—*Asclepias tuberosa*

C

Candytuft—*Iberis*
Cardinal flower—*Lobelia cardinalis*
Carpathian harebell—*Campanula carpatica*
Castor bean—*Ricinus*
Catmint—*Calamintha; Nepeta*
Cattail—*Typha*

Cedar, red—*Juniperus virginiana*
Celandine poppy—*Stylophorum*
Chamomile—*Chamaemelum*
Cherry—*Prunus* species
Chestnut—*Castanea*
Chinese plum yew—*Cephalotaxus*
Chives—*Allium schoenoprasum*
Chokeberry—*Aronia*
Christmas fern—*Polystichum acrostichoides*
Christmas rose—*Helleborus niger*
Cinquefoil—*Potentilla*
Columbine—*Aquilegia*
Coral bells—*Heuchera*
Cornelian cherry—*Cornus mas*
Cornflower—*Centaurea cyanus*
Crabapple—*Malus*
Cranesbill—*Geranium* species
Crape myrtle—*Lagerstroemia*
Creeping Jenny—*Lysimachia nummularia*
Cupid's dart—*Catananche*
Cushion spurge—*Euphorbia epithymoides*

D

Daffodil—*Narcissus*
Daylily—*Hemerocallis*
Dead nettle—*Lamium*
Dogwood—*Cornus*

E

Elderberry—*Sambucus*
Elm, Chinese—*Ulmus parvifolia*
Eulalia—*Miscanthus sinensis*
Evening primrose—*Oenothera*

F

False cypress—*Chamaecyparis*
False indigo—*Baptisia australis*
False spirea—*Astilbe*
Feather grass—*Miscanthus; Stipa*
Feather reed grass—*Calamagrostis*
Fennel—*Foeniculum*
Fescue—*Festuca*
Fetterbush—*Leucothöe*
Fir—*Abies*
Fir, Douglas—*Pseudotsuga menziesii*
Firethorn—*Pyracantha*
Flag—*Iris*
Flame grass—*Miscanthus purpurascens*
Flax, perennial blue—*Linum perenne*
Fleabane—*Erigeron*
Foamflower—*Tiarella*
Forget-me-not—*Myosotis sylvatica*
Fountain grass—*Pennisetum*
Foxglove—*Digitalis*
French pussy willow—*Salix caprea*
Fringe tree—*Chionanthus*

G

Gas plant—*Dictamnus albus*
Gayfeather—*Liatris*
Geranium, annual—*Pelargonium*
Germander—*Teucrium*
Globeflower—*Trollius*
Golden chain—*Laburnum anagyroides*
Golden rain tree—*Koelreuteria*
Goldenrod—*Solidago*
Grape—*Vitis*

H

Hawthorn—*Crataegus*
Heather—*Calluna*
Heath—*Erica*
Heavenly bamboo—*Nandina domestica*
Hemlock—*Tsuga*
Hen and chickens—*Sempervivum*
Hickory—*Carya* species
Holly grape—*Mahonia aquifolium*
Hollyhock—*Alcea rosea*
Hollyhock mallow—*Malva alcea*
Holly—*Ilex*
Honeysuckle—*Lonicera*
Horse chestnut—*Aesculus* species
Houseleek—*Sempervivum*
Hyacinth—*Hyacinthus orientalis*

I

Ice plant—*Delosperma*
Indian grass—*Sorghastrum nutans*
Indigo—*Indigofera*
Inkberry—*Ilex cornuta; I. glabra*
Interrupted fern—*Osmunda claytoniana*
Italian arum—*Arum italicum*
Ivy—*Hedera*

J

Japanese andromeda—*Pieris japonica*
Japanese anemone—*Anemone hybrida*
Japanese blood grass—*Imperata cylindrica* 'Rubra'
Japanese painted fern—*Athyrium niponicum* 'Pictum'
Japanese spurge—*Pachysandra terminalis*
Joe-Pye-weed—*Eupatorium* species
Johnny-jump-up—*Viola tricolor*
Juniper—*Juniperus*

K

Kentucky coffee tree—*Gymnocladus*

L

Lady's-mantle—*Alchemilla*
Lamb's ears—*Stachys* species
Larkspur—*Consolida*
Lavender cotton—*Santolina*
Lavender—*Lavandula*

Lavender mist — *Thalictrum rochebrunianum*
Lenten rose — *Helleborus orientalis*
Leyland cypress — × *Cupressocyparis leylandii*
Lilac — *Syringa*
Lily leek — *Allium moly*
Lily-of-the-valley — *Convallaria*
Lily turf — *Liriope*
Linden — *Tilia*
Locust — *Gleditsia; Robinia*
Love-in-a-mist — *Nigella damascena*

M

Maiden grass — *Miscanthus sinensis*
Maidenhair fern — *Adiantum*
Maidenhair tree — *Ginkgo*
Maltese cross — *Lychnis chalcedonica*
Maple — *Acer*
Marigold — *Tagetes*
Marjoram — *Origanum majorana*
Marsh marigold — *Caltha palustris*
Meadow beauty — *Rhexia virginica*
Meadow rue — *Thalictrum*
Mexican bamboo — *Polygonum japonicum*
Mexican hat — *Ratibida*
Mexican sunflower — *Tithonia*
Mist flower — *Eupatorium rugosum*
Mock orange — *Philadelphus*
Moneywort — *Lysimachia nummularia*
Monkshood — *Aconitum*
Moor grass — *Molinia caerulea*
Morning glory — *Ipomoea purpurea*
Moss pink — *Phlox subulata*
Mountain ash — *Sorbus*
Mountain cranberry — *Vaccinium vitis-idaea* var. *minus*
Mountain laurel — *Kalmia latifolia*
Mulberry — *Morus*

N

Nasturtium — *Tropaeolum*
Northern sea oats — *Chasmanthium latifolium*

O

Oak — *Quercus*
Oat grass — *Avena; Arrhenatherum; Helictotrichon*
Oregano — *Origanum vulgare*
Oregon grape — *Mahonia aquifolium*

P

Pampas grass — *Cortaderia*
Pansy — *Viola* species and hybrids
Pasqueflower — *Anemone pulsatilla*
Peach — *Prunus* species
Pear — *Pyrus*
Pecan — *Carya* species

Peony — *Paeonia*
Periwinkle — *Vinca minor*
Pickerel rush (Pickerel weed) — *Pontederia cordata*
Pincushion flower — *Scabiosa*
Pine — *Pinus*
Pinks — *Dianthus* species
Pitcher plant — *Sarracenia*
Plane tree — *Platanus*
Plantain lily — *Hosta*
Plumbago — *Ceratostigma*
Plum — *Prunus* species
Poplar — *Populus*
Poppy — *Eschscholzia; Papaver*
Pot marigold — *Calendula officinalis*
Prairie dropseed — *Sporobolus*
Prickly pear — *Opuntia*
Primrose — *Primula*
Privet — *Ligustrum*
Purple coneflower — *Echinacea purpurea*

Q

Quaking grass — *Briza*
Queen of the prairie — *Filipendula rubra*
Quince — *Chaenomeles; Cydonia; Pseudocydonia*

R

Ravenna grass — *Saccharum ravennae*
Redbud — *Cercis*
Red-hot poker — *Kniphofia*
Rose campion — *Lychnis coronaria*
Rosemary — *Rosmarinus*
Rue — *Ruta*
Russian sage — *Perovskia*

S

Sage — *Salvia*
Sedge — *Carex*
Serviceberry — *Amelanchier*
Shadbush — *Amelanchier*
Shooting star — *Dodecatheon meadia*
Shrub althea — *Hibiscus syriacus*
Silk tree — *Albizia julibrissin*
Silverbell — *Halesia*
Silver fleecevine — *Polygonum aubertii*
Silvergrass — *Miscanthus sinensis*
Snowball — *Viburnum* species
Snowbell — *Styrax*
Snowflake — *Leucojum*
Snow-in-summer — *Cerastium tomentosum*
Solomon's seal — *Polygonatum*
Sorrel tree (Sourwood) — *Oxydendrum*
Speedwell — *Veronica*
Spruce — *Picea*
St.-John's-wort — *Hypericum*
Stonecrop — *Sedum*
Strawberry — *Fragaria*
Strawflower — *Helichrysum bracteatum*

Sumac — *Rhus* species
Summersweet — *Clethra alnifolia*
Sunflower — *Helianthus*
Swamp pink — *Helonias bullata*
Sweet alyssum — *Lobularia maritima*
Sweet bay — *Magnolia virginiana*
Sweet box — *Sarcococca*
Sweet flag — *Acorus calamus*
Sweet gum — *Liquidambar*
Sweet woodruff — *Galium*
Switch grass — *Panicum*

T

Tansy — *Tanacetum vulgare*
Thrift — *Armeria*
Thyme — *Thymus*
Tree mallow — *Lavatera thuringiaca*
Trout lily — *Erythronium*
Trumpet vine — *Campsis*
Tulip — *Tulipa*
Tulip tree — *Liriodendron*
Turtlehead — *Chelone obliqua*

V

Virginia bluebell — *Mertensia*
Virginia creeper — *Parthenocissus*

W

Wake robin — *Trillium*
Wallflower — *Erysimum*
Walnut — *Juglans* species
Water lily — *Nymphaea*
Wild ginger — *Asarum*
Willow — *Salix*
Winterberry — *Ilex verticillata*
Winter creeper — *Euonymus fortunei*
Wintergreen — *Gaultheria procumbens*
Witch hazel — *Hamamelis*
Wormwood — *Artemisia* species

Y

Yarrow — *Achillea*
Yellowwood — *Cladrastis*
Yew — *Taxus*

Pronunciation Guide

Scientific names are the universal language for plants, but they are pronounced differently in various parts of the world, even among English-speaking countries. Because these names come from Latin and Greek, there is no absolute, approved, obligatory pronunciation for them—we say them as we choose. What follows is a list of the most-often-used ways to say the scientific plant names used in this book. Where two pronunciations are commonly used, both have been given.

A

Abelia—uh-BEE-lee-uh
Abies—A-beez
Acer—AY-ser
Achillea—ak-il-EE-uh
Adiantum—ad-ee-AN-tum
Ajuga—a-JEW-guh
Albizia—al-BIZ-ee-uh
Alcea—al-SEE-uh
Alchemilla—al-ke-MIL-luh
Allium—AL-ee-um
Alstroemeria—al-struh-MEE-ree-uh
Amaranthus—am-uh-RAN-thus
Amelanchier—am-el-AN-kee-er
Amsonia—am-SOWN-ee-uh
Anchusa—an-KOO-suh
Anemone—uh-NEM-oh-nee
Anisodontea—uh-nee-so-DONT-ee-uh
Anthemis—AN-the-mis
Aquilegia—ak-wuh-LEE-gee-uh
Arctostaphylos—ark-toe-STAF-il-oss
Armeria—ar-MEER-ee-uh
Aronia—uh-ROE-nee-uh
Arrhenatherum—uh-ren-uh-THER-um
Artemisia—ar-tuh-MEE-zee-uh
Arum—AY-rum
Aruncus—uh-RUN-kus
Arundo—uh-RUN-doe
Asarum—uh-SAR-um
Asclepias—as-KLEE-pee-as
Aster—AS-tur
Astilbe—uh-STILL-bee
Athyrium—uh-THER-ree-um
Avena—uh-VEE-nuh

B

Baptisia—bap-TIZ-ee-uh
Begonia—bee-GO-nee-uh
Berberis—BER-ber-is
Bergenia—ber-GEN-ee-uh
Betula—BET-yew-luh
Briza—BRY-zuh
Buddleia—BUD-lee-uh
Buxus—BUX-us

C

Caladium—ka-LAY-dee-um
Calamagrostis—CAL-uh-muh-GROS-tis
Calendula—kuh-LEN-dew-luh
Campanula—kam-PAN-yew-luh
Campis—KAMP-sis
Canna—KAN-nuh
Carex—KAY-rex
Caryopteris—kar-ee-OP-ter-is
Catananche—kat-uh-NAN-kee
Cedrus—SED-rus
Celosia—see-LOW-shee-uh
Centaurea—sen-TOR-ee-uh
Cerastium—ser-AS-tee-um
Ceratostigma—ser-at-oh-STIG-ma
Cercis—SER-sis
Chamaecyparis—kam-ee-SIP-uh-ris
Chamaemelum—kam-ee-MAY-lum
Chionanthus—kee-oh-NAN-thus
Chrysanthemum—kris-AN-the-mum
Chrysogonum—kris-OGH-oh-num
Clematis—KLEM-uh-tis
Cleome—klee-OH-mee
Colchicum—KOL-chi-kum
Coleus—KOH-lee-us
Comptonia—komp-TONE-ee-uh
Consolida—kon-SOW-li-da
Convallaria—kon-vuh-LAIR-ee-uh
Coreopsis—kor-ee-OP-sis
Cornus—KOR-nus
Cortaderia—kor-tuh-DEER-ee-uh
Corylus—KOR-il-us
Cosmos—KOZ-mos
Cotinus—koe-TIE-nus
Cotoneaster—kuh-toe-nee-AS-ter
Crambe—KRAM-bee
Crataegus—kruh-TEE-gus
Crocus—KROH-kus
Cryptomeria—krip-toe-MEER-ee-uh
× *Cupressocyparis*—kew-press-o-SIP-uh-ris
Cyclamen—SIK-la-men
Cyperus—sy-PEER-us
Cytisus—sy-TI-sus

D

Daphne—DAFF-nee
Darmera—DAR-mir-uh
Delphinium—del-FIN-ee-um
Deutzia—DOOT-zee-uh
Dianthus—dye-AN-thus
Dicentra—dye-SEN-tra
Digitalis—dij-i-TAHL-is
Dryopteris—dry-OP-ter-is

E

Echinacea—ek-uh-NAY-see-uh
Elymus—EL-im-us
Epimedium—ep-ee-MEE-dee-um
Erigeron—eh-RIJ-er-on
Erysimum—eh-RIS-i-mum
Erythronium—eh-rith-RONE-ee-um
Euonymus—yew-ON-uh-mus
Eupatorium—yew-pa-TOR-ee-um
Euphorbia—yew-FOR-bee-uh

F

Fagus—FAY-gus
Felicia—fee-LISS-ee-uh
Festuca—fes-TOO-ka
Ficus—FYE-kus
Filipendula—fil-i-PEN-dew-la
Foeniculum—fee-NIK-yew-lum
Forsythia—for-SITH-ee-uh
Fothergilla—foth-er-GILL-uh
Fragaria—fruh-GAIR-ee-uh

G

Gaillardia—gay-LAR-dee-uh
Gaultheria—gawl-THER-ee-uh
Genista—je-NIS-tuh
Geranium—jer-AIN-ee-um
Ginkgo—GINGK-go
Glyceria—gly-SEE-ree-uh
Gunnera—GUN-er-uh
Gymnocladus—jim-NO-kla-dus
Gypsophila—jip-SOFF-uh-la

H

Hakonechloa—huh-cone-ee-KLOH-uh
Halesia—hah-LEE-ze-uh
Hamamelis—ham-uh-MEE-lis
Hedera—HED-er-uh
Helianthus—hee-lee-AN-thus
Helichrysum—hee-lie-KRY-sum
  also hee-lie-KRIS-um
Helictotrichon—hee-lik-toe-TRI-kon
Heliopsis—hee-lee-OP-sis
Helleborus—hee-LEE-bor-us
  also hell-e-BOR-us
Hemerocallis—hem-er-oh-KAL-lis
Herniaria—her-ni-AIR-ee-uh
Hesperis—HES-per-is
Heuchera—HEW-ker-uh
Hibiscus—hy-BIS-kus
Hosta—HOS-tuh
Howea—HOW-ee-uh
Hyacinthus—hy-uh-SIN-thus
Hydrangea—hy-DRAN-gee-uh
Hypericum—hy-PER-i-kum
Hypoestes—hy-PES-teez

I

Iberis—eye-BEER-is
Ilex—EYE-lex
Impatiens—im-PAY-shiens
Imperata—im-per-AY-tuh
Indigofera—in-di-GO-fer-uh
Ipheion—IF-ee-on
Iris—EYE-ris

J

Juniperus—jew-NIP-er-us

K

Kalmia—KAL-mee-uh
Kniphofia—nip-HOH-fee-uh
Koelreuteria—koel-roo-TEE-ree-uh
Kolkwitzia—koel-KWIT-zee-uh

L

Lagerstroemia—lay-ger-STREE-mee-uh
Lamium—LAY-mee-um
Lavandula—la-VAN-dew-la
Lavatera—lav-at-TEE-ra
Leucothöe—loo-KO-tho-ee
Liatris—LIE-uh-tris also lie-AY-tris
Ligustrum—lye-GUS-trum
Lilium—LIL-ee-um
Linum—LYE-num
Liriodendron—leer-ee-oh-DEN-dron
Liriope—lee-RYE-oh-pee
Lobelia—low-BEE-lee-uh
Lobularia—lob-yew-LAY-ree-uh
Lonicera—lon-ISS-er-uh
Lupinus—loo-PIE-nus
Lysimachia—lye-sim-AK-ee-uh
   also lye-sim-MAY-kee-uh

M

Magnolia—mag-NOL-ee-uh
Mahonia—ma-HOE-nee-uh
Malus—MAY-lus
Malva—MAL-va
Mandevilla—man-duh-VIL-uh
Menispermum—men-iss-PERM-um
Mertensia—mer-TEN-see-uh
Microbiota—my-krow-bee-OH-tuh
Miscanthus—mis-KAN-thus
Molinia—mo-LEE-nee-uh
Monarda—moe-NARD-uh
Morus—MOE-rus
Myosotis—my-oh-SO-tis
Myrtus—MUR-tus

N

Nandina—nan-DEE-nuh
Narcissus—nar-SIS-us
Nepeta—NEP-et-uh
Nicotiana—ni-koe-she-AN-na

Nigella—nye-JELL-uh
Nymphaea—nim-FEE-uh

O

Oenothera—ee-no-THEE-ra
Opuntia—oh-PUN-tee-uh
Origanum—oh-RIG-uh-num
Osmunda—os-MUN-da
Oxydendrum—ox-see-DEN-drum

P

Pachysandra—pak-is-AN-druh
Paeonia—pee-OH-nee-uh
Panicum—PAN-i-kum
Papaver—pa-PAH-ver
Pelargonium—pel-ar-GO-nee-um
Pennisetum—pen-uh-SEE-tum
Penstemon—pen-STAY-mon
   also pen-STEE-mon
Perilla—per-ILL-uh
Perovskia—per-OV-skee-uh
Petunia—pee-TUNE-ee-uh
Phalaris—FAL-uh-ris
Philadelphus—fill-uh-DEL-fus
Phlox—FLOX
Photinia—foe-TIN-ee-uh
Physostegia—fie-so-STEE-gee-uh
Picea—PIE-see-uh
Pieris—pee-AIR-us
Pinus—PIE-nus
Platycodon—plat-i-KOE-don
Podophyllum—poe-doe-FIL-um
Polygonum—poe-LIG-oh-num
Polystichum—poe-LIS-ti-kum
Pontederia—pon-te-DEE-ree-uh
Portulaca—por-tew-LAK-uh
Potentilla—poe-ten-TILL-uh
Primula—PRIM-yew-luh
Prunus—PROO-nus
Pseudotsuga—soo-doe-TSOO-guh
Pyracantha—pie-ra-KAN-thuh

Q

Quercus—KWER-kus

R

Ranunculus—ra-NUN-kew-lus
Ratibida—ra-TIB-i-duh
Rhamnus—RAM-nus
Rhododendron—roe-doe-DEN-dron
Robinia—roe-BIN-ee-uh
Rodgersia—ro-JER-zee-uh
Rosa—RO-sa
Rosmarinus—rose-muh-RYE-nus
Rudbeckia—rood-BEK-ee-uh

S

Saccharum—SAK-kar-um
Sagina—suh-JEN-uh

Sagittaria—saj-it-TAY-ree-uh
Salix—SAY-lix
Salvia—SAL-vee-uh
Santolina—san-toe-LIE-nuh
   also san-toe-LEEN-uh
Sarcococca—sar-koe-KOE-kuh
Scabiosa—skab-ee-OH-suh
Schizophragma—sky-zoe-FRAG-ma
Scilla—SILL-uh
   also SKIL-luh
Sedum—SEE-dum
Sempervivum—sem-per-VIE-vum
Sisyrinchium—sis-i-RIN-kee-um
Solidago—sol-i-DAY-go
Sorghastrum—sore-GAS-trum
Spiraea—spy-REE-uh
Sporobolus—spor-OB-oh-lus
Stachys—STAY-kis
Stewartia—stew-ART-ee-uh
Stipa—STY-puh
Syringa—si-RING-guh

T

Tagetes—tuh-JEE-teez
Teucrium—TEW-kree-um
Thalictrum—tha-LIK-trum
Thuja—THEW-yuh
Thymus—TIE-mus
Tiarella—tee-uh-REL-luh
Trillium—TRIL-lee-um
Tropaeolum—troe-PEE-oh-lum
Tsuga—TSOO-guh
Tulipa—TEW-li-puh
Typha—TYE-fuh

U

Ulmus—UL-mus

V

Vaccinium—vak-SIN-ee-um
Valeriana—va-leer-ee-AH-na
Verbascum—ver-BAS-kum
Verbena—ver-BEE-na
Viburnum—vie-BER-num
Vinca—VING-kuh
Viola—VIE-o-luh
Vitis—VIE-tis

W

Weigela—why-GEE-luh
Wisteria—wis-TEER-ee-uh

Y

Yucca—YUK-ka

Z

Zamia—ZA-mia
Zelkova—zel-KOE-va
Zinnia—ZIN-ee-uh

SUBJECT INDEX

Italic page numbers refer to pages on which there are relevant photographs or illustrations. **Boldface** page numbers indicate charts, lists, or plans.

PLANT INDEX

Italic page numbers refer to pages on which there are relevant photographs. **Boldface** page numbers indicate charts, lists, or plans.

ACKNOWLEDGMENTS

Our thanks to the following for their contributions to the book:

Jerry Carrier, Glen-Gery Corporation, Shoemakersville, PA; Yunghi Choi Epstein, Lawson Carter Epstein Landscape Design, Washington, D.C.; Gordon Hayward, Putney, VT; Bob Larson and the National Atmospheric Deposition Program (NRSP-3)/National Trends Network (1998). NADP Program Office, Illinois State Water Survey, 2204 Griffith Dr., Champaign, IL 61820; Joanne Lawson, Lawson Carter Epstein Landscape Design, Washington, D.C.; Bob Nicholas, Crosstown Builders, Alexandria, VA; Ellen Pennick, Richmond, VA; Smitty's Building Supply, Alexandria, VA; Barbara Thorup, Charlottesville, VA; Sharon W. Waltman, U.S.D.A. Natural Resources Conservation Service, National Soil Survey Center, Lincoln, Nebraska.

Our thanks to the following for allowing us to show their merchandise in this book:

Barbara Butler; California Redwood Association; Campbell, Harrington & Brear; Dalton Pavillions, Inc.; William Fortington; Gardeners Eden; Garden Jazz; Gateways; Hadco® Outdoor Lighting; Lyngso Garden Materials; New Leaf Gallery; Nightscaping by Loran; Smith & Hawken; Solutions; The Thompson Company; Wind & Weather.

PHOTOGRAPHY CREDITS

The sources for the illustrations that appear in this book are listed below. Credits from left to right are separated by semi-colons; credits from top to bottom are separated by dashes.

Cover: Roger Foley, **Back cover:** Janet Davis-David Cavagnaro; Norman A. Plate; Janet Davis; Charles Mann-Alison Shaw, **Endpapers, hardcover edition:** Roger Foley, **1:** Alison Shaw, **2, 3:** Jerry Pavia **4, 5:** Nancy Rotenberg, **6:** Jerry Pavia, **9:** Jerry Pavia, **10, 11:** Roger Foley, **14:** Walter Chandoha-Jerry Pavia, **15:** Jerry Pavia-Leonard Phillips-Ken Druse, **18:** Karen Bussolini, **21:** Tom Wyatt, **22:** Philip Harvey, **24:** Alan and Linda Detrick, **25:** Ken Druse (2)-Karen Bussolini, Ken Druse (2), **26:** Ken Druse-Alan and Linda Detrick, **27:** Catriona Tudor-Erler, **28:** Philip Harvey, **30:** Carole Ottesen; Lynn Karlin, **31:** Charles Mann; Leonard Phillips-Karen Bussolini-Carole Ottesen; Charles Mann, **32, 33:** Carole Ottesen, **34:** Jerry Pavia, **35:** Alan and Linda Detrick; Roger Foley-Carole Ottesen; Roger Foley, **42:** Ken Cobb-Philip Harvey, **43:** Philip Harvey, **44, 45:** Philip Harvey, **46, 47:** Design by Lawson Carter Epstein Landscape Design, photography by M. Catherine Davis, **48, 49:** Nancy Rotenberg, **50, 51:** Nancy Rotenberg, **52, 53:** Nancy Rotenberg; insets: Nancy Rotenberg-Nancy Rotenberg; Lynn Karlin, **54–57:** Karen Bussolini, **58–61:** Virginia R. Weiler, **62, 63:** Jerry Pavia, **64, 65:** Lynn Karlin, **66, 67:** Dency Kane, **68, 69:** Ian Adams, **70, 71:** Ian Adams; insets: Ian Adams-Karen Bussolini; Alison Shaw, **72, 73:** Karen Bussolini, **74, 75:** Dency Kane, **76, 77:** Andrew Howard, **78, 79:** Lynn Karlin, **80, 81:** Andrew Howard, **82, 83:** Lynn Karlin, **84, 85:** Celia Pearson, **86, 87:** Karen Bussolini, **88–91:** Jerry Pavia, **92, 93:** Janet Davis, **94, 95:** Janet Davis; insets: Lynn Karlin; Derek Fell; Roger Foley, **96, 97:** Roger Foley, **98, 99:** Dency Kane, **100, 101:** Roger Foley, **102–105:** Catriona Tudor-Erler, **106, 107:** Ken Druse, **108, 109:** Alan and Linda Detrick, **110, 111:** Roger Foley, **112, 113:** Andrew Howard, **114, 115:** Roger Foley, **120, 121:** Roger Foley, **122, 123:** Roger Foley; Dency Kane; Roger Foley, **124, 125:** Roger Foley-Dency Kane; Roger Foley, **126, 127:** Leonard Phillips, **128–131:** Roger Foley, **132, 133:** Leonard Phillips, **134, 135:** Nancy Rotenberg, **136, 137:** Nancy Rotenberg; insets: Ian Adams, **138, 139:** Ian Adams, **140, 141:** Nancy Rotenberg, **142, 143:** Ian Adams, **144, 145:** Nancy Rotenberg, **146, 147:** Ian Adams, **148, 149:** Ken Druse, **150:** Derek Fell, **151:** Derek Fell-Saxon Holt; Peter O. Whiteley, **152:** Janet Davis-Saxon Holt, **153:** Peter O. Whiteley-Catriona Tudor-Erler, **154, 155:** Derek Fell; Ernest Braun-Karen Bussolini, **157:** Karen Bussolini-Janet Davis, **158:** Walter Chandoha, **159:** Charles Mann, **160:** Jerry Pavia; Karen Bussolini, **161:** Leonard Phillips; Dency Kane; Charles Mann-Ken Druse-Walter Chandoha, Michael Thompson, **162:** Karen Bussolini-Lynn Karlin; Dency Kane, **164, 165:** Walter Chandoha-Dency Kane, **165:** Dency Kane-Liz Ball; Jerry Pavia-Dency Kane, **166, 167:** Roger Foley; Derek Fell-Michael Thompson-Derek Fell, **169:** Dalton Pavilion Inc.-Walter Chandoha, **170, 171:** Derek Fell; Lynn Karlin (2)-Walter Chandoha, **172:** Karen Bussolini, **173:** Walter Chandoha-Liz Ball-Saxon Holt, **174:** Catriona Tudor-Erler-Karen Bussolini, **175:** Janet Davis-Karen Bussolini (2), **176, 177:** Teena Albert-Dency Kane-Teena Albert, **178:** Walter Chandoha, **179:** Jerry Pavia-Dency Kane; Karen Bussolini, **180:** Walter Chandoha; Janet Davis, **181:** Scott Atkinson, **182, 183:** Jerry Pavia; Karen Bussolini-Roger Foley, **184, 185:** Karen Bussolini; Derek Fell-Don Normark, **187:** Karen Bussolini, **188:** Derek Fell, **189:** Leonard Phillips, **190:** Walter Chandoha; Karen Bussolini-Karen Bussolini; Liz Ball, **191:** Karen Bussolini, **192, 193:** Walter Chandoha; Liz Ball-Leonard Phillips; Jerry Pavia, **194:** Walter Chandoha, **196, 197:** Jerry Pavia, **198, 199:** Walter Chandoha, **200:** Derek Fell, **204:** Dency Kane, **206:** Derek Fell-Liz Ball-Dency Kane, **208, 209:** Roger Foley; Derek Fell(3), **210:** Michael Thompson, **211:** Jerry Pavia, **212:** Ken Druse-Saxon Holt-Jerry Pavia, **214, 215:** Saxon Holt (3); Derek Fell; Leonard Phillips, **216, 217:** Jerry Pavia-Derek Fell; Mick Hales; David McDonald; Charles Mann-Saxon Holt, **218:** Derek Fell, **219:** Charles Mann; Jerry Pavia (2), **220, 221:** Ken Druse; Catriona Tudor-Erler-Saxon Holt-Peter O. Whiteley, **222, 223:** Tom Wyatt; Philip Harvey, **224:** Walter Chandoha, **226:** Kathleen Brenzel, **227:** Ken Druse-Leonard Phillips, **228:** Jerry Pavia, **229:** Jerry Pavia, **230:** David McDonald-Jerry Pavia-David McDonald, **232:** Jerry Pavia-Saxon Holt-Jerry Pavia, **234:** Jerry Pavia-Karen Bussolini-Jerry Pavia, **236, 237:** Nancy Rotenberg; Leonard Phillips; Ken Druse-Nancy Rotenberg (2); Ken Druse; Carole Ottesen; Walter Chandoha; Ken Druse, **238:** Charles Mann-Michael Thompson-Jerry Pavia, **240:** Marion Brenner-Saxon Holt-Derek Fell, **242:** Roger Foley; Philip Harvey (3), **243:** Philip Harvey-Philip Harvey; Michael Thompson-Saxon Holt-Jerry Pavia-Charles Mann, **246:** Charles Mann-David Cavagnaro-Walter Chandoha, **248:** David McDonald, **249:** David McDonald (2); Saxon Holt; Charles Mann, **250:** Dency Kane-Charles Mann-David McDonald, **252, 253:** Allan Mandell(3); Saxon Holt; Allan Mandell, **254:** Charles

Mann-Nancy Rotenberg-Carole Ottesen, **256, 257:** Karen Bussolini-Walter Chandoha; Jerry Pavia (2), **258:** Ed Carey; Lynne Harrison-Philip Harvey, **259:** Catriona Tudor-Erler-Jonelle Weaver-Janet Davis; Philip Harvey-Ed Carey, **260:** Norman A. Plate; Ken Druse, **261:** Janet Davis-Lynn Karlin, **262:** Connie Toops; Tom Wyatt (2), **263:** Jerry Pavia; Claire Curran; Jerry Pavia (2), **264, 265:** Roger Foley, **266:** Nancy Rotenberg, **267:** Kathleen Brenzel-Peter O. Whiteley; Philip Harvey; David Belda-Kathleen Brenzel; Karen Bussolini, **268:** Norman A. Plate-Philip Harvey; Nancy Rotenberg, **269:** Norman A. Plate-Norman A. Plate-Sean Sullivan (2); Norman A. Plate, **270, 271:** Alan and Linda Detrick; Dency Kane, courtesy of Carol Mercer/Design by Carol Mercer and Lisa Verderosa; Norman A. Plate-Philip Harvey, **272:** Mick Hales-Dency Kane, **273:** Jerry Pavia-Dency Kane; Carole Ottesen-Janet Davis, **274, 275:** Karl Petzke; Jonelle Weaver; Cheryl Fenton; Jim Sadlon; Cheryl Fenton(3)-Philip Harvey; Richard Rethemeyer; Norman A. Plate (3)-Karl Petzke; Richard Rethemeyer, **276, 277:** Norman A. Plate; Karen Bussolini; Sean Sullivan; Philip Harvey-Norman A. Plate; Peter Christiansen-Charles Mann; Carole Ottesen, **278:** Philip Harvey; Peter O. Whiteley-Peter Christiansen, **279:** Dency Kane; Janet Davis; Philip Harvey-Philip Harvey, **280, 281:** Roger Foley, **282, 283:** Philip Harvey; Deborah Jones; Jim Sadlon, Michael Bates garden; Peter O. Whiteley-Norman A. Plate; Philip Harvey, **284:** Robert Perron-Janet Davis, **285:** Richard Shiell, **286:** Hadco Lighting; Suzanne Woodard (2); Hadco Lighting (2), **287:** Nightscaping (2)-Hadco Lighting (4), **288:** Janet Davis-Sean Sullivan, **289:** David Belda (2); Philip Harvey-Jim Saldon; Karl Petzke; Jonelle Weaver-Jim Sadlon; Nancy Rotenberg; Philip Harvey, **290, 291:** Norman A. Plate; Peter O. Whitely-Carole Ottesen; Saxon Holt (2), **292:** Derek Fell-Catriona Tudor-Erler, **293:** Mick Hales, **294:** Jon Jensen; Victoria Pearson-Jon Jensen, **295:** Karen Bussolini; Carole Ottesen-Janet Davis, **296:** Walter Chandoha, **297:** Sean Sullivan-Peter O. Whiteley; Mick Hales-Deborah Jones; David Belda, **298, 299:** Dency Kane; Walter Chandoha; Norman A. Plate-Derek Fell; Catriona Tudor-Erler, **300, 301:** Karen Bussolini, **302, 303:** Jerry Pavia-Catriona Tudor-Erler; Derek Fell, **304:** Jerry Pavia-Catriona Tudor-Erler, **305:** Catriona Tudor-Erler, **306:** Lynn Karlin-Karen Bussolini; Rob and Ann Simpson; Andre Viette, **308:** Karen Bussolini-Walter Chandoha, **313:** Derek Fell-Karen Bussolini, **314, 315:** Karen Bussolini, **316:** Dwight Kuhn, **317:** Jerry Pavia-Tom Woodward, **318, 319:** Jerry Pavia; Dency Kane; Lynne Harrison-Karen Bussolini-R. Todd Davis, **322:** Niki Mareschal, The Image Bank-Robert Perron, **323:** Dwight Kuhn; Rob and Ann Simpson, **324:** Al Hamdan, The Image Bank-Catriona Tudor-Erler, **325:** Karen Bussolini, **326, 327:** Lynn Karlin, **328, 329:** Hank deLespinasse; Karen Bussolini; Jerry Pavia-Karen Bussolini, **330:** Darrow Watt; Norman A. Plate; Darrow Watt-Tom Wyatt, **331:** Norman A. Plate, **332:** Derek Fell; Jerry Pavia, **333:** Jerry Pavia, **334, 335:** Ken Druse, **360, 361:** Philip Harvey, **362:** Roger Foley, **363:** Philip Harvey, **364, 365:** Philip Harvey, **369:** Philip Harvey, **372, 373:** Philip Harvey-Peter Christiansen; Peter O. Whiteley, **374, 375:** Jerry Pavia-Darrow Watt; Alan and Linda Detrick; Tom Wyatt, **376:** Tom Wyatt, **377:** Janet Davis-Karen Bussolini, **378:** Jack McDowell (4)-Jerry Pavia, **379:** Philip Harvey, **382:** Tom Wyatt, **383:** Roger Foley, **389:** Walter Chandoha, **400:** Philip Harvey

ILLUSTRATION CREDITS

Back cover: Mark Pechenik, **7:** Mimi Osborne, **12, 13:** Reineck & Reineck, **16, 17:** Mimi Osborne, **20:** Reineck & Reineck, San Francisco, **20:** National Soil Survey Center Staff. 1999. Soil Reaction in the Southern United States. USDA-Natural Resources Conservation Service. National Soil Survey Center, Lincoln, Nebraska. Digital map product, **23:** Reineck & Reineck, **29:** Mimi Osborne, **36, 37:** Mimi Osborne, **38–41:** Reineck & Reineck, **152, 153:** Mark Pechenik, **156, 157:** Mark Pechenik, **160, 161:** Mark Pechenik, **168:** Mark Pechenik, **180:** Mark Pechenik, **181:** Lois Lovejoy, **186:** Mark Pechenik, **189:** Mark Pechenik, **195:** Mark Pechenik, **201:** Wendy Smith, **202:** Wendy Smith, **203:** Lois Lovejoy, **204, 205:** Wendy Smith, **206, 207:** Lois Lovejoy-Mimi Osborne, **212, 213:** Lois Lovejoy-Mimi Osborne, **218:** Wendy Smith, **219:** Wendy Smith, **229:** Wendy Smith, **230, 231:** Lois Lovejoy-Mimi Osborne, **232, 233:** Lois Lovejoy-Mimi Osborne, **234, 235:** Lois Lovejoy-Mimi Osborne, **239:** Wendy Smith-Mimi Osborne, **244:** Lois Lovejoy, Mimi Osborne **245:** Lois Lovejoy-Mimi Osborne, **246, 247:** Lois Lovejoy-Mimi Osborne, **250, 251:** Lois Lovejoy-Mimi Osborne, **255:** Mimi Osborne, **269:** Wendy Smith, **287:** Mimi Osborne, **299:** Wendy Smith, **305:** Erin O'Toole, **307:** Mimi Osborne, **309:** Mimi Osborne, **310–312:** Wendy Smith, **320, 321:** Mimi Osborne, **323:** National Atmospheric Deposition Program (NRSP-#)/National Trends Network. 1998. NADP Program Office, Illinois State Water Survey, 2204 Griffith Drive, Champaign, Illinois, 61820, **325:** Wendy Smith, **336–359:** Mark Pechenik, **366–371:** Rik Olson, **379–388:** Rik Olson, **390–397:** Rik Olson-Norman A. Plate (2) bottom, **397, 398–401:** Rik Olson